THE MAGIC FLUTE, MASONIC OPERA

THE MAGIC FLUTE, MASONIC OPERA

An Interpretation of the
Libretto and the Music by

JACQUES CHAILLEY

Translated from the French by
Herbert Weinstock

ALFRED A. KNOPF · 1971 · NEW YORK

THIS IS A BORZOI BOOK
PUBLISHED BY ALFRED A. KNOPF, INC.

Published in the United States by
Alfred A. Knopf, Inc., New York, and
simultaneously in Canada by Random House
of Canada Limited, Toronto. Distributed
by Random House, Inc., New York.
Originally published in French by Editions
Robert Laffont, Paris, France, 1968.
Library of Congress Catalog Card Number: 70-111248
ISBN: 0-394-43452-8
Manufactured in the United States of America
First American Edition

To Philippe Chabro

TRANSLATOR'S NOTE

My indebtedness to Miss Katherine Stechmann, whose copy-editing of the manuscript was carried out with talent equaled only by her patience, is most gratefully acknowledged.

H.W.

CONTENTS

ILLUSTRATIONS

(following page 146)

*Commentary on the Plates, with Sources,
will be found on pages 311–17.*

Part One

PRELIMINARY CIRCUM-VOLUTIONS

1

*What
Everyone
Knows*

An operagoer cannot help being puzzled at a performance of
Mozart's masterpiece. A jumpy, ill-assorted story in which the
sequence of situations is not guided by any apparent logic puts
him off as much as the marvelous variety of the incomparable
score enchants him. The first act begins as a fairy tale, continues as a *commedia buffa,* and ends in philosophic tirades.
The second act is even less comprehensible: we watch the
chief protagonists being subjected to unexplained trials of
astonishing arbitrariness and then suddenly learn that they
have earned the right to places of honor in the glory of Isis and
Osiris. A young prince in Japanese costume behaves in a cow-
ardly way when faced by a serpent, which three ladies kill for
him. And that exploit entitles him to be selected by the queen
to deliver her imprisoned daughter from an evil genius. Upon
seeing the girl's portrait, he falls in love with her and sets off to
free her. But when he reaches the evildoer's stronghold, he
begs for initiation into a Virtue concerning which not a word
has been whispered to him and completely forgets the beauty
he has come to win. Then one learns that the evil genius is

no less than the high priest of wisdom. And the imbroglio proceeds along those lines to its inexplicable final apotheosis.

A listener confused by so much that is arbitrary looks for guidance. To begin with, his program reminds him that *Die Zauberflöte* (together with the unfinished Requiem, which Mozart worked on simultaneously) is Mozart's last great work, that he attached special importance to it, and that he thought of it even upon his deathbed, looking at his watch and murmuring: "At this moment the Queen of the Night is coming onto the stage . . ." He learns too that the opera was commissioned by the director-actor of a suburban troupe, Emanuel Schikaneder, who played the role of Papageno; that it was played for the first time on September 30, 1791; and that it ran successfully through the winter season of 1791–2 at Vienna's Theater auf der Wieden. The program note adds that, like Mozart, Schikaneder was a Freemason, and that this detail doubtless explains the numerous obscure Masonic allusions sprinkled throughout the opera (and which the writer has been careful not to clarify).

Insufficiently enlightened, our operagoer turns to the analysis of the libretto. This is more or less what he reads:*

ACT I

Scene 1

The action is set in a wild, mountainous place.

Tamino, a Japanese prince, is being pursued by a serpent. Three veiled ladies, messengers of the Queen of the Night, kill the monster and gaze upon the beauty of the unconscious prince.

Papageno the Birdcatcher enters. Tamino mistakenly believes that this is his savior, and Papageno boasts of his prowess. But he has misbehaved: the three Messengers punish him for lying. They hand Tamino a portrait of the Queen's daughter, whom the evil

---

* This résumé is an approximately exact translation of the anonymous analysis supplied for a performance by the Vienna Opera at Brussels in 1954, but any analogous analysis could have been chosen.

genius Sarastro holds prisoner. Tamino is infatuated by her beauty
and promises to free her. The Messengers give him a magic flute,
Papageno a set of magic bells.

Scene 2

The action is set in a room in an Egyptian palace.

Three slaves rejoice over Pamina's flight, but she is brought back
by the Moor Monostatos, who desires her. Papageno enters. The
Birdcatcher informs the girl of her liberator's arrival.

Scene 3

The stage represents three temples, marked respectively
Temple of Wisdom, Temple of Reason, and Temple of Nature.

Three boys guide Tamino toward the temples, where he seeks the
enemy of the Queen of the Night. He is greeted by an old priest,
and learns that Sarastro is not the malevolent being as which he
has been painted. Tamino interrogates the stars. Voices encourage
him. The sound of his flute is answered by Papageno's whistle; the
Birdcatcher enters, accompanied by Pamina. Monostatos chases
them, but Papageno's magic bells bewitch the Moor, forcing him
to flee.

Sarastro enters with his retinue. He punishes the Moor for his
misdeeds and, after having seen Tamino and Pamina united, separates them so that they can triumph through trials.

ACT II
Scene 1

The action occurs in a grove of palms at the Egyptian pyramids.

Sarastro asks the gods to grant wisdom to the young couple. Tamino and Papageno are led to the subterranes of the temple, where
they are subjected to various temptations to be overcome in silence. Tamino obeys. Papageno finds it almost impossible to remain silent.

Scene 2

The action takes place in a garden.

Monostatos tries to seduce Pamina. The Queen of the Night gives
her daughter a dagger with which to kill Sarastro.

The Moor takes the dagger and threatens Pamina. Sarastro

stops him and drives him off. Tamino and Papageno are subjected
to trials. Papageno remains attached to worldly pleasures; Sarastro
gives him a companion of his own kind: Papagena.

Scene 3
The action takes place in the temple caverns.

Tamino, accompanied by Pamina and playing on his magic flute,
passes the trials by water and by fire. He is worthy to win his beloved. The powers of Night are vanquished. The opera ends with
a hymn to the Sun.

"That is all very well," our operagoer says to himself, "but
what does it mean?"

I have undertaken this book because I have asked that question many times without receiving an answer.

2

Traditions and
Misunderstandings

That the most celebrated and most admired of Mozart's operas practically never has been explained satisfactorily is a paradox. To hear the action of *Die Zauberflöte* described as a jumble of stupidities still is common despite the opposing testimony of Goethe and that of Mozart himself—who recounts the scorn with which he treated as a Papageno a man who spoke that way. When this subject comes up, the most serious books habitually take refuge in prudent generalities.

That lack of understanding doubtless originates in the very nature of the opera itself, which makes use of Masonic traditions often unknown to the uninitiated. Very possibly, explanation of them has not always been desired by their guardians. "It is enough," Goethe says, "that the crowd should find pleasure in seeing the spectacle: at the same time, its high significance will not escape the initiates." [1] Goethe was a Freemason; he held *Die Zauberflöte*, its libretto included, in such high esteem that at one time he considered writing a sequel to it.* A very significant passage occurs in *Hermann und Dorothea*, when Hermann recounts a visit to some neighbors:

Minette was at the piano. The father was there; he was listening to his daughter's singing, and he appeared enchanted. I did not understand all the words that she sang, but it was largely a matter of Pamina and Tamino. Not wanting to sit there saying nothing, as soon as the singing ended I asked questions about the text and the two characters. Everyone remained silent and smiled. Then the father said: "Well then, my friend, doesn't one know anyone except Adam and Eve?"

Quoting that scene, Otto Jahn saw in it only "testimony to the success of the work," [3] but it is typical of the attitude of the "initiates"—an attitude resulting from reticence about explaining the symbols, but also from satisfaction over the idea that those symbols, while being divulged sufficiently to awaken interest, are not being clarified in the eyes of the "profane": the idea that Masonic lodges reproached either Schikaneder or Mozart for having betrayed their secrets seems not to be supported by any serious testimony.† Such reticence has lost some

---

* He actually began this projected sequel, a fragment of which was published in 1802. Further, Christian August Vulpius, who was Goethe's brother-in-law, edited a revision of the libretto which was performed at Weimar in 1794.[2]

† One of the widespread legends concerning *Die Zauberflöte* is that Mozart died of poisoning—not by Antonio Salieri, as in another legend, which we need not discuss here[4]—but by Freemasons in revenge for his disclosure of some of their secrets. Launched in Nazi Germany,[5] this thesis would not deserve attention if it had not been brought up again in 1958 by a Viennese illustrated publication[6] and repeated in 1964 by an eminent Mozartean, Otto Erich Deutsch, during a public lecture delivered at Salzburg.[7] I have a copy of a brochure published in 1961[8] which also supports the theory and emphasizes that the poisoning must have been with mercury. It points out curious coincidences regarding mercurial symbolism in Mozart's destiny. The portrait that pictures him, at the age of seven, at a harpsichord is decorated with a quotation from the Homeric Hymn to Mercury; the frontispiece of the *Zauberflöte* libretto (Plate 33) bears on the left-hand stela eight allegories of Mercury (eight is Mercury's number), as does the commemorative forty-groschen stamp issued by Austria in 1956 for the Mozart bicentennial! Remember that though the Masonic character of *Die Zauberflöte* is so patent that it cannot be denied

of its importance because of the numerous publications that have become accessible to the uninitiated. Undoubtedly there still is much that an "outsider" like myself could add to what he would have to know in order to understand *Die Zauberflöte* completely. At least, I am conscious of that limitation. Only with assistance for which I want to thank several writers[9] have I been able to propose an explanation that I hope will finally prove coherent (without daring, let it be clear, to assert that every detail in it will be irreproachable). I wish, however, to specify that though their advice has been not only valuable, but in fact indispensable, to me, I will not in the course of this book divulge any "secret" that is not accessible to a properly oriented researcher and that is not to be found in some work within the reach of an outsider.[10] That fact makes all the more surprising the general poverty of the musicology dealing with this subject.

A second cause of the common lack of understanding unquestionably results from a legend that has for a long time excessively comforted exegetes conscious of the precariousness of their commentaries. *Die Zauberflöte*, this legend says, originated as only a harmless fairy tale, but its plan and intention were altered as it was worked upon. The entire beginning is a pure fairy tale unrelated to what follows, for the Masonic section begins only with the first-act finale. Nothing is to be looked for, then, except in the evidently initiatory scenes, which were stuck on later without relation to the rest, so that the story will yield up only puerile images devoid of logic and significance. That musicologists as eminent as Georges de Saint-Foix, Edward J. Dent, and Hermann Abert rallied to this lazy thesis in no way reduces its improbability. Its historical inaccuracy was proved in 1901 by Egon von Komorzynski,

---

in good faith (it never has been), nevertheless it was not openly proclaimed at the time of the opera's première.

and again in 1959 by Jean and Brigitte Massin.[11] I propose shortly to discuss this question with the reader in the hope of demonstrating the inanity of that thesis by internal analysis of the opera.

Two other traditions, on the other hand, though not verified —what is more, they are unverifiable—coincide perfectly with analysis of the libretto, the character of which they explain very well. The first is that the plan and large outlines of the opera were discussed and established at the bedside of Ignaz von Born, a master of Masonic symbolism and an authority venerated by all Viennese Masons. During the creation of the opera, Born died, and it is often supposed that Schikaneder and Mozart were thinking of him when they created the character of Sarastro. The second tradition—based upon belated assertions by the person involved—leaves to Schikaneder (outside of his having suggested the subject and supervised the whole) responsibility only for the Papageno episodes; it assigns the rest of the opera to his collaborator, Johann Giesecke, who later became a professor of mineralogy at the University of Dublin. That division of labor would explain the evident disparity between the serious scenes and Papageno's buffooneries, between the lofty symbolic speculations and the rest of Schikaneder's production.

Nothing of all this is very simple, and it is impossible to approach a study of Mozart's last opera without having tried beforehand to clarify not only those questions, but also others related to the historic, religious, and social contexts of the opera. To do that is the aim of this first part.

3

The Libretto: How Many Authors?

The name of only one writer appears both on the poster announcing the first performance and in the first published libretto: that of Emanuel Schikaneder, director of the Theater auf der Wieden, where *Die Zauberflöte* was first staged. He had kept the role of Papageno for himself: the frequently reproduced engraving of that character in the feathered costume of a birdcatcher, in the first edition of the libretto, is probably intended to represent him.*

Schikaneder was forty-three years old at the time of *Die Zauberflöte*. He had known Mozart for a long time. They had met in Salzburg in 1780; there the former itinerant violinist, become an actor and the director of a traveling troupe, had rented the municipal theater for some weeks to present varied spectacles four times each week, alternately tragedies and comedies, operas, lyric comedies, and ballets. He was then playing youthful leading roles (his most celebrated part was Hamlet), and his stagings were known for their originality, which sometimes was stigmatized as extravagance. Schikane-

* Regarding this, see Plate 11 and the commentary on it.

der was not, then, a professional singer, a fact that is not without interest in explaining the style in which Mozart composed the role of Papageno. At Salzburg, he had asked Wolfgang to compose for his troupe some songs or pieces (notably a lost aria, "*Warum, o Liebe*," K.365a), in return for which the Mozart family was given free permanent admission to his spectacles, a privilege of which they almost always took advantage. Thus their friendship was established, and Schikaneder even joined the archery society to which the Mozarts belonged.[1]

Mozart and Schikaneder have been described as lodge brothers, which is only half correct. Schikaneder certainly was a Freemason. But on May 4, 1789, he had been expelled from the Ratisbon Loge Karl zu den drei Schlüsseln because of his free ways. He had not yet passed beyond the degree of Companion, and despite various self-contradicting assertions to the contrary,[2] the most recent historians tend to think that he was never readmitted into any Viennese lodge.[3] It was not, then, for Masonic reasons that Mozart was first called upon to see Schikaneder in Vienna. They met with as much pleasure as before, as the actor had come to be a promoter of that "German opera" of which Mozart never had stopped dreaming. That project had been on the verge of being carried out several times, but Schikaneder, still directing his ambulant troupe, had failed to bring it to reality since 1786. The plan finally came to fruition, but only in 1790 was the troupe able to establish itself in the capital, its director having obtained the management of the Theater im Starhembergischen Freihause auf der Wieden, shortened to Theater auf der Wieden. It was, Dent says, "a flimsy erection which had been run up in one of the numerous courtyards of what is still called the 'Freihaus', a huge block of low yellow buildings south of the Naschmarkt. In those days it was outside the fortifications of the city, just on the right hand of the road leading out of the Kärntnerthor." [4] It was, then, an outlying, if not a suburban, theater.

Faithful to his ambition to promote "German opera" (we shall discover later what that meant), Schikaneder made the Singspiel the basis of his Vienna repertoire. He was encouraged by the success obtained at the competing Theater in der Leopoldstadt by his colleague Marinelli, a specialist in burlesques and magic shows of which the hero was often the popular comic Kaspar or Kasper. On November 7, 1789, Schikaneder established the formula of his own "magic" operas with an *Oberon* inspired by Christoph Martin Wieland. He had one of the actors in his troupe, Giesecke, write for it a libretto that—Komorzynski says—was a shameless plagiarism of another *Oberon* recently written by Friedrich Sophie Seyler. He entrusted the music to the Konzertmeister of the Vienna Opera, Paul Wranitzky, a Mason and a former violinist for Count Esterházy.[5] The success earned by that story of a magic horn certainly led to the selection of *Die Zauberflöte* as the subject of Schikaneder's next spectacle. But that success had also put Marinelli on guard, with results that we shall see shortly.

———

In connection with *Oberon*, I mentioned a curious person who later was to get himself much talked about in relation to the libretto of *Die Zauberflöte*. A supporting actor who appeared as a member of the chorus and in "utility" roles, he was singularly polyvalent and much better educated than the majority of that epoch's theatrical people: on occasion, he was dramatist, jurist, and mineralogist: Johann Georg Metzler, called Giesecke. In 1788, he had translated into German the libretto of an opera by Pasquale Anfossi. Then, taking his inspiration entirely from Wieland, he had written that of *Oberon der Elfenkönig*, which Schikaneder had ordered from him in 1789. He belonged to Schikaneder's troupe, and his

name appeared on the poster announcing the first performance of Die Zauberflöte as taking the inconspicuous role of
the first slave. But he had still another job: he was stage manager.[6] He too was a Freemason, but as in Schikaneder's case,
his Masonic career remains mysterious, at least in the 1790's.
It is not attested to by the archives until much later.[7]

In 1794, Giesecke more or less gave up the theater for
mineralogy, and thereafter he traveled here and there, becoming a professor at the University of Dublin in 1813 and a member of the Royal Academy of Ireland in 1817. In 1818, returning to Vienna after a long absence for the purpose of making
a gift of a scientific collection to the Imperial Museum, he
was recognized in a restaurant one day by a former theatrical
comrade who was dining there with other theater people,
among them a prominent tenor and operatic director, Julius
Cornet. It was the latter who, publishing in 1849 a book on
opera in Germany,[8] related the conversation that took place
there that evening, in the course of which Giesecke gave the
most unexpectedly specific details about his collaboration with
Schikaneder. He asserted that, though Schikaneder had signed
the libretto and directed the production, the only dialogue
that he had written was that of the episodes involving Papageno, the role that he had played. All the rest, he said, he himself had written.

Giesecke's claims naturally were doubted, one argument
against them being that a long time had elapsed between the
events and his revelation of them. That was, furthermore, all
the easier because Mozart and Schikaneder, the only men who
could have confirmed or denied them, were by then both dead.
Otto Jahn, in his famous book, which appeared in 1856–59,
accepted Cornet's testimony. His editors modified the passage
in posthumous reprintings. Although the opinions of Mozarteans remain divided, on the whole they are very hostile.[9] I do
not intend to join the debate, but to reject everything in this

matter may be excessive despite the validity of the objections offered. The Papageno scenes clearly are different in spirit from the rest of the libretto, and that disparity could be explained more satisfactorily that way, seeing that mineralogy, by way of alchemy, was a domain open wide to the symbolism with which *Die Zauberflöte* is crowded and that Born, the *deus ex machina* of whom I shall speak shortly, was a master in that science when Giesecke was taking his first steps in it. Therefore it is very tempting to imagine Born suggesting the ideas, Schikaneder theatricalizing them and drawing up the comic scenes, Giesecke providing him with the serious scenes —and all in close collaboration with Mozart. Is that what really happened? It would be hazardous to say so. The objections to Cornet's narrative are not final,[10] but they are solid, and one of the most worrisome is that, with a single exception (that of Neukomm's confidences to Jahn, mentioned in a note), the story is nowhere supported. Even Seyfried's letter, of which I shall speak again in the next chapter (Seyfried was, according to Cornet, one of those at the restaurant in 1818), a letter that takes into account the author's friendship with Giesecke, shows his collaboration with Schikaneder in a much more modest light. But that does not mean that it was any less real. Even if, as is possible, Cornet "inflated" the role of the actor-mineralogist, it is very probable that Saint-Foix, the illustrious Mozartean, was correct when he declared that the author of the libretto was less Schikaneder than what he calls "the Schikaneder firm." [11]

The third person involved in the story, Baron Ignaz von Born, did not, however, belong to the "firm." He reigned over much loftier spheres. Born in Transylvania in 1742, a former pupil of the Jesuits and then of the University of Prague, he had studied philosophy, law, and the natural sciences. In 1776, his reputation as a mineralogist had led the Empress Maria Theresia to call him to Vienna to continue his studies there.

Becoming one of the champions of the Enlightenment, having reached one of the highest degrees in Freemasonry as general secretary of the Grand Lodge of Austria, he was one of its leaders during the difficult hours of the "reform" imposed by Joseph II, of which I shall speak. He was also one of the theoreticians most listened to; his attention was particularly directed toward problems of ritual, and especially toward the restoration to honor of what—on the basis of various doubtful writings, the most celebrated of which was Terrasson's *Sethos* —was honestly believed to be the tradition of the ancient Egyptian mysteries. In 1784,[12] he published in the *Journal für Freymaurer* a long article of which the staging of *Die Zauberflöte* seems a veritable illustration.

Born was the Grand Secretary of the Vienna Loge zur wahren Eintracht (True Unity), which he had founded. Joseph Haydn was initiated in that lodge on February 11, 1785, and Mozart attended the ceremony. Although Mozart belonged to another lodge, the Loge zur Wohltätigkeit (Charity), the frequency with which his signature appears on the register of the lodge directed by Born attests to the attraction that the older man exercised upon him.[13] That feeling appears to have been reciprocal, as Born subscribed to works by Mozart. It was in his honor that, on April 20, 1785, Mozart composed his cantata *Die Maurerfreude* (Masonic Joy, K.471), in the Masonic key of E-flat major. One can therefore take for granted the existence between the two men of personal relations beyond the area of official contacts.

Ignaz von Born died in July 1791, during the rehearsals of *Die Zauberflöte*. Rumors spread that he had inspired it, and that the librettist and composer had portrayed him in the personage of the wise Sarastro. What can one think? It is hard to say. Written documents shed little light, as the notion did not appear at all until 1866, and then in the very moot *roman à clef* interpretation put forward by Zille (which I shall examine on p. 48). But of all the *roman à clef* readings put forward Zille's is by much the most, if not the only, plausible one. A Masonic portrait of the Philosopher (Plate 2) shows him accompanied by attributes that are certainly those of his degree, but which nonetheless serve to evoke the character of Sarastro very closely. On it one sees the lion pulling his chariot; the sphinx of the "mysteries of the Egyptians"; the palm of the Initiates, whose deliberations open Act II of *Die Zauberflöte*; not to mention such other symbols as the acacia branch opposite the palm, the serpent biting its tail, with its head turned toward the East, the symbol of the eternal life of the dead, and—in a ray-surrounded oval recalling the Sun, of which the Queen of the Night says that the High Priest "bears the circle on his breast"—an eight-pointed star, doubtless a degree symbol, but also the symbol of the union of Man and Woman in the Couple (3 + 5) in the teaching propounded (as we shall see) in the finale of the opera. The eight-pointed star, furthermore, figures in the seventeenth arcanum of the ancient tarot (replaced in the same irradiating oval by the five-pointed star of the pentagram in the tarot of Etteilla, of which I shall speak in Chapter 12).

To deduce from all this that the creators of *Die Zauberflöte* intended, in putting Sarastro on the stage, to describe Born personally would be excessive. The resemblance became inevitable because they wanted to present a sage of high degree, and Born answered to that requirement; but Sarastro would no doubt have been the same if Born had not existed. Sarastro represents the ideal sage whose characteristics Born's admirers had attributed to him. But tradition has not ceased to link the great man's name to the opera, which, in addition, was closely inspired by his writings. Although nothing can be asserted positively, what remains completely probable is that he participated personally in its elaboration, under the conditions that we shall see shortly, and the imprint of his personality should suffice to render suspect the smirks of those who speak condescendingly of the action in Die Zauberflöte as "one of the most absurd specimens of that form of literature in which absurdity is regarded as a matter of course." [14]

A fourth person remains who was involved in the matter, and he not the least of them: Mozart himself. No document tells us in black and white what his role in it was outside of the music, but it is known that his correspondence was in all likelihood "purified" of everything related to his Masonic activity by Constanze and her second husband, Georg Nikolaus Nissen. We are thus practically reduced to conjectures. But they turn out to be singularly harmonious.

The first certain fact is that Mozart did not work on Die Zauberflöte as a musician indifferent to the significance of his libretto, but as a true "believer" in relation to its contents. One piece of eloquent testimony has reached us despite the censorship: his letter to Constanze of October 8–9, 1791, in which he says that before taking "Mamma" * to the performance the next day, he has given her, to begin with, the libretto to read; after which he recounts in a fury the denseness of a man who, sitting beside him in a loge, did not understand the action at all. "At first I was patient enough to draw his attention to a few passages," he writes. "But he laughed at everything. Well, I could stand it no longer. I called him a Papageno and cleared out. But I don't think that the idiot understood my remark." I have italicized "a few passages" because when Mozart wanted Die Zauberflöte to be appreciated, he did not emphasize a modulation or a detail in the orchestration, but the words of the libretto. The Massins have even observed that the big, solemn scene in the second act, especially picked out by Mozart as helpful to the foolishness of the man involved, is, uniquely, almost wholly spoken, nearly devoid of music.[15]

* Frau Weber, Constanze Mozart's mother.

Mozart, then, "believed" in his libretto; in the minute care of his musical exegesis we shall see that he understood its symbolism completely. But that symbolism—who had been capable of enriching the work with it? Born, beyond doubt; but Born was too lofty a personage, and above all was then too gravely ill, to have been able, beyond the large outlines, to supervise details of its elaboration. Schikaneder, as I have already said, was little disposed toward the handling of large abstractions; also, driven from his Regensburg lodge and not reinstated at Vienna, he was no longer, so to speak, "in the swim," and could not have entered it again except under a determining influence. As for Giesecke, his role remains problematic; it is not even certain that he was a Mason at the time. Consequently, only one answer appears plausible: the constant personal intervention in the libretto of Mozart himself. A Mason as assiduous as he was convinced, initiated into the third degree, he certainly did not himself write any of the text —that was Schikaneder's affair, whether or not he was helped by Giesecke or someone else—but we can take it as morally certain that he watched over it very closely, serving as permanent intermediary between the too-remote philosopher and the too-light theatrical man.

Later on, we shall encounter several confirmations of that hypothesis. We shall see that earlier than Die Zauberflöte Mozart had never written a Singspiel without a moralistic arrière-pensée, and that, according to a source that I shall discuss, his first reaction to the proposal of a fairy tale inspired by the Zauberflöte in Wieland's collection was precisely to recoil before the novelty for him of its unpretentious genre. Apparently it was he, and not Schikaneder, who had personal rapport with Born. And we know from the famous letter "on death" that he wrote to his father on April 4, 1787, that he meditated deeply on metaphysical problems. I shall shortly have reason to quote and comment upon that letter; I restrict myself here to recalling its testimony, in which the celebrated "you know what I mean," escaping the posthumous censorship, emphasizes the covert initiate significance.

That is why I am convinced that Mozart was not merely the musician of the enterprise, but also the collaborator because of whom *Die Zauberflöte*, almost alone of its species, went beyond that formless condition of innumerable Singspiels into which, at first, it was destined to fall, and became, not only by the splendor of its music, but also by the ambitions of its libretto—and despite whatever there is in it of clumsiness in realization—one of the durable monuments of the human spirit.

4

The Legend
of the Revised
Libretto

We still are commonly told that *Die Zauberflöte* consists of two interlaced plays that have little relation to one another, or even are contradictory, in that the Queen of the Night represents Good at the beginning, Evil at the end, and so forth. This legend says that Schikaneder began his libretto with the idea of writing a harmless fairy story, after which, having learned that a competitor had preceded him in adapting the same story, he simply went on with his work on the basis of another scheme, starting at the point he had already reached. Mozart, we are told, mechanically composed his score to the text thus furnished him, not bothering about what the words meant, and the resulting opera—words and music—was a "fable cut from Harlequin's cloak," the result of that senseless coupling. Truly a strange history, a very helpful excuse for not trying to understand. It will be worthwhile to look at the matter more closely.[1]

For almost half a century, no one seems to have puzzled over all this. Not that no attention was paid to the opera, which had enormous success everywhere and was translated and adapted in every possible manner. In 1801, there even appeared, issued by Alberti, a dialogue in verse entitled *Mozart und Schikaneder*,[2] anonymous at first, but later included in *Theatralische Gespräche um die Zauberflöte* by Perinet, who had written the famous competitive play: nothing about our problem is touched upon in it.

The first known reference appeared about 1840 in a letter from the composer Ignaz von Seyfried, apparently replying to an inquiry.* In fact, at about that time, a journalist named J. P. Lyser had stirred up malicious echoes regarding the relationship between Schikaneder and Mozart, and a controversy on that subject had been running its course. As Seyfried had been orchestral director for Schikaneder (who had died in 1812) from 1797 on, it was natural for his memories to be called upon.

These details present the legend in its first state. Let us sum them up: as his preceding spectacle, Schikaneder had given an *Oberon* adapted by Giesecke from a tale in Wieland's *Dschinnistan*: Seyfried specifies that the two men had worked together in plundering that collection, and that Schikaneder had set aside another story, *Lulu, oder Die Zauberflöte*, as a source for a successor to *Oberon*. He had begun to adapt the latter, but at the moment when the *libretto* was completed up to the first finale, the competitive Theater in der Leopoldstadt had presented a play by Perinet derived from the same source: *Die Zauberzither, oder Kaspar der Fagottist*. Thereupon Schikaneder *refashioned the entire plan*. Later Seyfried says that the score was all but complete when Mozart left for Prague, that he orchestrated and completed it upon his return, ending with the March of the Priests and the Overture, the parts for which, the ink on them still wet,† reached the players' desks at the dress rehearsal.

* A complete translation of this letter appears in Appendix 1.

† This is confirmed by Mozart's autograph catalogue: *cf.* the facsimile in Jean and Brigitte Massin, *W. A. Mozart*, p. 1152.

Seyfried's letter, retailing events that had occurred forty years earlier, is not firsthand evidence, and is not presented as such. In 1791, he had been only fifteen years old, and despite the pride with which he asserts that he had seen Mozart at work in the *"Zauberflöte Häuschen,"* Mozart certainly would not have dreamed of making a confidant of him then. His letter contains excusable errors, but they set the limits within which his testimony can be accepted: those same limits must be set for confidences that Seyfried may have collected.*

According to Seyfried, therefore, what happened was not a "break," but a complete recasting of the libretto. Mozart was not involved, having composed his score only after that recasting was complete—and, naturally, to the final version of the libretto.

All of that is perfectly plausible except for one detail: the play at the Leopoldstadt was presented on June 8. Theaters of that sort were not adapted to long months of preparation and never confided their projects to their competitors, and it is hard to believe that Schikaneder knew about the play before the beginning of May, at the earliest. Well, on June 11, as we know from a letter to Constanze, Mozart had composed the music as far as the duet of the two priests in the second act (No. 11 in his score).† Because it was his custom to compose sequentially, saving only the overture and any stage music for the last, one would have to suppose that in less than five weeks Schikaneder had been able to refashion his libretto entirely, rewrite it completely from beginning to end, and give it to his musician, who in turn had been able to compose two thirds of the score. The first seems possible, but as for the second,

---

* Seyfried was a pupil of both Mozart and Leopold Koželuch, but only for piano. He was not required to know that Schikaneder and Mozart had met at Salzburg; likewise, his documentation on the Vienna lodges is very fantastic, but he himself specifies that he knew on the subject only what he had from Giesecke's recounting.

† In his letter of June 11, Mozart says that "out of sheer boredom" he has just composed an aria for the opera—and quotes a verse of this No. 11.

there are limits to credibility even when one is dealing with Mozart.

And then, what a curious story, that of a writer specializing in plagiarism (not at all an outrage to the ethics of the period) who is suddenly seized by panic at the idea that his next production will resemble that of a competitor, this when he has just achieved an enormous success with an *Oberon* that (according to Komorzynski) was an unblushing plagiarism of a piece by Seyler inspired by the same source and staged only a short time before under the same title!

We can believe, then, that the Leopoldstadt matter had nothing to do with the real reason for a change of plan that actually seems to have occurred. If a change there was, it must have been decided upon much sooner, and for a reason that Schikaneder did not want to confide to Seyfried. In any case, for Seyfried it was not a question of the famous "break": the work had been foreseen and started on one level, but the libretto had been remade later on another. That it bears traces of that transformation may be; but everything was reshaped to fit the second plan. That is what Seyfried tells us, and it is what analysis of the opera will demonstrate.

Seyfried's letter bears neither a date nor an addressee's name; but as its contents are reflected in an article published in 1841 by a literary man named Treitschke* in a short-lived review called *Orpheus*, there is every reason to think that it was addressed to him and shortly preceded the writing of his article.

Treitschke, who did not limit himself to this story alone, was not content merely to transcribe the items of information he had received: being a good journalist, he "arranged" and

---

* He should not be confused with the well-known historian of the same name, Heinrich von Treitschke. Our Georg Friedrich Treitschke is unknown except for the matter we are dealing with and for having redone the libretto of *Fidelio* after Joseph von Sonnleithner. His article is entitled *"Die Zauberflöte, der Dorfbarbier und Fidelio."*

embellished them. According to him, not only had the "libretto" been drafted in part when the Kaspar matter came up, but also Mozart "had composed the first scene" by then. And doubt begins to arise: what became of the sections already written? Destroyed, adapted, or juxtaposed? The published version leaves room for all the hypotheses.

Treitschke's article slumbered for sixteen years. Then, one day in 1857, the *Monatsschrift für Theater und Musik*, a review issued by Josef Klemm, published a sensational unsigned article entitled *"Die Entstehung der Zauberflöte"* (The Genesis of *Die Zauberflöte*), which was little less than a new treatment, still further embellished, of "unpublished" details. "Mozart," we read, "had scarcely composed the first pieces when Joseph Schuster, one of Schikaneder's actors,* appeared to announce some bad news to Schikaneder: he had accidentally been present at a rehearsal of a new magic opera at the Leopoldstadt, Perinet's *Kaspar der Fagottist, oder Die Zauberzither*, with music by Wenzel Müller. He was sadly certain that Perinet—like Schikaneder—had found the subject in A. J. Liebeskind's story *Lulu, oder Die Zauberflöte*, in Wieland's collection: the characters and the action were the same as those of *Die Zauberflöte*. Nothing to do, then, but to abandon (*umwerfen*) what had been done and give the opera another direction." [3] The legend had been born, and it became tenacious. Almost all books and references to *Die Zauberflöte* hark back, whether consciously or not, to that anonymous 1857 article (translated complete in Appendix 2).

To catch the writer in flagrant offenses of inconsequence or ignorance is easy at every turn, however. Following Treitschke, he describes Schikaneder's financial distress and his going to beg Mozart to save him from bankruptcy by accepting the commission. But historians recall that in 1791 Schikaneder was in full financial euphoria after the success of

---

* No actor of this name appears in the first cast of *Die Zauberflöte*.

Oberon, whereas, on the contrary, Mozart was in terrible need, ready to accept any way of earning a living, even that of composing a boring *opera seria* to a libretto (*La Clemenza di Tito*) by Metastasio. He evokes Mozart's trip to Prague in connection with that opera, but places it in March, whereas it took place in August-September. He speaks of the assistance of Süssmayr, saying that he composed a large part of *Die Zauberflöte*, thus confusing the history of that opera with that of the Requiem. As for the "terrible snowstorm" on the day of Mozart's funeral, we shall see later (pp. 72–3) the inanity of that equally tenacious legend, which had been mentioned for the first time only one year earlier, in 1856.

The story of the "break" cannot survive those inconsequences. Can one imagine that as irascible a composer as Mozart, obliged by a competitor to destroy and recompose his work, would—between details about a servant's tardiness and about a missed café rendezvous—have told his wife about his first meeting with the nuisance in these terms: "To cheer myself up I then went to the Kasperle Theater* to see the new opera 'Der Fagottist,' which is making such a sensation, but there is nothing in it at all" (*aber gar nichts daran ist*).[4] If that "nothing" had been the cause of his having to toss his music into a wastebasket, his recriminations would have resounded; and it would not have been to cheer himself up that he would have gone to the theater—three days after the first performance, what is more. Actually, on the day of that première he had peacefully gone to see Constanze in Baden.

All of that makes the 1857 story very hard to believe. Also, the original version of it has been altered little by little, in variations that each subsequent writer repeats, imitating his predecessors without returning to the sources. Dent's descrip-

---

* This refers to the Kaspar in the title. He is the traditional comic personage of Viennese comedy. The phrase has a contemptuous nuance, something like "I went to see a Grade B movie."

tion, already referred to, gives the more or less standard present state of the story:[5]

The initial idea of *Die Zauberflöte*, then, was to be more or less as follows: the hero makes the acquaintance of the fairy queen, who gives him a portrait of her daughter and sends him to rescue her from captivity in the castle of a wicked magician, which he will be able to do by the help of the magic flute. For some reason *which has never yet been satisfactorily explained* [italics mine], the whole plot was completely changed at this stage. The wicked magician was made the agent of good, and the fairy queen the representative of evil. Some of the music was already written, but Schikaneder *was not going to have that wasted* [italics mine], so the join was covered up as well as could be managed.

Thus one can measure out the road traveled after Seyfried's letter. He spoke of a libretto re-begun; Treitschke and the anonymous writer replaced "libretto" with "music." Dent, in turn, interpreted *umwerfen* as meaning to save and juxtapose the pieces already begun!

Thus legends are born. This one is wholly inconsistent. One further detail will suffice to put it out of court: *Die Zauberflöte* opens with the "episode of the serpent," the source of which was not *Lulu*, but *Sethos*—that is, the most Masonic of the sources for the work. Further, it is Dent himself who tells us so.[6]

Ought we, then, to reject everything in that legend? There is no smoke without fire, above all if we prudently remember the amount of smoke given it in the oldest version.[7] To sum up: Marinelli's theater had presented, before Schikaneder, an adaptation of the Wieland-Liebeskind *Lulu, oder Die Zauberflöte*; that much is incontestable. That after *Lulu* Schikaneder reshaped his partly written play so as to transform the fairy tale into a morality full of Masonic symbolism is altogether believable. That the relation between those two occurrences was that of cause and effect is strictly possible, but is an assertion that must be examined cautiously. What is certain is that in no case can we consider the libretto as we have it to have been formed by soldering together two independent sections. The later idea was grafted as much upon the first scenes as upon the last, even if the first scenes preserve more visible traces of the abandoned first writing. At once miscellaneous and homogeneous, the opera is the one and the other at the beginning as much as at the end. And of Mozart's music as we know it, we can affirm that not a single eighth-note was composed to the possible first version of the libretto.

5

Sources of
the Libretto

We have seen that in assuming direction of the Theater auf der Wieden in 1789, Schikaneder had selected the course of entering into direct competition with the Leopoldstadt theater directed by Marinelli, which presented a repertoire of German lyric comedies of fairy-tale, popular nature. Success with *Oberon der Elfenkönig* in 1790 certainly had confirmed him in that orientation.

Oberon had been written and signed by Giesecke, who—Seyfried tells us—had joined Schikaneder in raiding the collection by Wieland from which he had extracted the story. That work is well known: it is an anthology of Oriental tales by various authors published in 1786 and entitled *Dschinnistan*. It does in fact include an *Oberon* of which the author doubtless was Wieland himself, and which Weber would take up again in 1826. In the story, which was inspired by the French *chanson de geste Huon de Bordeaux*, an important role is played by a magic horn that performs miracles. At the end of the first act, Oberon appears in his cloud-chariot and, playing on the horn, involves the menacing Mussulmans irresistibly in a dance that renders them inoffensive. In that scene one can recognize the scene of Monostatos and the glockenspiel.*

That Schikaneder should have thought of mining the same lode for his next spectacle is not surprising. In the same collection there was another story of the same sort: *Lulu, oder Die Zauberflöte*, the author of which was not Wieland but Liebeskind. This time, Prince Lulu rescues the beautiful captive and the horn is replaced by a flute, but the basis of the story is the same. It does not move beyond the limitations of a fairy tale. Thus it is very plausible that Schikaneder's first notion should have been, as Seyfried said, to make from *Die Zauberflöte* a fairy-tale play analogous to *Oberon*, taking the basic idea from Liebeskind's tale. The only difference— it is a sizable one—was that he selected not Wranitzky, but Mozart, to compose the music. Later we shall see the consequences of that decision.

Here is the plot of *Lulu* as summarized by Jahn:[1]

The good fairy Perifirime, called the Radiant Fairy, lives in an old enchanted castle in the Kingdom of Khurasan. During a hunt, Prince Lulu, son of the king, ventures near the castle, a place normally avoided. There the fairy appears to him in all her splendor and promises him a large reward if he will submit to her orders. She confides to him that the evil magician Dilsengbuin, helped by his perfidious servant Barsin, has stolen her finest talisman from her: a fiery golden sword that all the spirits and elements of all countries obey because every being struck by its sparks at once becomes an obedient servant of its possessor. But only a young man who has never known the power of love could, by guile, take possession of the talisman. The fairy designates Lulu as her savior and promises to give him the most precious of her possessions if he will only obey her instructions. They refer to the beautiful Sidi,

* The scene also appears in Weber's *Oberon*, where it has been moved to a different place. It is the valet Scherasmin who plays before the stake being prepared for Huon and Rezia. The source was the same. James Robinson Planché, Weber's English librettist, was a London Frenchman, exactly as the librettist of Marinelli's *Kaspar der Fagottist* was a Vienna Frenchman, Perinet.

her daughter, whose father is Sabalem, King of Kashmir, then under the control of the magician. The latter overwhelms Sidi with his attentions, but she defends herself thanks to the power that has been given her, which allows her to resist all outside power as long as her heart is not touched by love. The fairy gives Lulu two magic gifts: a flute that conquers the hearts of all who hear it, awakes or calms all passion as desired, and a ring that, when it is merely turned, allows its possessor to change himself into the personage of his choice. Furthermore, when the ring is thrown to the ground, it brings the fairy to the help of whoever has so thrown it down.

Lulu, thus equipped, transforms himself into an old man and approaches the magician's castle, built on a rock; at once, by the sound of his flute, he attracts the forest animals, then the magician himself, who leads him into the castle, where he will try to awaken the love of the reticent beauty. Lulu succeeds in winning the confidence of the magician and of his son, the dwarf Barka—whose mother is none other than Barsin—and also wins the love of the beautiful Sidi. During a feast, he succeeds in putting both of them to sleep and seizing the sword. With the help of the spirits, and finally thanks to the appearance of the fairy, he overcomes all the obstacles set by the magician, who flees in the form of an owl, his son taking on that of a barn owl. The fairy demolishes the castle on the rock and takes the lovers in her chariot to her own castle, where the kings of Khurasan and Kashmir bless their union.

Reading that, one sees that the resemblances to Die Zauberflöte are real, but summary and wholly external, becoming smaller as we proceed. Seyfried's version, according to which Schikaneder entirely rewrote his play after having prepared up to the first finale a first version inspired by that story, is quite believable.

This would explain why the libretto is called Die Zauberflöte though that accessory plays only a very secondary role in it, and one could easily discover in the story of the hunter lost in the fairy's domain the point of departure from which Schikaneder, having decided to alter the meaning of the play, would have developed his new idea, under influences that were totally different. But what is certain, I repeat, is that, contrary to the legend of the "break," this second scenario was revised from the first scene on, that the entire play is homogeneous from this point of view, and that Mozart's music was written from beginning to end in view of the final drama, not in view of the fairy story originally envisaged.

We have also said that it seems unbelievable that the matter of the rival theater could have been the real cause of that change of direction. We saw that argument undermined by an examination of the calendar. That impression is confirmed if one examines Perinet's play, of which in turn Jahn gave this résumé:[2]

While a member of a hunting party, Prince Armidoro, whose servant is called Kaspar Bita, wanders into the kingdom of the fairy Perifirime. She sends him to the home of the magician Bosphoro, giving him a zither having all the powers of the magic flute. Through a small sprite named Pizichi, who knows how to be helpful in difficult moments, he sends Kaspar a magic bassoon, which gives rise to jests in doubtful taste. The magic power of the ring, which is capable of transforming the prince, now into an old man, now into a young one, is presented naïvely to the spectator, who must appeal to his imagination if the desired effect is to be obtained. Zumio is the magician's fat servant. He eyes the young girls and becomes amorous of Palmyre, companion of the beautiful Sidi, who in turn becomes amorous of Kaspar. After Armidoro and Kaspar have succeeded, thanks to the magic instruments, in winning the sympathy of Bosphoro and Zumio, they finally enter the castle and win the love of the young girls, but not without awakening the distrust of the men, who try to get rid of them so as to take possession of the instruments. Perifirime saves them during a boatride. Thanks to Pizichi's warnings, an attempt at poisoning fails. Finally, during a dinner, Armidoro succeeds in putting them to sleep, thanks to the magic instruments, and lays hold of the fiery sword. Then he can subject all the spirits to his power. In the midst of all that, Perifirime appears, punishes Bosphoro, and takes the lovers back to her palace.

That, then, was the play staged by Marinelli on June 8, 1791, at the Theater in der Leopoldstadt, the play over which Schikaneder is said to have worried so much that he gave up a direct adaptation of Liebeskind's tale. One notes that, contrary to what the anonymous writer asserted in 1857, Perinet's libretto made so free with the original that his competitor need not have felt pangs of conscience, especially if, as is probable, his conscience reasoned only in terms of commerce.

However that may be, it is certain that, starting from the groundwork supplied by the story, Schikaneder—alone or in collaboration—imagined an entirely different development, and that for it he must have turned to a literature of a completely different sort. What could it have been?

In the first place, it seems evident that Mozart must have talked to him about two earlier dramas of Masonic illumination upon which he had collaborated: *Thamos, König in Ägypten*, and *Zaide*, whole scenes of which one finds transplanted into *Die Zauberflöte*. *Thamos* furnished, in the Egyptian framework dear to the Freemasons, the notions of the conflict between Light and Night, of the symbolic kidnapping carried out by the priests of the Sun, of the final marriage with an initiated prince. The characters are faithfully parallel: the Queen of the Night is called Mirza; Pamina, Saïs; and Sarastro, Sethos—all as in the novel that I shall discuss shortly. As for *Zaide*, at least one scene was brought over from it more or less verbatim: the episode of the portrait, which furthermore was almost hackneyed in the literature of the period. The source can be discovered in one of Klopstock's odes, *Die frühen Gräber*, which Gluck set to music about 1770. In *Zaide*, the unfinished Singspiel that Mozart had begun in 1779, the slave Zaide, coming upon the sleeping Gomatz, falls in love with him at first sight and places her portrait beside him. Waking up and seeing the portrait,

Gomatz immediately falls in love and sings of his love in an aria resembling Tamino's.

If Mozart really suggested the transmutation of *Die Zauber-flöte* into a Masonic play, he did not take his friend Schika-neder off guard. Although the subject never had been treated with the allusive precision that one encounters in *Die Zauber-flöte*, it was "in the air." Marinelli, Schikaneder's rival, had in his repertoire a *Megära, die fürchterliche Hexe* (Megära, the Terrible Witch) by Philipp Hafner (1761), in which "wicked women and greathearted magicians" rubbed shoul-ders, and during the preceding year (September 1790) had presented a big spectacle opera by Wenzel Müller, *Das Sonnenfest der Braminen* (The Sun Festival of the Brah-mins), with ceremonies very like Sarastro's. Also in 1790, Schikaneder himself had written, for Benedikt Schack, his future Tamino, *Der Stein der Weisen* (The Philosopher's Stone), which brings us still closer to the final version of *Die Zauberflöte*. In it, a magician explains how he was initiated into the Egyptian mysteries, one sees a trial by fire and water, and the comic companion of the two chief protagonists has a certain relation to Papageno.[3]

Vienna was not the only place in which these subjects were the order of the day. Lessing, considered an authority on Masonic matters, had written *Nathan der Weise*, a play along the same lines. About 1770, the Foire Saint-Ovide at Paris had presented a vaudeville entitled *Arlequin Franc-Maçon*, in which Harlequin, unable to marry Columbine because he has no money, decides to be initiated so as to achieve profit-able relations, but lets himself become the victim of two swindlers who arrange a parodistic scene of initiation.[4]

In 1784, the Stadttheater at Vienna presented a three-act *Lustspiel* in praise of the Freemasons entitled *Die Freimaurer*; it was unsigned, but the music has been attributed to Christian Jacob Wagenseil.[5] One could unearth numerous other examples.

But *Die Zauberflöte* goes well beyond all of its predecessors both in seriousness and in detailed Masonic information. As such seriousness was neither the dominant trait of the suburban theater nor, as is known, Schikaneder's essential quality, and as Giesecke's role in its writing remains subject to cautious treatment, one can only think that some other influence is manifested in it. I have already said that it seems logical to attribute that influence to Mozart, possibly supported by Born.

The latter, we have seen, had published in 1784, in the Vienna *Journal für Freymaurer*, an article entitled *"Über die Mysterien der Ägypter."* That the librettist of *Die Zauberflöte* made free use of it is certain. But he seems also to have had direct access to the work that the philosopher had utilized most, and which figured among the Masonic "classics"—an enormous French novel issued anonymously in 1731, the work of the Abbé Jean Terrasson, a translator of Diodorus Siculus and professor of Greek and Latin philosophy at the Collège de France: *Sethos, histoire ou vie tirée des monuments, anecdotes de l'ancienne Égypte . . . traduit d'un manuscrit grec.* Dent sums it up by saying that Sethos "is an Egyptian prince, born in the century before the Trojan War. The first part of the book deals with his education and his initiation into the mysteries; the second part describes his travels in Africa as universal lawgiver for savage tribes; finally, he returns to Egypt and retires into a college of initiates for the rest of his life." [6] Translated into many languages—into German first in 1732 and again in 1778—Terrasson's novel passed until the nineteenth century as a historical authority on the Egyptian mysteries.

It was clearly a hoax, but the hoax of a well-read man nour-

SETHOS,

HISTOIRE OU VIE

Tirée des Monuments, anecdotes de l'ancienne Egypte ;

Ouvrage dans lequel on trouve la description des Initiations aux Myſteres Egyptiens, traduit d'un manuſcrit Grec.

LIVRE · PREMIER.

L E S Egyptiens , qui font remonter l'an-
cienneté de leur origine juſqu'à des temps
où notre hiſtoire n'atteint pas , diſent que
les dieux ont été leurs premiers rois. Ils en
comptent ſept : Vulcain , le Soleil , Agatho-
démon , Saturne , Oſiris , Iſis & Typhon.
Par Vulcain , auquel ils n'aſſignent point
de commencement , leurs philoſophes en-
tendoient le feu élémentaire répandu par

Tome I.   **A**

First page of the novel *Sethos*, edition of 1767.
Collection Roger Cotte.

ished on early writers and knowing how to make use of them: one finds traces in it of Diodorus, Plutarch, Apuleius, and Heliodorus' *Ethiopica*.[7] The working-out could easily be superimposed upon that sketched after *Lulu*, and one clearly sees the transfer from one to the other: the Queen of the Night, a transformation of the fairy Perifirime, notably borrowed her chief characteristics from Daluca, Sethos' mother-in-law, "a lady who herself was rather disreputable, and [who] being desirous of becoming omnipotent at court, did her best to get rid of the wise philosophers who had frequented it in the days of the late queen," which she attempts to accomplish by giving " 'the sole empire of conversation to such ladies of the court as she had observed the most vain.' " [8] The Three Ladies and many details that we come upon while reading *Die Zauberflöte* came directly from *Sethos*.

But all of those "sources" (undoubtedly one could locate others) remain very secondary. The essential source, almost the only true one, was above all the Masonic ritual considered not only in its literal sense, but also in the very essence of its symbolism and of the initiate traditions that supported it. In our analysis, we shall see that the entire libretto, sustained by the music, was fashioned upon it. That is unquestionably why, in a society impregnated with avowed or latent Masonry, and independently of the exceptional quality of its music, the destiny of *Die Zauberflöte* has remained unique in its genre.

6

History of the Libretto and Its Growth

We have a miraculously exact statement about the beginning of this history: "It was on March 7, 1791, at eight o'clock in the morning . . ." Unhappily, we already have seen what little faith that romantic story deserves (it can be read in Appendix 2 by anyone particularly interested).

In fact, it is probable that the project was started somewhat earlier: a letter from Schikaneder to Mozart, dated September 5, 1790, certainly seems to refer to it.[1] Mozart probably began to work at the beginning of March 1791, so that a six-month interval is not excessive for all that had to precede the composing if the two preceding chapters are correct: discussions between Schikaneder and Mozart, the start on the first version of the libretto, its abandonment, the search for a new plan, and finally the preparation of the libretto as we know it.

Because the Leopoldstadt affair almost certainly must be dismissed, no document tells us dependably what occurred during that time. But conjecture is easy. In fact, one can easily imagine Mozart's reaction when Schikaneder came to him to propose his fairy story. The writer of the anonymous 1857 article noted it with his customary clumsiness, but doubtless with some relation to what Mozart actually said: "I have never written a fairy-tale opera." As we shall see in Chapter 7, the mature Mozart never had composed for the theater without a governing moral or social idea. There was none in *Lulu*. And one can easily imagine his effort to persuade the director-writer to give his opera some more substantial content. Magic-religious stories were in the atmosphere, as we have seen, and Mozart was a practicing Mason. Schikaneder, though doubtless less fervent after his Ratisbon experiences, was nonetheless also a Freemason. The relationship of the two men was sufficiently close so that they could agree to deal with Masonic materials, above all if Mozart was able at that time to present Schikaneder to Born, whose influence was considerable. Born would probably have urged them to reread carefully the sources of the initiate literature, notably his own 1784 article and the novel *Sethos*. For his part, Mozart certainly would have spoken of his earlier music for *Thamos* and for *Zaide*. The Marinelli affair undoubtedly took place a little later. And it was very probably thus that the libretto of *Die Zauberflöte* was brought to its final form.

That different libretto must have been completed, or at least put in condition to serve the composer, toward the end of February 1791. We have no indication that Mozart did any work on the score until then. On January 5, 1791, he completed his Piano Concerto in B flat, K.595, and then devoted himself above all to a multitude of minor, but gainful tasks: carnival dances for the court, fantasies for mechanical organs, etc. His financial situation was alarming, and one cannot read without distress the letter that he wrote on April 13 to his "Friend and Brother" Puchberg to beg for a loan of twenty florins, and the one written at the end of the month, in which he excuses himself for still not being able to repay it. Just as harrowing is that petition to the city of Vienna, in which the glorious court composer humbly begs the municipality for the honor of being named, without stipends, assistant to and substitute for Kapellmeister Hoffman, "who is very old"—this in the hope of obtaining the Cathedral Kapellmeistership when Hoffman finally dies.[2]

From March on (and this would seem to explain why that month has been named), Mozart's collaboration with Schikaneder took on tangible form. One after another, Mozart set, to words from Schikaneder's repertoire, an aria (*Per questa bella mano*, K.612) for his friend Thaddäus Gerl, a singer in Schikaneder's troupe who later would be Sarastro, and composed, on a theme—*"Ein Weib ist das herrlichste Ding"* —by Benedikt Schack (the future Tamino), from a Schikaneder Singspiel, *Der dumme Gärtner*—a set of piano variations (K.613) of which the Massins noted the curiously "Papagenoish" character.

A gap in Mozart's catalogue to the end of July signifies that he was working above all on the opera. Nevertheless, in those four months, he composed not only more than half of *Die Zauberflöte* (with several successive versions of some of the numbers), but also the String Quintet (K.614) in E-flat major (April 12), the Adagio and Rondo for harmonica, flute, oboe, viola, and cello (K.617, May 23), the celebrated *Ave Verum* (K.618), two Masonic cantatas, and several other works that have been lost.

Early in June, Constanze, who was pregnant, went to Baden for a cure, taking her elder son, Karl. Her husband, driven by work on *Die Zauberflöte*, unwillingly had to let her travel alone, for Schikaneder and he considered it necessary to meet almost every day (another fact that interestingly supports our hypothesis). Remaining in the empty apartment in Vienna, Mozart struggled on amid domestic cares, of which his correspondence gives daily accounts. Despite that, he worked intensively. In order to make his comings and goings less numerous, Schikaneder shortly placed at his disposition, as a place in which he could work peacefully, a small wooden structure near the theater. Gossiping tongues babbled, but that did not matter. The cabin still survives. Dismantled at the time of the demolition of the Theater auf der Wieden, it was taken to Salzburg and is now in the garden of the Mozarteum.

On June 11, Mozart reached the second-act duet of the priests (No. 11). Also on that day, returning from one of his many trips to Baden, he became aware for the first time, with the indifference noted, of that famous *Kaspar* which, according to the 1857 article, caused him to redo entirely a section of what he had already composed. His son Franz Xaver was born on July 26, and at the end of that month he could foresee the end of his work on the opera.

Then, suddenly, two commissions materialized to distract him. One, received at the end of July, has given rise to many legends that do not concern us here: it was the famous Requiem, with its "messenger in gray," so freely romanticized later. The other, more immediate, is of no great artistic interest, but has some importance as underlining the musician's shaky social position. It was the composition of the *opera seria* to be performed in connection with the coronation of Leopold II at Prague—*La Clemenza di Tito*, which he tossed off in less than a month, but which nonetheless was a drain at an inopportune moment.

On about August 15, Mozart left Vienna for Prague, whence he did not return until about September 15, only two weeks before the première of *Die Zauberflöte*, which was still not finished. The autograph catalogue does not mention the completion of the Overture until the evening of the dress rehearsal, September 28, or of the March of the Priests until after that event. Two days later, September 30, with Mozart himself conducting, the E-major chord was sounded before the lowered curtain of the Theater auf der Wieden.

The anonymous writer of the 1857 article, whom there is no reason to doubt in this, said that Mozart was in the pit only for the first three performances, but we know that he returned very often, with friends or with important individuals, to hear the opera. We even know about a joke that he played on Schikaneder one day, taking the place of the glockenspiel-player in the wings (see p. 125). According to the same writer, the reception of the opera was hesitant at first, but finally became enthusiastic, and thereafter never diminished. Nevertheless, no Vienna periodical took notice of it: it was being performed in an outlying theater of no importance. Later, in 1793, a Berlin periodical asserted that the performance had been mediocre and that the music had been massacred.[3] But, as the Massins observed, if that had been the case Mozart probably would have complained and would not have taken such pleasure in returning to hear the opera every time he could.

An infinitely precious document has survived from those performances: it is a series of six colored engravings representing, with the precision of theatrical drawings, moments in Schikaneder's original production. It must be admitted that they do not flatter the production, which was praised greatly by its contemporaries, and that they often seem to us singularly puerile. What can one think, for example, of Sarastro's lions (Plate 17) in patched paper?

These designs, by Josef and Peter Schaffer, appeared in 1794 in the *Allgemein-Europäische Journal*, Brünn. No doubt of their authenticity is possible:[4] the Birdcatcher's costume is in every detail that of the 1793 edition of the libretto (slightly modifying that of 1791). Not only does one observe various symbolic details of rubrics that were quickly forgotten in later stagings (e.g., in Plate 15, the serpent cut into three pieces), but also one is struck by Papageno's characteristic profile, with its low forehead and prominent chin, a profile that corresponds exactly to the silhouette of Schikaneder as it appears in several portraits (*cf.* Plate 24). On the other hand, one may be more reticent about the likeness of the celebrated portrait of Papageno so often reproduced without reservation, which ornaments the first edition of the libretto—and that despite its being dated 1791 and despite a notice in the handbill offering for sale "the libretto containing two prints representing Herr Schikaneder in his role of Papageno and in his true costume" * (Plate 11). At best (our man was then forty-three), it portrays Schikaneder as singularly rejuvenated and beautified.

Die Zauberflöte held the boards until well after Mozart's death. A second edition of the libretto, resembling the first, but ornamented with a frontispiece and a supplementary tailpiece, had to be printed in 1793. A third, different in typography, was produced at Berlin in 1794. The success, in fact, rapidly expanded beyond the walls of the Theater auf der Wieden. On February 24, 1801, the Kärntnertortheater staged the opera in new décors, enraging Schikaneder, who was excluded, his name not even being mentioned. He in turn took revenge by organizing another production, of great splendor, in the new Theater an der Wien, successor to the old Theater auf der Wieden, adding to Papageno's entrance aria topical couplets addressed to the audience:

> *Der Papageno ist zwar da*
> *Doch singt er noch nicht hopsasa . . .*

"Papageno certainly is here, but he is not yet singing *hopsasa*; only one victory will rejoice him, that of your judgment. Long ago I promised to make the magic flute sing and

---

* There are in fact two prints, only one of which represents Papageno; the other is the frontispiece representing the Trial by Earth.

resound, but painter, costumer, and machinist demanded this long delay."

In 1810, it was the Theater in der Leopoldstadt, the former rival, which gave Die Zauberflöte, and in 1812 the two theaters played it simultaneously.

Outside Vienna, we find Die Zauberflöte performed in Prague in October 1792, in Frankfurt-am-Main in 1793, in Berlin in 1794. Hamburg was more hesitant: it was only after many tergiversations that Mozart's masterpiece finally was played there in 1793. In that year, too, the opera was performed at Braunschweig, but with the libretto refashioned by Vulpius, and in French—and also in Dresden, in the original version. There were also productions in Dutch, Swedish, Danish, and Polish. Die Zauberflöte was welcomed enthusiastically everywhere but in Italy and England, where there was long delay in accepting that "musica scelerata." In London, it was heard first in Italian (1811), then in German (1833), and finally in English (1838), this last with the libretto translated by James Robinson Planché, librettist of Weber's Oberon.

In Paris the fortunes of Die Zauberflöte were extremely curious. It appeared there in 1801—or at least there appeared in its place a work that the producers had the effrontery to present as a French translation of it "revised" by Ludwig Wenzel Lachnith, a Czech musician living in Paris, to a text by Étienne Morel, called Morel de Chédeville. Morel was the brother-in-law of the all-powerful Baron de la Ferté, who had been intendant of the Menus-Plaisirs until 1790; he had made his debut as an "arranger" in 1782 by reshaping Quinault's Thésée libretto for Gossec's use. Fortified by his connections, he received as many orders for librettos after the Revolution as before it, and succeeded in being named accountant of the Opéra in 1802, a fact that doubtless explains the obstinacy with which every attempt to make known the original of Die Zauberflöte rather than his arrangement of it was rejected.

It would be difficult to imagine a more shameless massacre than that scandalous version, which was even rebaptized *Les Mystères d'Isis*. Not only were the action transformed, the characters modified, the order of the numbers changed, but also some numbers were suppressed and others borrowed from other operas (notably from *La Clemenza di Tito*). More serious, Mozart's music was thoroughly "corrected": Monostatos's aria was assigned to Papagena (who was called Mona), duets became trios, etc. In the Overture, the ritual rhythms in the middle of the fugue were modified to be like those of the beginning. Two measures of plain tonic chords were added to the terminal cadence, and so forth (*cf.* Plates 39 and 40).[5] Even the French critics of that day were scandalized (the production was referred to punningly as *Les Misères d'ici*), and the most amusing thing is to find among the chorus of protesters the name of the most famous emulator of Lachnith, Castil-Blaze, the perpetrator of *Robin des Bois*, which was to be to Weber's *Der Freischütz* what *Les Mystères d'Isis* had been to Mozart's *Die Zauberflöte*.

That did not prevent the "work" of the Opéra's accountant from being played 130 times between its première (August 23, 1801) and 1827. As late as May 1, 1836, Berlioz took account of it in the *Journal des débats* in these terms: "It was thus, dressed up as an ape, got up grotesquely in cheap finery, with one eye gouged out, an arm withered, a leg broken, that they dared to present the greatest musician in the world to this French public, so delicate, so demanding, saying to it: 'Look—Mozart,' etc. O miserable . . . etc." [6]

Not until February 23, 1865, did Paris finally have its own faithful version of *Die Zauberflöte*, the translation by Charles Truinet, called "Nuitter," and Alexandre Beaume, called "Beaumont," staged at the Théâtre-Lyrique (a troupe from Aachen, however, had played the opera in German at the Théâtre-Italien as early as 1829). In 1909, the Opéra-Comique

LES MYSTÈRES D'ISIS

ACTE PREMIER.

*Le Théâtre représente les Portiques qui entourent l'enceinte habitée par
les Prêtres d'Isis. On voit, d'un côté, l'entrée du Palais de Myrrene; de l'autre,
celle des souterrains qui conduisent à la demeure des Prêtres et au Temple d'Isis.
Plus loin, un Pont sur un Canal du Nil: on découvre dans le fond diverses Pyramides,
et dans le lointain la vue de Memphis. Au lever de la Toile, les Prêtres et Prêtresses sont
rangés sur le Théâtre, où ils attendent l'heure fixée pour offrire un sacrifice à Isis (il est nuit)*

SCÈNE PREMIÈRE.

First scene of *Les Mystères d'Isis*.
Collection Institut de Musicologie, Paris.

performed *La Flûte enchantée* in a fresh translation by Alexandre Bisson and Paul Ferrier—and in 1922, the Opéra replaced the Nuitter-Beaumont version with one by J.-G. Prod'homme and Jules Kienlin which had been sung in 1912 at the Théâtre de la Monnaie, Brussels.*

Not only was *Die Zauberflöte* performed often; it also was the object of innumerable parodies, imitations, and "sequels," [7] and Schikaneder never relinquished the dream of repeating its success. Alas, Mozart no longer was there. In 1797, Schikaneder fabricated an uninteresting new mixture under the title *Babylons Pyramiden,* dividing composition of the music between Georg Anton Gallus (Johann Mederitsch) and Peter von Winter. In 1798, it was a "second part" of *Die Zauberflöte* which he announced as *Das Labirint, oder Der Kampf mit den Elementen,* also with music by Winter. As for Goethe, after patronizing a staging of *Die Zauberflöte* at Weimar in 1794—with the libretto rewritten by his brother-in-law, Vulpius—he projected a sequel, the plan and some fragments of which have survived.[8]

Goethe's enthusiasm for *Die Zauberflöte* unquestionably depended more upon the initiate value that he recognized in the libretto than upon love for the music. That value, nonetheless, was very slow to be recognized. At the time of the première, naturally, nothing had been said or printed concerning the Masonic significance of the work. The initiates were counted upon to understand it by themselves; there was no question of explaining it to the profane. The first attempts at exegesis appeared in 1794, and then proved contradictory. Under the title *"Allegorie aus der Zauberflöte,"* in the *Journal des Luxus und der Moden* IX, published at Königsberg, Ludwig

---

* The Prod'homme-Kienlin translation has been published. Remarkably faithful in the spoken prose scenes and very adroit in the sung verse, it is, on the other hand, highly fantastic in its translation of the rubrics and stage directions, which refer to the production at the Opéra, not at all to Schikaneder's libretto.

von Blatzko, the earliest, spoke of the struggle between Light
and the Shadows and of the allegory of Good and Evil.[9] But
in that same year, in a pamphlet entitled *Göttersprache gegen
die Jakobiner*, Johann Valentin Eybel put forward an entirely
different explanation. For him, it was a political *roman à clef*:
the Queen of the Night represented the tyranny of Louis XIV
(!); Pamina was Liberty, daughter of despotism; Tamino was
the people; the Three Ladies represented the deputies of the
Three Estates, etc.[10] Not until 1857 was the word "Freemasonry" spoken clearly in connection with *Die Zauberflöte*—by
Leopold von Sonnleithner.[11] He, however, following the details of the anonymous article appearing in that same year and
dealing with the change of plan in midstream, had the Masonic references begin only at the end of Act I. Once that departure had been made, all subsequent commentators fell
more or less under its influence. In 1861, in the fourth number
of his journal *Aus der Mansarde*, Georg Friedrich Daumer developed Blatzko's *roman à clef* idea in an anticlerical way: because Sarastro represented the Kingdom of Light, the Queen
of the Night must be Superstition (in which term he included
Religion); her Three Ladies represented the three religions—
Jewish, Christian, and Islamic, and so forth.[12] Five years later
(1866), a Leipzig theologian and Freemason, Moritz Alexander Zille, again took up Eybel's historical thesis, but set it in
the context of the period of the opera's composition: Sarastro
was Ignaz von Born, Tamino the Emperor Joseph II, Monostatos a certain Hoffmann who was known as a renegade
Mason, etc. As for Pamina, she was the Austrian people whom
her mother, Maria Theresia (the Queen of the Night) wished
to set up against the Freemasons.[12] Later hypotheses all were
more or less inspired by one or another of those mentioned.
In 1914, Maurice Kufferath was undoubtedly the first to call
attention, though still very prudently, to the relationship of
the libretto to aspects of the Masonic ritual.[13] Paul Nettl, in

several works, and notably in his short book entitled *Mozart und die königliche Kunst,* furnished, unsystematically, more numerous examples; I have already cited the considerable contribution of Jean and Brigitte Massin. Finally, I had completed preparation of the present book when I had the satisfaction of finding, in a little-known work prefaced by an incontestable Masonic authority, confirmation of the correctness of my point of departure and of some of the comparisons that I had suggested without having located the earlier model (among others, that of the subterranean scene with the Cabinet of Reflection).[14] The convergence of all these inquiries is significant. I believe that I have gone much farther than my predecessors, but I have had to render homage to their labors, and if I have fallen into error along the way, I hope that my temerity will be excused.

7

Mozart
and the
Singspiel

Mozart's attitude toward the Singspiel, already referred to, requires further discussion because it involves not only his individual position, but also an increasingly general tendency that touches the history of *Die Zauberflöte*, of ideas, of the lyric theater, and of the theater as a whole.

Further, one may object to the well-established usage of the German term in a foreign language as though it dealt with a specific genre and were untranslatable. The Singspiel is very simply the German equivalent of the French *opéra-comique*. One may disagree with the usual cliché asserting that *opéra-comique* is a "specifically French" form, the Singspiel "specifically German," for the latter manifestly derives from the former and both show the influence of the Italian *opera buffa*.

However that may be, at the end of the eighteenth century, the *opera seria*, stationary in its formulas and its ennui, no longer interested anyone except a small, isolated audience of aristocrats. The Italian *opera buffa* too came to the point of revolving in its eternal stories of deceived dotards and disguised soubrettes. The attempt to revitalize the lyric theater came more and more to be concentrated within the framework of the *opéra-comique*.

France set the example. In 1752, Jean-Jacques Rousseau's *Le Devin du village*, creating the prototype of the genre,[1] adumbrated its ambitions: slender as it was, the action took on, in the context of the period, a philosophic value as an apology for "Nature" which one searches for vainly in its models: "In town they are more lovable; in the village they know better how to love." With Philidor's *Le Jardinier et son seigneur* (1761), the tone was raised, though still tentatively, to that of social satire: "These gentlemen here have only one finger for doing good; they have nine fingers for doing evil." Monsigny in 1762, with *Le Roi et le fermier* (and above all with *Le Déserteur* in 1769), then Philidor in 1765 with *Tom Jones*, and later Grétry with *Lucile* (1769) and Dalayrac with *Nina, ou La Folle par amour* (1786), went on to follow the literary tendencies of the new "tearful comedy" of La Chaussée, Sedaine, and the later Beaumarchais: their *opéra-comique* no longer wanted merely to amuse, but aimed at arousing emotion, freed of having to introduce into the action an episodic supernumerary like the dragon Montauciel in *Le Déserteur*, the Viennese response to which was the various avatars of "Kasperl," whether called Pedrillo or Papageno.

The German Singspiel followed the French example only after some twenty years, but was not long thereafter in trying to go beyond it. Not content with arousing emotion, it wanted to make its audience think, and *Die Zauberflöte* was to be the strongest expression of that ambition. Let us take a single example, that of Mozart. He first handled the genre in 1768, when he was twelve, in a simple German adaptation of the libretto of Favart's *Bastien et Bastienne*, a vaudeville parody of Rousseau's *Le Devin du village*. In view of the guidance given the boy, the choice was significant. The little work has been smothered in its composer's catalogue under the avalanche of Italian titles of the *La Finta Something* sort, which, like all of his confreres, he turned out. Despite his many enthusiastic declarations in favor of "German opera" (by which he meant, above all, *opéra-comique*),* we have to wait until about 1780 to see him take action. But his purpose was constantly reaffirmed from then on, as can be proved by simply enumerating the theatrical works in German which he composed after that.

Nothing survives of the "melodrama" *Semiramis* that Mozart projected and began at Mannheim in 1778 on his return from Paris. But conjecture is easy. It must have concerned an adaptation of Voltaire's tragedy by Baron Otto von Gemmingen, who is well known to us. A great friend of Wolfgang's, Gemmingen became his first Venerable[2] when he was initiated in 1784. J. and B. Massin very astutely sniffed out the scent of mystery in this regard in the correspondence between Mozart and his father. They deduced that if it seemed necessary to be secretive about *Semiramis*, that was because, like its model, it contained "many ideas of the *Aufklärung* which could be useful for Masonic propaganda."[3]

A similar atmosphere surrounded Mozart's collaboration with Baron von Gebler. In 1773, Gebler, having unsuccessfully sounded out several musicians (Gluck included) who were Freemasons like himself, had entrusted to the seventeen-year-old Mozart the task of composing incidental music for

* I am surprised by Dent's interpretation (pp. 28–9) of a remark made by Mozart in a letter to his father on February 4, 1778, about a man who "perhaps thinks that people remain twelve years old for ever." According to Dent, this referred to Mozart's indignant refusal to participate in the founding of a German opera: ". . . the Emperor intended to establish a permanent German opera at Vienna, but . . . he [Mozart] knew that it meant comic opera, and he had put that away with childish things." Reading the original letter suffices to see that this was not at all the reason. Mozart refused to compose a comic opera for which no performance was guaranteed, and was vexed because the imperial intendant had written to Leopold Mozart about "*ihr Sohn*" instead of "*der Herr Sohn.*" The cited clause from Mozart's letter referred solely to that point.

his "heroic drama" *Thamos, König in Ägypten.* In 1786, Gebler too would be Mozart's Venerable.[4] His script already contained in essence all the themes of the *Zauberflöte* text. Mozart must have been aware of that, for he used motives from the *Thamos* music in *Die Zauberflöte,* and he must have thought well of the earlier work, as he took it up again in 1779 to reshape and improve it.

The series of great Singspiels opened with the incomplete *Zaide* of 1780. The discovery, about 1940, of its complete libretto[5] permits us to follow its action up to the dénouement. And, as the Massins subtly demonstrated, that dénouement transmutes a banal story of stylish *"turquerie"* into a veritable thesis piece in the line of the *Lettres persanes* and Voltaire's *contes.* Through the influential Joseph von Sonnenfels, Aulic councilor and president of the Academy of Fine Arts, but also secretary of the Loge zur wahren Eintracht, Mozart had become aware of *Nathan der Weise,* the play then being completed by Sonnenfels's close friend Lessing. The theme of *Nathan der Weise* was very close to that of *Zaide,* and in it the "noble representative of the philosophy of the Enlightenment . . . takes up in the form of an apologue one of the chief precepts of his *Gespräche für Freymaurer"* (Massin): a protest, by means of an idyllic depiction of the greatness of the Oriental soul, against "the Christian pretension to a monopoly of the high moral values of humanity."

Zaide, the actual title of which no doubt was *Das Serail,* and which also includes a prefiguration of the portrait aria in *Die Zauberflöte,* was to some degree a rough draft of *Die Entführung aus dem Serail.* In that third of Mozart's Singspiels, composed two years later, we find the same themes reinforced. The superficial aspect of the anecdote should not mask the background revealed in the final vaudeville: "Nothing is more odious than vengeance. On the contrary, to be humane, to have a good heart, and to pardon without personal resentment—that alone is characteristic of great souls." Basically, this is already Sarastro's aria: in form, it resembles very closely all the moralities in *Die Zauberflöte*. And it all derives from the same current of thought, the one to which Montesquieu's *Lettres persanes* (1721) had given impulse and which had been transferred to the lyric stage in *"Le Turc généreux,"* * the first *entrée* of *Les Indes galantes*, by Fuzelier and Rameau (1735).[6] Was Rameau a Freemason? No decisive document supplying a definite answer has been found, but that he was has been presumed more than once,[7] and the analogy of conception between Rameau's *Zoroastre* (1749) and Mozart's Sarastro has often been noted.

Die Zauberflöte was Mozart's last Singspiel. Between *Die Entführung* and it, he composed the amusing but rather insignificant *Schauspieldirektor*, which need not detain us; it is less a Singspiel than an occasional skit composed to a subject furnished personally by Joseph II to poke fun at the little oddities of theatrical singers. Also, in this rapid review, I have not mentioned the comedies in Italian, the choice of texts for which counted less with the composer than did those for the "German operas," each word of which had significance for the audience. Nevertheless, once the distressing period of those *Finta Somethings* was past, can one say that this preoccupation disappeared? Absolutely not. The choice of Beaumarchais as source for *Le Nozze di Figaro* (1786) was significant, even though Lorenzo Da Ponte may have blunted the piquancies of the French play somewhat. *Don Giovanni*, the *dramma giocoso* of the following year, testifies to the preoccupations so often referred to,[8] and the stupidity of the action of *Così fan tutte* does not prevent it from presenting a well-defined social message, if only in its title: that of proclaiming

---

* Fuzelier pointed out as his source, not Montesquieu, but an article in the *Mercure de France* (1734) about the Grand Vizier Topal Osman, "so well known for his excessive generosity."

the moral fragility of the fair sex, a theme that *Die Zauber-flöte*, as we shall see clearly later on, in turn took as its mission to develop, at the same time proceeding to the conclusion and corrective that had been lacking.

So it would seem, as I have already suggested, that in his maturity Mozart never "wrote for no reason." And that idea is perhaps the key to the problem examined in Chapter 4.

8

---◆◀◎▶◆---

Freemasonry in Vienna in the Eighteenth Century

Everything said up to this point has led toward the same point of convergence, the Freemasonry that *Die Zauberflöte* seeks to glorify by means of transparent symbols. For those who know that movement only from descriptions by its adversaries or the picture that it was possible to offer in the time of the minister Combes, it may be useful to describe it by appealing to its own historians. The political and often anticlerical evolution that it underwent during the past century, at least in France,[1] the virulence of the polemic slogans that it aroused, the repeated condemnations that it has suffered at the hands of successive popes, the scandals, finally, with which its enemies, in both good faith and bad, have not ceased trying to involve it—all that is of a nature to give to one of today's "profane" a false picture of what, in Mozart's time, was a movement ruled by ideas that brought together in scarcely conceivable proportion everything that Europe could count of intelligence and generosity, and which sustained in Mozart, as in so many others, the proselytizing enthusiasm to which *Die Zauberflöte* offers us spirited testimony.

The veritable tidal wave that constituted the history of Freemasonry in the eighteenth century is one of those compensatory, inevitable, periodic phenomena which follow every weakening of the great traditional spiritual values. Schisms, heresies, great exercises in moral improvement are only various aspects of this phenomenon, with which the history of the Church is studded, and which made Cathari, Franciscans, and Lutherans into neighbors with differing destinies. In the eighteenth century, once again the Church in many places was only a political institution or framework empty, or almost empty, of spiritual substance. The originality of Freemasonry lay in not rebelling against those lacks but pretending to ignore them and in itself offering to its members a substitute responsive to the aspirations of its time.

Fundamentally, it appealed to the humanitarian teaching of the philosophers of the Enlightenment, intending to go beyond the particularism of the standard rites and religions. Then, when not only the Christian world of Europe, but even the Germanies themselves were profoundly divided by the scission of the Reformation—on one side Catholic states, including Austria, on the other Protestant states, including most of the German lands—it became for many a real relief to ignore those barriers. In a time of expanding, beckoning horizons, a period into which the existence of other worlds provided with other religions had begun to seep, Montesquieu's "How can one be a Persian?" took on the value of a question of conscience for all reflective men—and there was much reflection during the eighteenth century. Resolutely religious, but placing in parity on its altars the Bible, the Koran, the Vedas, and several other "Books of the Sacred Law," Freemasonry proclaimed each of its members free to adhere to the faith of his choice. For its own part, it limited itself to extracting a sort of synthetic dogmatic minimum: belief in a Creator-God, the "Great Architect of the Universe," in whatever form

He might present Himself. But it was beyond Him (whence the reticence of, and then the condemnations by, the Roman Church) that it preached the properly human virtues, in the name of which the French Revolution would arise and which it believed could assure the happiness of future society: that happiness of which *Die Zauberflöte*, through the voice of Sarastro, sings the idyllic ideal.

In its form, Freemasonry believed itself the successor of various initiate traditions, the survivals of which it applied itself to collecting and revitalizing. There were, to begin with, those of the medieval confraternities, principally that of the "masons" and architects, of which it took itself to be the direct descendant—whence not only its name,* but also the distinction between the older, "operative" Masonry of the stone artisans and the "speculative" Masonry of its successors, which preserved from the former only symbols and rites.[2] Proceeding from there, it created a veritable mythology founded upon, among other sources, the legend of Hiram, architect of the Temple of Solomon (I shall speak of that in connection with the character of Monostatos), and a meticulous, complicated ritual, the gestures and symbols of which it attempted, not always successfully, to keep secret. The "trials" in *Die Zauberflöte* are a sufficiently faithful evocation so that initiates could recognize them in passing, sufficiently altered so that the grand law of secrecy would not be broken too openly.

Freemasonry was not long in wanting to rise still higher from its corporative traditions, to the ancient Oriental mysteries of antiquity whence, it was believed, the traditions had come. Pythagoras was known to have collected in Egypt the initiative material that he later carried to Greece, so Egypt

---

* On the (disputed) significance of the word Free in "Freemason," see Jean Palou, *La Franc-Maçonnerie*, p. 24, and Paul Naudon, *La Franc-Maçonnerie*, p. 21, etc. According to some, it referred to ancient exemptions related to rights or servitudes; according to others, it related to the quality of the stone that was worked.

became the object of the most febrile investigations, from which numerous charlatans knew how to profit. That can explain the prodigious success of so gross a fraud as, in our eyes, the novel *Sethos,* which for a long time was one of the books found in the lodges. Born took inspiration from it for the study on the Egyptian mysteries which he published shortly before *Die Zauberflöte,* which is in some places a direct emanation from it (certain phrases are even reproduced from it textually). Some more or less dubious "reformers" like the celebrated Cagliostro* also sought to "Egyptianize" Freemasonry. With the assistance of Napoleon's Egyptian campaign, "Egyptian rites" [3] proliferated enormously during the nineteenth century; perhaps, also, the very success of *Die Zauberflöte* helped.

The libretto of *Die Zauberflöte,* however, was not the first to find inspiration in *Sethos.* Gebler's drama *Thamos, König in Ägypten,* for which Mozart composed in 1773 the incidental music that he recast in 1779, and which he recalled at several points in *Die Zauberflöte,* had been derived from it, as had an Italian *Osiride* that Johann Gottlieb Naumann had set in 1781 for a princely marriage at Dresden. Naumann was a Freemason. Da Ponte was in Dresden at that time, and he collaborated there with the librettist Caterino Mazzolà: Nettl suggests that it was not impossible that the librettist of *Le Nozze di Figaro* should have been "the first to give Mozart the idea of a Masonic opera." [4] A plausible but footless supposition: that all those librettos have a common background

---

* The charlatanism of Cagliostro (1743–95) has always been taken for granted. Nevertheless, one must note an attempt to rehabilitate him made in 1912 by Dr. Marc Haven, in his book *Le Maître inconnu, Cagliostro,* which was followed in 1947 by the publication of his ritual in the edition of the Cahiers Astrologiques de Nice under the title *Rituel de la Maçonnerie égyptienne.* The seal of Cagliostro reproduced on p. 122 was taken from this latter work. It represents an S-shaped serpent with an apple in its mouth and transfixed by an arrow: one inevitably thinks of the first scene of *Die Zauberflöte.*

should not surprise us, for they all go back to the same source, the history of which I should now sketch.

Organized in regular form in England early in the eighteenth century (the founding in 1717 of the London Grand Lodge is considered its official birth), Freemasonry counted 30,000 brothers in France alone in 1776, and 70,000 initiates of all degrees in 1787.[5] As for the Grand Lodge of Austria, constituted in 1742 at the instigation of Schaffgotsch, count-archbishop of Breslau,[6] in 1784 it consisted of sixty-six lodges, eight of them in Vienna, in the seven provinces of Austria, Bohemia, Galicia, Lombardy, the "Siebenbürgen," Hungary, and the Lowlands.[7] The order already had been the target of several condemnations by the Church of Rome,* the first and most important of them by Clement XII in 1738. But before pontifical acts could be put into effect, they had to be promulgated by the civil authority, and in several countries the targets of excommunication included persons too highly placed to allow that authority, favorable or not, to run the risk of ensuing scandals. In Austria, Maria Theresia was hostile to the order, but for ill-defined reasons it was only during the reign of Joseph II (1765–90) that the question of promulgating the papal bull of 1738 was posed. Despite the influence that the Empress, Joseph II's mother, kept until her death in 1780, he constantly opposed the promulgation, as much out of sympathy with Masonic ideas as because of highly placed personages to be "protected." Contrary to what occurred in Florence, Venice, Sardinia, Poland, Spain, and Portugal—but exactly as in France, where the Parlement had refused to register the pontifical bull—Catholics in the Austrian states then faced no official interdiction making obedience to the Church incompatible with membership in Masonry. The re-

---

* No less than twelve condemnations were drawn up from 1738 (Clement XII) to 1902 (Leo XIII). The list can be found in Serge Hutin, *Les Francs-Maçons*, p. 20.

sult was the extremely large number of ecclesiastics, often of high rank, who frequented the lodges (Colloredo himself, archbishop of Salzburg and "patron" of Mozart, was perhaps among them*). To see Freemasons attending religious services officially and in regalia was not rare. As a Catholic, Mozart could, in all security of conscience, work simultaneously on the Requiem and *Die Zauberflöte*.

The year 1785, lighted for Mozart by the first ardors of a neophyte, was also the last year of Austrian Masonry's golden age. Joseph II, who had been protecting it, undertook to "reform" it, as in 1781 he had wanted to reform the Catholic Church in his dominions. On December 11, 1785, he prescribed a whole series of measures chiefly aimed at regrouping the lodges in the hands of responsible men known to him over whom he would be able to exercise control.[9] Many lodges were closed and reconstituted, merged with others under different names. Mozart's lodge, the Loge zur Wohltätigkeit, was thus merged with the Loge zur gekrönten Hoffnung and the Loge zu den drei Feuern to form the Loge zur neugekrönten Hoffnung. Born's lodge, the Loge zur wahren Eintracht, was joined to the Loge zu den drei Adlern and the Loge zum Palmenbaum, becoming the Loge zur Wahrheit, of which Born remained the Venerable, being solemnly installed on January 6, 1786. Although Joseph II had not acted in a spirit of hostility, this disturbance was to prove catastrophic for the order. In a brief period, the official number of Masons in Vienna fell from more than a thousand to three hundred and sixty.[10]

Joseph II died in 1790. Opinion is divided concerning the

* According to Carl de Nys (communication to the Société de Musicologie on December 13, 1966), Colloredo belonged to the Apollo Lodge. Further, several members of his cathedral chapter were affiliated with the "Enlightened." Richard Koch asserted that the archbishop did not belong to the Apollo, but to the Loge zür Fürsicht, in which Mozart, his father, and Schikaneder had figured as visitors (this seems rather surprising, as we shall see in the next chapter[8]).

attitude toward Freemasonry of his brother and successor, Leopold II, who reigned only two years—the years of *Die Zauberflöte*. J. Kuéss, historian of Austrian Freemasonry, presents him as a benevolent protector holding elevated ideas analogous to those of the order, the result of his education.[11] The Massins, on the other hand, describe his reign as the precursor of the unhappy affliction that fell upon the Freemasons under his successor, Francis II (1792–1835), which they called the *Hochmitternacht* (High Midnight). In any case, it is very probable that the events in France, notably involving the fate of the Emperor's sister, Marie Antoinette, made Leopold's court very receptive to the rumors, repeated more and more insistently, about the real or supposed responsibility of international Freemasonry; furthermore, public opinion confused without much distinction several more or less parallel sects, among them the "Bavarian Illuminati," who were politically restless and very influential in Vienna. Some people have asserted that Mozart was one of them, and the question deserves investigation.

Because of the rapid and prodigious growth of Freemasonry, its history could not develop without jerkiness and dissension. The flexibility of the organization in leaving a wide margin of initiative to each nation could only favor a certain dispersion, to the point at which it might be said with some exaggeration that what existed was not one Freemasonry, but several juxtaposed Freemasonries.*

* This is still true, as certain divisions have a clearly religious tendency, whereas others are freethinking and sometimes anticlerical. In France, several "obediences" exist independently of one another while communicating more or less: Grande Loge de France, Grand-Orient de France, Grande Loge Nationale, etc.[12] Those who knew the Boy Scout movement before World War II (that of today is very far from the principles upon which it was founded) can compare the two organizations. The founder of the Boy Scouts, Lord Baden-Powell, was very closely inspired by the Masonic model, a fact that allowed the "French Boy Scout" organization to preserve its unity while grouping together Catholic, Protestant, Jewish, and lay associations.

I do not intend to tell that history, which the reader can find in all the specialized works. Their divergences, furthermore, bear but little on what concerns us here, as they involve above all the higher degrees, and the symbolism of *Die Zauberflöte* does not, in that respect, go beyond that of the first degree, which is much the same everywhere. The Vienna lodges of Mozart's time adhered chiefly to the rite of the Strict Observance,[13] founded in 1763 by Baron de Hund, which claimed to return to the traditions of the Ordre du Temple suppressed by Philippe le Bel in 1314. Jean Palou[14] is not gentle with the Strict Observance: it was, he writes, "a very bizarre mixture of Masonic symbolism, alchemical practices,* and Rosicrucian traditions." † But, again, these details involve chiefly the higher degrees. An entirely different matter is the sect called the "Illuminati of Bavaria," to which some have tried to link the Masonic activity not only of Mozart, but also of all the great German-speaking Masons of the eighteenth century: Goethe, Herder, Born, etc.

Based upon Freemasonry, but outside it, the order of the "Illuminati of Bavaria" ‡ had been founded in 1776 by Weishaupt, doyen of the Ingolstadt law school, who meant it to be a weapon in the war against the Jesuits, whose influence re-

* It will be recalled that both Born and Giesecke were involved with mineralogy, a science in constant relation to alchemy.

† Like the Illuminati, the Rosicrucians, founded in Germany about 1756, were at first outside Freemasonry, but then were received into it in a more or less inextricable mixture, above all in Vienna, where they were established in 1775. They claimed to have grown out of the Templars, and cultivated alchemy and theosophy. Several rival orders appeared: the Clerks Templar, occultists and para-Catholics; the Swedish System of Zinnendorf, an alchemist and spiritualist; and the Strict Observance, which was wholly integrated into regular Masonry. The Rosicrucians were violently opposed to Illuminism: they could not accept either its anticlericalism or its political aspect. The pseudo-resurrection of the Rosicrucians in the nineteenth century by "Sâr" Péladan, with which Erik Satie was involved, bore almost no relation to the authentic eighteenth-century movement.

‡ It goes without saying that the German word *Illuminaten* has not the pejorative connotation that clings to the related French and English terms.

mained preponderant despite the theoretical suppression of 1733. Its spirit was very different from that of official Masonry. Cynically enough, Weishaupt asserted that against the Jesuits he wanted to use their own weapons, which consisted, according to him, of "an iron discipline joined to the constant employment of falsehood and dissimulation for pedagogical purposes." [15] For that reason, the "revelations" of each degree consisted essentially of disavowal of those of the preceding degree. The initiates were divided into three degrees: *novice*, *minerval*,* and *illuminatus minor*. Public readings in assembly were planned to include Masonic writings (such as Lessing's *Gespräche für Freymaurer*), works about the Egyptian mysteries (*Sethos* among them), and extracts from French or German philosophers. Not until after the foundation of his order did Weishaupt enter regular Freemasonry. With the help of the poet Adolf von Knigge,† he then completed his organization by creating (1782), beyond the three existing degrees, which became a "class" called *Pépinière*, other classes to follow it. The first of the new classes was Freemasonry itself, considered only in its three lowest degrees: apprentice, fellow, and master. Thence, in his relations with Freemasonry, arose imbroglios that were inextricable and, what is more, intentional.

A particular target because of its political aims, Illuminism, together with the mass of secret societies, was forbidden in Bavaria in June 1784 by the Elector Karl Theodor. It continued to exist in Austria, where it seems to have been protected by Archbishop Colloredo. By reducing the number of

---

* Should one, with the Massins (p. 1184), evoke Papageno in noting that "the emblem of the *minerval* is a bird with a man's head"? Later we shall see the Birdcatcher and his costume have a much more coherent explanation in the framework of *Die Zauberflöte*. The Illuministic emblem is doubtless only the inversion of the Egyptian gods with bodies of men and heads of birds.

† Knigge (1752–96) was also a composer. Among other works, he published through André in 1781 *Six Sonates de clavecin seul* (title in French). André was also the "arranger" as a separate piece of the Overture to *Die Entführung aus dem Serail*.

lodges, Joseph II's reform undoubtedly contributed to its absorption into regular Freemasonry. "From 1785 to 1790," the Massins say (p. 1188), "Illuminism was only sporadically active; from 1788 to 1790 it died out." In other words, its influence upon *Die Zauberflöte* could have been no more than that of an indirect memory.

In 1911 Richard Koch published a small book in which he tried to make of Mozart, among many others, not only the regular Mason that everyone knows him to have been, but also an adept of Illuminism; that thesis has been repeated often since then.[16] Mozart's supposed entry into Illuminism would have occurred well before his regular initiation in 1784, and that would explain the abundance of the somewhat "para-Masonic" works which he composed before that event. This thesis seems to have been received with skepticism in well-informed circles. Having no competence to judge it, I limit myself to mentioning it without expressing an opinion. I am, however, very much inclined to share the skepticism. Koch's book seems not to be scholarly in its handling of information,* and Mozart's enthusiasm at the moment of his real initiation was not at all the attitude of a man for whom that initiation would not be a fulfillment. Rather, that enthusiasm evokes the reactions of a neophyte overwhelmed by the revelation, a fact that excludes any such preparation. Nevertheless, his initiation seems to have climaxed a long series of events, which we must now examine.

---

* One example among many: Richard Koch gives (*Br.˙. Mozart, Freimaurer und Illuminaten, nebst einige freimaurerischen kulturhistorischen Skizzen*, p. 17) a facsimile of what he calls "Mozart's diploma as a Freemason," giving it in French, and the transcript referred to on p. 16 in German translation. In that translation, note in large letters Mozart's name and his title "K. K. Kammerkompositeur": in the original document, the space foreseen for such information remains blank. *Cf.* Plate 37.

9

---◆---

Mozart and
Freemasonry

Mozart was officially admitted into Freemasonry by initiation on December 14, 1784. Nonetheless, it is permissible to say that his whole career had developed in an environment that was in some part para-Masonic and was marked by a series of significant occurrences in that respect.

At the age of eleven, Wolfgang, saved from the disfigurations of smallpox, sent as a token of gratitude to his physician, Dr. Joseph Wolf of Olmütz, an arietta (*An die Freude*, K.53); one notes with surprise that so early a composition was set to a Masonic text. Who had supplied the boy with that text? The Massins suppose that it was the physician himself; but Carl de Nys suggests that the parish priest at Olmütz may have been a Mason and involved in the matter.[1] When, the next year, Mozart composed *Bastien und Bastienne,* the little work was performed in the gardens of Dr. Anton Mesmer, the apostle of "animal magnetism." Mesmer was also a Freemason; later, he even created a schism bearing his name (Mesmerism), which in 1783 led "to the establishment of a Masonic society which was formed in Paris under the title 'Ordre de l'Harmonie universelle,' and which was intended to purify adepts by initiation" [2] by confirming them in the founder's doctrines. At sixteen (1772), Mozart composed an aria on the words of a ritual hymn, O heiliges Band.* The next year (1773), he was chosen, as we know, by Gebler to compose the incidental music for the Masonic drama Thamos after the defection of Gluck and another Masonic musician. The resemblance of its subject to that of Die Zauberflöte has long been remarked, and he revised it in 1779. When he left for Paris in 1778, he had in his pocket a letter of recommendation from Gemmingen to the Parisian Masons, and in particular to those of the Loge Olympique, the concerts of which were closely related to those of the Concert spirituel,[4] directed by Le Gros, who was a member of the Loge Saint-Jean d'Écosse du Contrat Social.[5] Gemmingen awaited him on his return to Mannheim to propose Semiramis, which we have already discussed. His advisers were Baron Gottfried van Swieten and Joseph von Sonnenfels long before he became aware of their high functions in Viennese Masonry. And the list continues. Clearly, for Mozart, Masonic initiation was not a coup de théâtre, but the outcome of a long evolution, which he would undertake to retrace symbolically in Act I of Die Zauberflöte.

Mozart took the decisive step on December 14, 1784. In the Loge zur Wohltätigkeit (Charity), the Venerable of which was his Semiramis librettist, Otto von Gemmingen, he was initiated into the degree of Apprentice, undergoing, with a conviction to which all his later work[6] testifies, the ritual

---

* K.148. The date 1772 was contested by Saint-Foix and Wyzewa (W. A. Mozart, etc., II, p. 426), but their reasoning was circular, their objection having been precisely that Masonic aspect which seemed to them anachronistic. René Dumesnil gives another argument, of a musical nature: it points out the relationship of the accompaniment to Sarastro's prayer in Die Zauberflöte.[3]

trials that he would present in stylized form in the second act of his opera.

Mozart's Masonic fervor is indicated by "advancement" that was rapid, though not exceptional, for the period: three months at most after his entrance, he was initiated into the degree of Fellow (before March 26, 1785), and a month later into that of Master (April 22). During the remaining six years of his life, he seems not to have gone beyond the degree of Master, but it should be noted that the third degree was the highest of the first group in the hierarchy. Beyond it began the "high degrees," conferred parsimoniously.

Mozart was not satisfied with merely "practicing"; to his proselytizing is attributed the "conversion" of his father and—it should probably be added—that of Haydn.[7] Leopold Mozart was initiated into the same lodge three months after his son (March 1785), and he also advanced swiftly: Fellow on April 6, Master on April 22, three days before he left Vienna to return to Salzburg.

That was the last meeting of father and son, and one can accept only with skepticism Richard Koch's statement that they, as well as Schikaneder, were "visitors" in a Salzburg lodge on an unspecified date.[8] But, as the Massins say,[9] Wolfgang probably did not stop discussing Masonic questions with Leopold in writing: it is from this precise moment forward that later owners of the letters destroyed them almost without exception. The only one to survive has become famous: it is the renowned "letter about death," which Wolfgang wrote to his father on April 4, 1787, the essential passage in which (italics mine) is:[10]

As death, when we come to consider it closely, is the true goal of our existence, I have formed *during the last few years* such close relations with this best and truest friend of mankind, that his image is not only no longer terrifying to me, but is indeed very soothing and consoling! And I thank my God for graciously granting me the opportunity (*you know what I mean*) of learning that death is the key which unlocks the door to our true happiness.

Leopold was to die less than two months later.

That letter, in which we see that the Lodge had been more successful than the Church in bringing Mozart—a member of both—serenity in the face of the Beyond (for in 1787 that was the meaning of his words "during the last few years"), singularly resembles another letter, written thirty-eight years later by another great Viennese musician, Schubert, to his father: "If only he [his brother Ferdinand—"I suppose that he still crawls to the 'Cross' "] could once see these heavenly mountains and lakes, the sight of which threatens to crush or engulf us, he would not be so attached to puny human life or regard as other than good fortune that of being confided to earth's indescribable power of creating new life." [11] Was Schubert a Freemason? This is not the place to discuss that question, but it may be noted in passing that, as with Beethoven, the question has at least been raised.[12]

It has been considered equally possible that Mozart instigated Haydn's rather belated initiation: in any case, he attended it. It occurred less than two months after his own—on Saturday, February 11, 1785, at the Loge zur wahren Eintracht (True Unity), of which the Venerable was Ignaz von Born, the future inspirer of *Die Zauberflöte*. It does not seem to have been noted * that on that same evening (February 11) there occurred the celebrated scene recounted by Leopold to his daughter Nannerl, in which Haydn, having joined the Mozarts to hear Wolfgang's latest quartets, uttered the famous sentence: "I say to you before God and as an honest man, that your son is the greatest composer I know personally

---

* In fact, Leopold says nothing about it in his letter: he had arrived in Vienna the preceding day and had not yet been initiated. Had Wolfgang not reached the stage of confiding in his father, or was Leopold already applying the law of discretion to his relations with his daughter?

or by name." May not the emotion aroused by the ceremony that had just been completed have played some part in that famous incident?

As we have seen, Mozart appears to have attended Born's lodge almost as assiduously as his own. Nevertheless, that reason does not suffice to underwrite the claim, made later by Seyfried on the basis of Giesecke's tales, that the latter lodge was nothing but a *"Fressloge"* (guzzling lodge) in which Schikaneder and he enjoyed themselves all day long. The suggestion, a malicious deformation of the then current practice of Masonic banquets, probably reflects some rancor on Giesecke's part toward his onetime director; it is not repeated in any other source.

When the regrouping of the lodges imposed by the reform of Joseph II took place at the end of 1785, Mozart became a member, not of Born's new lodge, but of the one that administratively absorbed his own: the Loge zur neugekrönten Hoffnung (Hope Newly Crowned). The name of his new Venerable differs in different sources, but almost certainly[13] was Gebler: Mozart thus exchanged the librettist of *Semiramis* for the librettist of *Thamos*.

This panoramic view should not be completed without recalling that Masons were very numerous in Mozart's immediate circle: his brother-in-law Josef Lange, his publisher Artaria, Johann Michael Puchberg—the man from whom he constantly borrowed money—were Masons.[14] Even outside Vienna, the Br.·. (*i.e.*, Brother) Mozart enjoyed lofty, active Masonic friendships. When he went to Prague for the last time (1791) while completing *Die Zauberflöte*, a solemn reception in his honor was given there by the Loge zur Wahrheit und Eintracht (Truth and Unity). Truth and Unity—the words, as the Massins remark, that in 1783 figured in the name of the lodge founded in Vienna that year and then directed by Born: the Loge zur wahren Eintracht. And "from

that fact one can surmise," the writers conclude, "why the
initiative of inviting Mozart to Prague was taken." [15]

The death of Joseph II marked a painful alteration in
Mozart's social position at court, and the new sovereign's ambiguous position vis-à-vis Freemasonry may have been one of
the causes. We have seen that, notably in the salons, unpleasant remarks about it were being repeated with increasing frequency, and Die Zauberflöte contains at least one scene—that
of the Three Ladies in Act II—in which the allusions are very
transparent. They undoubtedly served the purpose of allowing
Tamino to let the audience know, through Mozart's music,
the Masons' evaluation of that gossip: "It is the idle talk of
women, conceived by hypocrites and spread by liars." * We
have seen that this reply and other, similar remarks so struck
the intellectuals that the Leipzig theologian Alexander Zille
tried in 1866 to convert the entire libretto into a pièce à clefs.[16]

Disregarded by the court to the insulting extent of not being
invited to festivities that his official title gave him the right to
attend, was Mozart equally disregarded by the Church, and
for the same reason? Toward the end of his life, his youthful
faith unquestionably cooled off notably,† and it was without

---

* [Translator's note.] Lines in English from the libretto of Die Zauberflöte
are quoted verbatim or slightly adapted from Robert Pack and Marjorie
Lelash, eds., Mozart's Librettos, New York, 1961.

† The evolution of the religious feelings of the four great classic Viennese
musicians seems a faithful image of Freemasonry itself in this respect. Haydn
remained a fervent Catholic all his life. Mozart remained one superficially.
Beethoven proclaimed himself a deist while detaching himself almost completely from the Church. Schubert, finally, who was raised in the strictest
religious practice, reacted violently and in the end turned to a fierce anticlericalism occasionally tinged with a vague remnant of sentimental religiosity.
(Cf. my study "Le Winterreise de Schubert, est-il une œuvre ésotérique?"
Revue d'Esthétique, 1965, pp. 113–24.) Haydn and Mozart were both convinced Freemasons. One cannot be certain about Beethoven and Schubert,
whose membership would have begun during the Hochmitternacht and the
period of scarce archives, but all appearances point to their having been
Masons too. (Cf. my study of Beethoven in Natalicia Musicologica, dedicated
to Knud Jeppesen, Copenhagen, 1962.)

his knowledge that, on December 4, 1791, his sister-in-law
Sophie went out to ask a priest to come up "at all costs" to see
the dying man. But that fact was insufficient cause to justify
the bad grace with which the parish clergy carried out that
mission.[17] Should it be explained by the musician's notorious
Masonry? That is, in fact, the Massins' opinion. But this time
they seem to have allowed their avowed anticlericalism to lead
them too far: they assert that in the end the priests did not
trouble themselves. But all we know is that at last they promised unwillingly; we are not told whether they kept their word
or stayed away. But in the latter case, Sophie, who was already
strongly against them, would not have failed to include that
supplementary complaint when telling the story. It is more
reasonable to think, with Bernhard Paumgartner, that "it is
probable, but not certain, that Mozart received the Holy
Sacraments." [18]

That Mozart, because he was a Freemason, had been listed
as excommunicated, to the point of being refused the final
Sacraments, seems inadmissible. To begin with, such excommunication was illegal because, as we have noted, the German
states had not promulgated Rome's decrees regarding Freemasonry, which therefore were not juridically applicable. It
may be objected that an isolated ecclesiastic could have known
about them and wanted to demonstrate his personal zeal. Perhaps, but in that case the religious obsequies would also, *a
fortiori*, have been denied. But they took place in St. Stephen's
Cathedral—in a side chapel at three o'clock in the afternoon,
it is true. But that was the classic burial of the poor, leading to
the common burial ditch at the end.

Here again it would be tendentious to deduce ecclesiastical
malice toward a Mason. It was Baron van Swieten in person,
a lodge brother, who advised Constanze to have the most
economical funeral possible.

A tenacious legend grew up regarding that funeral, so tenacious that one finds it retold by the most eminent Mozarteans: Paumgartner, Erich Schenk, Roland Tenschert, the Massins, etc. (not to speak of earlier writings): ghastly weather, a blizzard, the procession dispersed. None of that occurred. We have the meteorological bulletins on the Vienna weather on that day: "mild weather with frequent mist" and a temperature varying between 37 and 38 degrees Fahrenheit, with a "light east wind." *

What remains is the neglect of Mozart's tomb by his widow. But that is another story.[20]

* The source of this legend slightly antedated the one of the change of plan in midstream for *Die Zauberflöte*, but it is of the same sort: an anonymous article in the *Wiener Morgenpost* of January 22, 1856. In reality, there was nothing anomalous about Mozart's funeral. Vienna had been suffering from a cholera epidemic, and the police regulations concerning burials were strict. A body was accompanied to the grave only if the cemetery was near the church, which was not true of the Cemetery of St. Marx.[19]

10

Freemasonry
and Feminism in
Die Zauberflöte

When examining *Die Zauberflöte*, we shall not be long in perceiving that the problems it raises almost all revolve around a central idea referred to by the title of this chapter. It will therefore be useful, before we go to the heart of the matter, to look at the state of this question as it could have been posed at the time when Mozart was composing.

We shall soon see, in fact, that Mozart took a very precise position on the subject. One year earlier, in signing *Così fan tutte*, he had proclaimed, in a disenchanted tone of jocularity, a scorn of the fair sex which was, at bottom, shared by the entire eighteenth century concealed under the appearance of a feigned gallantry. That scorn will be the point of departure for the text of *Die Zauberflöte*, the violently antifeminist declarations of which have often been remarked. But—and this has been noted less often—through the rise of Pamina and her final glorification in priestly vestments beside Tamino, the final outcome will, on the contrary, be a proclamation of the redemption of Woman and her rise to equality with Man in the Mystery of the Couple.

The idea was audacious, frankly revolutionary at that time. Taking up again in a more serious tone what *Così fan tutte* had set forth lightly, it brought to the thesis of Woman's inferiority a corrective much less usual than the thesis itself. That corrective looks even bolder when it is examined on the Masonic and religious plane of its presentation, for it touched upon a delicate, fundamental problem in the thought and discipline of the lodges at the time when Mozart was writing.

Every religious society, particularly at its beginning, tends more or less toward masculine domination, or at least to separation between men and women, with, in a large majority of instances, the exclusion of women from any initiate or assimilated access. No more than the Catholic Church was Freemasonry an exception to this rule.* Article 3 of Anderson's Constitutions (1723) limited admission to "men of good reputation" and excluded "slaves, women, and immoral or disgraced men," [1] and even in 1929 the Grand Lodge of England included among the "fundamental principles" demanded for recognition by it "that the Grand Lodge and the separate lodges must be composed entirely of men" and must "not maintain any relationship, Masonic or of any other nature, whatever it may be, with mixed lodges or with groups that admit women as members." [2]

Such lodges, in fact, were not long in being formed. Many of them were neither more nor less than fantastic parodies, the very names of which reveal their futility. At least one of those institutions, however, was serious enough to raise acute problems for regular Masonry, and these are reflected in *Die*

---

* In the Church, not only has access to Holy Orders always been forbidden to women (the few exceptions always are of subaltern nature), but also their participation, even now, has never been accepted without more or less avowed reservations. Not until the instruction *Musicam sacram* (1967) were women outside convents given the right to sing the Office (a practice that had been forbidden was then no more than "tolerated"). Also even in that recent document, their presence brings with it prohibition against stationing the chorus in the choir of the church.

Zauberflöte. It was a veritable female, more or less parallel Masonry which, despite the obligatory presence of male officers in its hierarchy, formed the basis of the "Adoption Lodges" exclusively for women and "arising out of masculine lodges with the mission of carrying on charitable works." [2] That institution, which took the name Order of the Mopses [*des Mopses*],* had its own ritual, which I shall mention again in connection with *Die Zauberflöte.* It became important enough to be recognized officially by the Grand-Orient de France[3] in 1774, the year after its foundation (1773), but the expediency and even the legitimacy of its existence never ceased to be food for bitter controversy. Its historian, G. O. Vat, asserts that "it was born in Vienna about 1737 and spread from there to France and Holland, some say even to England," [5] but that claim seems very dubious,† as the Grand Lodge of Austria was constituted only in 1742.[6] More believable is the opinion of Naudon, according to whom the idea was launched in France about 1744 by the Chevalier de Beauchêne; it would be about 1760 that the separate lodges

---

* The name "Mopses" is obscure. If one puts aside the possibility of a witticism in bad taste, the word evoking the argot "little dog" (there were witticisms of the same stripe in the affair: Ladies of the *Bouchon* (Cask-Bung), Order of the Honey Bee, etc.[4]), it may have referred to the augur Mopsus (Mopsoš in Greek), but the connection is unclear. Two augurs of that name exist in mythology. One, "son of Apollo and of Manto, daughter of Tiresias, was a famous augur and great captain; he was honored at Claros with his father's priesthood and delivered prophecies; after his death, he was revered as a demigod, and was celebrated as an oracle at Malée [*sic*] in Cilicia." The other, "son of the nymph Chloris and of Amycus, for which reason he was sometimes called Amycides, was an Argonaut and augur who was also given divine honors after his death and spoke as an oracle on the gulf in which Carthage later was built" (Fr. Noël, *Dictionnaire de la fable*, 1815, p. 426). Vivaldi composed a cantata on Mopsus.

† Vat's book may be unreliable about dates: on the same page he speaks of the closing of the lodges "in 1736, the time at which the Papal Bull excommunicating the Freemasons appeared," thus erring by two years on the date of a particularly well-known event.

became important enough to justify their being included in the plot of *Die Zauberflöte.*

The problem of a female Masonry took on a new aspect when, about 1784, the renowned adventurer Cagliostro founded, as the "Egyptian rite," his own Freemasonry made up of lodges admitting both sexes and mixing magical rites with alchemy, spiritualism, and witchcraft. He had taken the title of "Grand Copt" and had promoted his companion, Lorenza Feliciani, to the rank of Grand Mistress of feminine initiations under the name of "Queen of Sheba." Cagliostro did not do away with the hierarchical differences between male and female lodges, but modified the presentation: in lieu of an "ordinary" masculine Masonry (blue Masonry) more or less tolerating alongside it a sort of inferior feminine para-Masonry, the "Grand Copt" wanted to raise the latter to the level of ordinary Masonry and treat the former as a sort of superior Masonry of high degrees, increasing to seven, for example, the degrees of Apprentice.[7] Perhaps *Die Zauberflöte* owed to Cagliostro's ritual the idea of the final scene presenting Tamino and Pamina in "priestly vestments." When Cagliostro, who had spent time successively at Bordeaux and Lyon, found himself disavowed in Paris in 1785 by the Convent des Philalèthes, from which he had sought recognition of his doctrines, his rupture with regular Masonry became reciprocal hostility, and it is very likely that the resulting resentments increased still more the defiant attitude of real Masons toward societies of that type. That defiance also found additional fuel in the indiscretions that unfortunately added to the ladies' reputation for garrulity. *Die Zauberflöte* does not fail to recall that on every occasion: "Women do little but they chatter much," the Old Priest says to Tamino during his first instruction. The Masonry of Adoption had scarcely been founded when there appeared at Amsterdam (in 1742, according to

Vat[8]) a malicious brochure published by the Abbé Pérau under the title *La Franc-Maçonnerie trahie et le secret révélé des Mopses*, which unquestionably contributed to reinforcing the Freemasons' skepticism about the discretion of their sisters.

In fact, after a brilliant period around 1780, the Masonry of Adoption seems to have declined with the approach of the French Revolution, to be reborn later, more or less sporadically, through the influence of the Empress Joséphine, herself Grande Maîtresse of the Loge d'Adoption Sainte-Caroline,[9] and again at the beginning of the nineteenth century, when an independent female Masonry was created for the first time.[10]

However that may have been, the relations between regular lodges and Lodges of Adoption certainly were often strained, the former remaining constantly on the alert to keep the latter in a subaltern position, the latter naturally seeking to achieve equality, the idea of which could only confuse the initiates. "Masonry," an 1841 report says, "which can propagate itself only by persuasion, has need of women if it is to flourish; far from having them as auxiliaries, it is obliged to struggle against them constantly." [11]

That sentence well expresses the context in which the action of *Die Zauberflöte* unfolds. The Queen of the Night, as her name indicates, reigns only over darkness. Her Three Ladies, however, are initiates (see Chapter 14), but of an initiation forever incomplete, beyond which their sex cannot pass. Their presence defiles the Temple and motivates the thunder of the grand anathemas, and their final assault is only the supreme attempt to wring from men the Royal Secret that they alone possess, which is symbolized by the Solar Circle bequeathed only to Sarastro.

However, the librettists of *Die Zauberflöte* were more liberal, not only than the librettist of *Così fan tutte*, which by its very title excludes every exception to its scorn, but even than the 1841 writer cited above. The latter's solution consisted of giving women the illusion of doing something without letting them touch anything serious—in the organization "two or three times a year . . . under your direction, in their special rite," of harmless "little festivities." *Die Zauberflöte* sees the matter in loftier terms. The pretensions of the Queen of the Night will be nullified by rejection, but Pamina by her merits will earn the redemption of her sex.

Thus we have approached the great esoteric teachings that *Die Zauberflöte*, both in its libretto and in its music, means to inculcate. And now we can approach the second part of this book.

Part Two

IN PURSUIT
OF THE
HIDDEN
MEANING

11

Exegesis of Five Chords

At the beginning, I spoke of the curious deficiency revealed in the enormous Mozart bibliography when one approaches exegesis of *Die Zauberflöte*. I am not aware of more than a single monograph in French, that of Maurice Kufferath (1914–19). It contains valuable information, particularly in its comparison of the score with that of Wranitsky's *Oberon*—but at the date of its writing it could not hope to give a full explanation. Among the works in various languages which I have read, and they are numerous, I have encountered only two that have aimed at explication of *Die Zauberflöte* in the manner intended here: the *Mozart* of Paul Nettl and that of Jean and Brigitte Massin.

Their exegeses go considerably beyond those of their predecessors, but are not wholly satisfactory. Nettl still accepts the notion that the libretto was written at two times. The Massins had the wisdom to abandon that theory, but did not progress beyond the old idea that the Queen of the Night was wholly the incarnation of the Spirit of Evil. They also speak of a "shift" in the middle of the libretto. Formerly attributed to a change of plan made during the writing, it is, they say, a subjective illusion: the facts are presented to the audience, not as they really are, but as seen by Tamino, who, not yet an initiate, at first believes the Queen's lies.[1] An ingenious if somewhat anachronistic idea, closer to Pirandello and the cinema of Alain Resnais than to a suburban Viennese theater of the eighteenth century.

Ought we, then, abandon all attempt to understand? I was much disposed to think so when, some years ago, a chance discovery made during research brought me an unexpected solution to an analogous problem.[2] That dealt with the "Dissonant" Quartet, K.465: I had occasion to demonstrate that the harmonic peculiarities in its introduction, inexplicable up to then, continued a well-established tradition for describing darkness and chaos, a tradition going back at least to the *Elemens* (1737) of Jean-Fery Rebel, who explained it at length in his own commentary. That tradition was continued in such works as Handel's *Israel in Egypt* (1739); it recurred after Mozart in the introduction to Haydn's *Die Schöpfung*. The adagio introduction of the "Dissonant" Quartet could only have been looked upon at that time as an image of chaotic darkness, and it was violently opposed to the contrary depiction of order and clarity which bursts forth so soon in the allegro: *Ordo ab Chao*, as one of the most important Masonic mottoes expresses it.[3] That quartet, dedicated to Joseph Haydn two months before he was led to the portal of the Temple "by the hand of friendship"—that of Mozart (who must have spoken to him of this project often at that time)— was one of the first works that Mozart composed after his initiation in December 1784, and one, therefore, in which he would have felt most strongly, if he felt it at all, the profound impression produced by that event. In the course of that ceremony, as is well known, the postulant is introduced with his eyes blindfolded; then the blindfold is brusquely removed and he is dazzled by the brilliant lights. These symbolize the sudden illumination of Knowledge, coming immediately after the night of Ignorance. Everything seems to indicate an analogous evocation in the quartet, which, for this and other reasons, appears to be an indisputably Masonic work.*

Recalling my earlier work, I was struck by the similarity of the plan of the Overture to *Die Zauberflöte*—the Masonic character of which was publicly acknowledged—to that of the opening of the "Dissonant" Quartet. I became convinced that its adagio introduction had a significance like that of the quartet, of which it showed all the characteristics. Like the quartet introduction, then, it was meant to represent darkness and ignorance so as to oppose them to the solid architecture of the succeeding fugue. But to what did the darkness correspond?

The answer to that question was obviously to be found in the opening chords, which commentators had not failed to discuss. Without any exception known to me, all of them echoed one another in commenting upon those "three chords." Nettl even went so far as to specify that they represent the proclamation of the Apprentice degree, which "consists of rapping out three knocks in anapestic rhythm . . . the three ascending chords [indicating] the increasing strength of the three knocks." [4] But then why that description of darkness evoked by an initiative knocking? The contradiction was flagrant.

From the first, it seemed to me evident that the key to the problem lay in the fact that the knocking, which is regular in the middle of the fugue, where it takes on the rhythmic form

* In my dissertation, I also asserted the Masonic character of Beethoven's seventh quartet. Later, I revealed analogous probabilities in Schubert's *Winterreise* (cf. p. 321). No archive document allows us to say that Beethoven and Schubert were Freemasons (or members of a similar organization), but the period was the full *Hochmitternacht*, and out of prudence the archives were often more than discreet. Further, Masonic ideas could have circulated outside the direct dependencies of the Grand Lodge of Austria, and doubtless did so.

(in the traditional Masonic notation*) of oo-o, oo-o, oo-o—
the three anapestic blows described by Nettl—was not regular
at the beginning of the adagio. There are, to be sure, three
groups, but not at all the "three chords" usually described.
Further, the three groups are irregular, the first having only
one chord, attacked without anacrusis.

I had entertained other hypotheses, none of which had satisfied me fully, when a singular revelation came to me, that of
the apparently insurmountable difficulty of counting up to
five. For, after all, these chords, so important to understanding the work, are not 3, as Nettl said, nor 3 x 2, as in *Thamos*,
nor 3 x 3, as in the middle of the fugue. They are *five*, presented in regular rhythm of alternating long and short notes
(L-SL-SL) or, according to Masonic notation, o-oo-oo. And
the number 5 has a very precise meaning.[5] In the symbolism
adopted by Masonry, it is opposed to the number 3 of the male
principle, and thus represents its opposite, the female principle.

That significance of Five demands detailed study that can be
touched upon only lightly here. "In arithmology, or the mystique
of the Number," Matila Ghika wrote, "[the Pentad, or characteristic of the Five] . . . is also the *Gamos*, the number of Aphrodite
as the goddess of fecundating union, of generative Love, the ab-
stract archetype of generation. Five, in fact, is the combination of
the first even number, feminine, maternal, schizogenetic (Two,
dyad), and the first uneven number (male, asymmetric)—that is,
complete (Three, triad [6])."
Five, then, will be feminine because of its generative principle,
but feminine in the Couple, as the isolated feminine belongs to
the Two. It is possible that the notion of Five, the fecundated
feminine, passed by derivation to that of Five, the initiated female
principle. In the same way, in Roman Catholic iconography, the
Virgin often is haloed with five-pointed stars, whereas the head of
God the Father, whose beard expresses virility, is surrounded by

* This notation indicates the knock by an o; the hyphens between the o's
show the groupings of connected knocks.

an isosceles triangle. The triangle is usually explained by the Trinity; but that explanation will serve only when all Three Persons are enclosed. Very often only the Father is triangulated.

Although Five is the feminine number only under the above-mentioned aspect, it also has other meanings. It is what notably leads to the five-pointed star so often honored in Masonic iconography, "the eternal pentagram, Pythagorean, Mediterranean," which, having become the 'flaming star' already present on the acts of the last operative English lodges of the seventeenth century, takes the post of honor on a majority of the Free-Masonic documents, properly so called, of the eighteenth century and glows above the throne of the Master of the Lodge or the altar, always with the enigmatic G at its center . . ." [7] exactly as it glows in the center of the symbolic composition that forms the frontispiece of the original edition of the *Zauberflöte* libretto.* The pentagram is also the geometric stylization of the harmonious proportions of the human body. As for the Five, one also finds it in certain degrees of masculine Masonry, but always in the degrees of which the symbolism evokes the presence of a female element. The latter, often of lunary nature, is in fact the necessary complement of the solar, masculine principle. That is why the Perfect Couple Tamino-Pamina undergo together the two trials by Fire (masculine sign) and Water (feminine sign), whereas in the case of the imperfect couple, Papageno refuses the Water and Papagena does not confront the Fire. Sarastro's initiates invoke Isis and Osiris together.[8]

It is nonetheless true that eighteenth- and nineteenth-century rituals are explicit: Five is the feminine knocking par excellence, replacing the Three blows everywhere that the masculine initiates would have used them.† Often the Sisters would put five dots in a quincunx after their signatures as the Brothers put three points

---

* Plate 33. See also Plates 3, 8, 10, and 32.

† *Cf.* the following facsimile of a page from a book dated 1787. On the rhythm of this rapping in five we are unhappily uncertain, as its usage has been abolished and the documents that I have been able to consult do not spell it out. Therefore I cannot say whether or not the rhythm presented at the beginning of Mozart's Overture, the rhythm encountered again in other parts of *Die Zauberflöte*, has a ritual significance. A different rhythm, referred to as "five little blows" or "five equal blows," is sometimes mentioned.[9] It evokes the fluting of Papageno and other allusions in the score which I shall touch upon in the analysis.

LA VRAIE

MAÇONNERIE

D'ADOPTION.

OBSERVATIONS

SUR LES LOGES D'ADOPTION.

Ces Loges, qui font très fréquentes,
mais pas encore autant qu'elles devroient
l'être, ne font jamais convoquées que par
des Grands-Maîtres Francs-Maçons. On n'y
admet aucun convive, qu'il ne foit au moins
Compagnon. Tous ceux qui ont des Grades
font obligés d'en donner les ornemens aux
Sœurs, fans rien réferver qui puiffe leur
laiffer quelque diftinction de rang fur celles
qui feront reçues. Tout le commandement
fe fait par cinq coups de maillet; ouverture,
clôture de Loge, tant celle de Réception, que
celle de Table; de même que les fantés,
demandes & interrogations extraordinaires.

in a triangle.[10] Quinary symbols abound in the ritual of Adoption. Such is the apple cut in half, a reminder of the Edenic Tree of Genesis, which has a pentagram in the center of its core: "Bite into this apple without attacking the core, which is the germ and source of all our vices," the Inspectress charged with this role says to the new member at the moment of receiving her into the degree of Companion.[9] In the eighteenth-century engraving reproduced in Plate 26, which represents an initiation into that degree, the halved apple can be seen on the table.

The opening knocking, then, is not a useless statement of the one that occurs a little later, in the middle of the fugue. It establishes the female order described by the introductory adagio, just as the second establishes the male order described by the fugue. The former is depicted amid elements commonly employed for this purpose in the eighteenth century, such as the Kingdom of Darkness and Chaos (the "Kingdom of the Night"), the latter as that of order and constructive labor. We are full in the area of the scornful motto *"Così fan tutte."*

The masculine knocking certainly has the anapestic rhythm described by Nettl. It is not the rapping of the Apprentice degree, but that of the Master degree, it being triple whereas that of the Apprentice is single.* Further, that is logical, for that same knocking is echoed in the stage music of the second

---

* However, the triple knocking is intended as a sign of joy as early as the first degree on certain occasions. Cf. a Masonic song of the First Empire:

> *Buvons donc, mes frères, buvons,*
> *Par trois fois trois en vrais Maçons.*[11]
> (So drink, my Brothers, drink,
> Three times three, as true Masons.)

(on facing page)
The Five Beats in the Ritual of Adoption. Extract from *"La Vraie Maçonnerie d'Adoption,"* in *Recueil précieux de la Maçonnerie Adonhiramite à Philadelphie, par un Chevalier de tous les Ordres Maçonniques (Louis Guillemain de Saint-Victor), à Philadelphie chez Philarèthe,* 1787. Collection Alain Serrière.

act, in the midst of the Council of the Initiates. It will be heard three times, and here it is presented in 3 x 3 with the rhythm oo-o adopted by most of the rites (but not by the Scottish Rite, which uses equal beats).[12] One will encounter the same knocking again three years after *Die Zauberflöte*, in the "sequel" put together by Schikaneder and Winter, *Das Labirint, oder Der Kampf mit den Elementen*. Thus one sees the persistence of the tradition and of its interpretation.

One also sees the foolishness of the sad Lachnith of *Les Mystères d'Isis*, who, doubtless having believed Mozart negligent in having two different knockings—that in the beginning and that in the middle—coldly "corrected" the latter by tying two half-notes in such a way as to produce three regular double blows, oo-oo-oo. Probably without realizing it, Lachnith thus reproduced the rhythm that Mozart had introduced at the beginning of the final symphony of Act I of *Thamos*. At that time, Mozart had not been initiated; doubtless he then knew the ritual knockings at second hand well enough to want to use them, but not well enough to reproduce them correctly.

We also find that knocking, in chords, at the beginning of Philidor's *Carmen Seculare*; but simultaneously with it, the woodwinds give it without the anacrusis, and the brasses, taking up the number 3 as Mozart himself will do, repeat it several times. The *Carmen Seculare* is indisputably a Masonic work, but this detail apparently has never been pointed out.*

We note that the "masculine rapping" in the fugue, as in its reappearance in Act II, is orchestrated in a special way: with the instrumentation of "winds" appropriate to the "wind-instrument columns"—that is, of the instrumental ensembles

---

* Its first performances were given three "nights" in a row, February 26, 27, and 28, 1779, at the Grand Lodge of London (Freemasons Hall), for which it seems to have been written. Roger Cotte told me that an imposing majority of Freemasons figures in the list of subscribers printed at the beginning of the work, and the text—not usual in the period—is made up, despite the misleading title, of verses by Horace chosen because of their possible Masonic interpretation. The *Carmen Seculare* properly speaking is only the final section of the work (4th section, p. 133; the preceding sections consist of: as a pro-

that participated in the lodge ceremonies,* whereas the initial "feminine rapping" is orchestrated without special character, in ordinary orchestral *tutti*. That may signify that the feminine Order of the number 5 does not attain to the initiate knowledge reserved to adepts of the number 3. We already have seen how reluctantly the masculine lodges accepted the existence of the Lodges of Adoption. In details of this sort— and the score abounds in them—it may well be that Mozart has let us know in his way his opinion on the matter.

At the same time, a striking contrast is made between the first measures of the opera and the last, in which, returning to the same key (the initiatory E-flat major), with Tamino and Pamina arrayed in priestly paraphernalia, the glorification of the Mystery of the Couple† will break forth at the Woman's elevation into the light with her husband as the kingdom of their original ignorance collapses.

With that background, and led by Mozart himself, we can now approach the study of his last work in a new spirit.

---

logue, p. 23, the 1st strophe of Ode III, 1; as Part I, p. 26, strophes 8–11 of Ode IV, 6; as Part II, p. 37, strophes 1–7 of the same Ode; as Part III, p. 100, Ode I, 21).

* In the French lodges, the usual constitution of the "wind-instrument columns" was the wind sextet: 2 oboes, 2 bassoons, 2 horns.[13] At Vienna it seems to have been less fixed, but was always composed of winds. A special instrument, the basset horn (a sort of alto clarinet), played a specific role there (Mozart introduced it into several initiatory scenes in *Die Zauberflöte*).

Not only were many Masonic works written for wind instruments, but also that special sonority often was employed by initiate musicians for covert homage. When I studied orchestral direction with Pierre Monteux, he pointed out to me one day—doubtless without having in mind any connection of this sort—that all of Beethoven's symphonies include in their development at least one episode for winds alone. There has been much discussion of the role played by the trombones in the scene of the Commendatore in *Don Giovanni*, as in the oracle in *Idomeneo*: here one sees its significance, as well as that in the Hades scene in the *Orfeo* of Gluck (a Freemason). That significance, further, is related to the tradition of infernal brasses of the eighteenth century (*cf.* Monteverdi's *Orfeo*).

† This will also be the finnale of Haydn's very Masonic *Die Schöpfung*.

12

The Cosmogony
of the
Libretto

As we have begun to understand from what already has been said, the action of *Die Zauberflöte* turns essentially on the struggle between two antagonistic ideas symbolized by Day and Night, Sarastro and the Queen of the Night, Man and Woman. To say, as is common, that their struggle is that of Good and Evil, of Freemasonry and its enemies, is a simplification so excessive as to approach nonsense.

Nowhere, in truth, is it said that the Queen of the Night represents Evil. Night is darkness, not wicked in itself. But it is the opposite of Day, and if the conflict becomes sharp, the creators well know where their sympathies lie. *Die Zauberflöte* is essentially a symbolic illustration of that conflict between two worlds,* the Masculine and the Feminine, the conflict to

* It will be useful, in order to put an end to that famous legend of the "shift" during the creation, to emphasize that the terms of the conflict are established coherently in the first scenes. That the Queen and her Ladies should speak of Sarastro as an "evil genius" is normal: he is their enemy. But from the beginning his domain is presented as a superb castle in contrast to the shapeless rocks of his adversary; the Ladies immediately brush aside as blasphemous (No. 3A) the idea suggested by Tamino that Sarastro could be capable of carrying Pamina off to ravish her.

be resolved, after the necessary purification, by the new, perfect union in the Mystery of the Couple.

But to reduce this analysis entirely to a sexual problem would be excessive. It is only one aspect of a view of the world which calls upon old traditions of esoterism.

The capital passage for understanding the libretto is the speech made to Pamina by the Queen in Act II—and the fact that it is often deleted in performance underlines the general incomprehension. It should be read complete:

Your father, who was the Master here, voluntarily cast off the seven-aureoled Sun in favor of the Initiates of Isis. Another now bears the powerful solar emblem upon his breast: Sarastro. Shortly before your father's death, I reproached him about this matter. Then he said to me severely: "Woman, I am soon going to die; all the treasures that were my private property I leave to you, to you and your daughter." "And the Solar Circle, which encompasses the universe and penetrates it with its rays, to whom do you leave that?" I asked sharply. "Let it belong to the Initiates," was his reply. "Sarastro will be the MANLY guardian, as I myself have been up to this day. [*Sarastro wird ihn so* MÄNNLICH *verwalten, wie ich bisher.*] Ask me not one word more. These matters are not accessible to your woman's spirit. Your duty is to submit yourself completely, and your daughter also, to the direction of these Wise Men."

The revelations of that passage must be "translated." As is clear, they make no sense except in relation to an esoteric tradition implicitly referred to but not explained: the writers here touch upon one of the "secrets" that they would not expound clearly on the stage of a suburban theater. It is not impossible that the tradition, connected with the Egyptian context in which the action is taking place, was closely linked to the world of alchemy. We find that illustrated strikingly by a card or "lamina" of the Masonic tarot of Etteilla, an anagram of Alliette, contemporary with *Die Zauberflöte*, or about 1790 (Plates 3 and 4). Unlike some other tarot pictures that ignore this symbol (Plates 5 and 6), it represents the XIXth major arcanum, which must be the Sun, and which here takes the number 2, in the form of blinding light produced, not by the Sun itself, the masculine symbol, but by a five-pointed star, a symbol with many meanings, among which, as we have seen, figures the feminine signal linked to the number 5, the star-pentagram that Lucian revealed as the sign of recognition of Pythagorean initiates[1] and which dominates the frontispiece of the 1791 edition of the libretto of Die Zauberflöte. On the lamina, the traditional two children play naked under the steps of the Alchemical Furnace upon which the fire burns. Their sex is still indeterminate, and they await the completion of the Great Work to receive their attributes. The explanatory booklet gives this lamina the explicit name "Masonry of Hiram," and no less clearly denominates as "Order of Mopses" the next tarot, on which, in a nocturnal water scene, the two traditional dogs bay at the Moon.

To return to the revelations of the Queen of the Night, the reign of Pamina's father symbolizes the anterior, still unformed state of matter, in which the differentiation of the sexes had not yet appeared. When it occurred, the power of the world was divided between men and women: to the latter went the "treasures that were my private property." They are not enumerated, but it is very clearly specified that they do not include Wisdom, which is symbolized by the Solar Circle, symbol of Fire and of masculinity, "which encompasses the universe and penetrates it with its rays." That had been withheld from what had been left her as the wife of the Master. Deprived of the Sun—that is, of wisdom—she therefore became queen of the nocturnal feminine kingdom, thereafter separated from the solar masculine kingdom. Of this latter, the guardian will be Sarastro, who will guard it in a "manly" (männlich) way. These mysteries are inaccessible to a woman's spirit (*dem weiblichen Geiste*). The duty of women is to submit themselves entirely to the direction of the wise men.

That final prescription will be repeated often throughout *Die Zauberflöte* (Nos. 9A, 11, 12), and it will not be, as it has often been called, a formless patchwork of "antifeminist tirades" inserted without reason, but the very foundation of the libretto. At every turn during their long initiation, Tamino and even Papageno will be reminded that the final aim is to act as men—"man" here being *Mann*, not *Mensch*.

The Queen of the Night's great error has been not to accept that predominance of men over her sex. She is proud, Sarastro never ceases to recall, and would like to abolish that supremacy. On the day when her own daughter will be taken from her to participate with the elect Man in his rise and to form the Perfect Couple with him, her fury will be unbounded. In the beginning, she will count upon her daughter to establish the domination of women over Man (the order to murder Sarastro); then, deceived in that hope, she will become deranged to the degree of wanting to penetrate into the Temple so as to destroy it (irreverently, one might say that the basis of the story is the rebellion of the mother-in-law). Naturally, she will be overcome and her power finally destroyed.

Nothing appears, then, in the behavior of the Queen of the Night of the legendary change in the subject, no alteration, but instead an altogether normal psychological progression if one considers both the *parti pris* of the symbolic action and the theatrical exaggeration. Thus the unity of the libretto is reestablished, it having been questioned only because of faulty interpretation of what the Queen signifies.

The subject thus moves gradually toward the conflict between the sexes, a conflict that will reach a harmonious outcome in the Couple. The Man and the Woman must first seek one another. Then, having come together, they must pass beyond their first state through a series of trials which will render them worthy of their new one. For the Man, these trials at first are individual: they lead him to the threshold of the symbolic Temple, but he cannot open its doors unaided. Those who have preceded him in discovering Wisdom (that is to say, the Freemasons) must, by imposing their own ritual trials upon him, help him to achieve the supreme stage.

The Woman undergoes a still greater transformation because by nature she belongs to an inferior world symbolized by Night and because she resents being led. Before anything else, she must be pulled away, even against her will. In the Kingdom of Love, she will at first experience disillusionments (Monostatos). But if she knows how to resist, she will shortly be allowed to contemplate the Elect. He, in his labor of purification, will make her suffer without ceasing to love her: she must keep her faith, for the moment will come when, hand in hand, they will be enabled to confront the most fearsome trials together. They will emerge victorious, and will be fit to dominate the world.

Thus a third era will be born. The crisis of the sexes was unknown to the reign of Pamina's father. It was born from their division (the world divided between the Queen of the Night and Sarastro).* Through the union of Tamino and Pamina, the conflict will be resolved and a new Age of Gold can open for the world.

That, in synopsis, is the scheme of Die Zauberflöte. But

---

* Although the identity is not complete, one can compare this doctrine to the legend of the androgynes cut in two by Zeus, of which Plato speaks in The Banquet (190 ff.). One discovers numerous strange analogies: an initiate character announced in preamble; connection of the male with the Sun and of the androgyne with the Moon (here the female is connected with the Earth); rebellion of pride against the gods; finally, reunion of the two halves in the final Couple, "in such a manner," Hephaistos says, "that from being the two beings that you are, you will become a single being . . . ; then, after your death, down there in Hades, instead of being two, you will again be a single being, the two of you having died a common death."

before approaching the unfolding of the story, we must first examine its protagonists. We shall see that considerable mature thought was given to the cast of characters, and that this is far from being the "naïve tale" that Mozart has been accused of condescending to set to music.

13

The Principal Characters: Two Heavenly Bodies, Four Elements

The conflict that pits the Queen of the Night against Sarastro is only one element in the fundamental dualism of the esoteric cosmogony. That dualism is symbolized at the entrance to a Masonic temple by two columns, denominated J and B (Jakin and Booz), which recall the two brass columns built by Hiram at the gates to the temple of Solomon; and each of them is meant to represent one of the elements in its multiple figurations:

JAKIN	BOOZ[a]
Osiris	Isis
Masculine	Feminine
Sun	Moon
Day	Night
Fire	Water
Gold	Silver
Active	Passive
Number 3	Number 5
Red	Black or white

[a] In certain rites, notably in France, these columns are sometimes reversed, doubtless because those who copied the rituals saw the columns of the Temple of Solomon as interior, whereas they were exterior.[1]

(JAKIN)	(BOOZ)
Elucidation	Discourse
Bull	Twins
Masonry of Hiram =	Order of Mopses =
traditional masculine	feminine "Masonry
Masonry	of Adoption"

That table will play a large role in the symbolism of the libretto. We have mentioned the Day-Night opposition. One could as well choose the example of the Sun-Moon dualism, given that Sarastro "bears the Solar Emblem on his breast" whereas it is by moonlight that, in Act II, the Queen of the Night appears to her daughter, Pamina.

Thus, Sarastro/Queen = Sun/Moon. In the hermetic cosmogony, man's life is dominated by the alternation of these two heavenly bodies, the "two luminaries" of the "Masonic Apprentice Table," [2] which in Nature are closest to him and which alone are visible on a suprastellar scale. This universe, in turn, is made up of Four Elements, themselves grouped by the tradition into two complementary dyads: Fire and Water on one hand,* Air and Earth on the other. As the table shows, Fire and Water, related respectively to the Sun and to the Moon, also represent Man and Woman. They will evidently be Tamino and Pamina. Then there is the other dyad, Air and Earth. We can easily see which of its specific characteristics determines the apparently singular aspects of two of the other principal protagonists, Papageno and Monostatos.

Let us look at the former: a catcher of birds, which inhabit the air, himself so covered with their plumage that Tamino mistakes him for one of them, player of the flute (a wind instrument), as light and featherbrained as the winged animals, Papageno possesses all the characteristics of the Kingdom of the Air. His symmetric opposite is Monostatos, black symbol

---

* Contrary to appearances, Fire and Water are considered, not incompatible, but complementary: without Fire, Water would be frozen.[3]

of chthonic darkness, guide of the Queen and her Ladies through the subterranean places familiar to him, drunk with the idea of burdening the entire world with chains forged in the underground cave of some Vulcan.*

To sum up: Papageno and Monostatos are the Air and the Earth; Tamino and Pamina are Fire and Water. Above them, with the required relationships, Sarastro and the Queen of the Night represent the Sun and the Moon; the traditional cosmogony is faithfully presented.

We may clarify all this by the following table, which clarifies the relationships among the personages in the story:

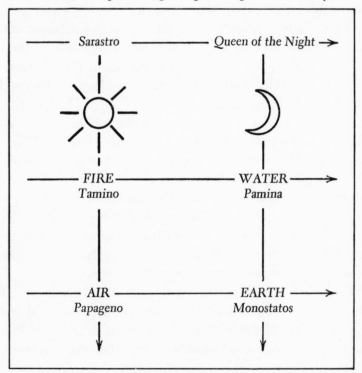

* Chains or ropes signify whatever holds the candidate to the profane world he is leaving. In certain rites, a postulant is brought in in chains that are then removed.[4] This is particularly true of the feminine initiation (*cf.* Plate 26).

We note that at the beginning of the action, Papageno and Monostatos are inverted with reference to this table: Papageno is serving the Queen of the Night, Monostatos is serving Sarastro. The action has as its precise consequence that of restoring each of them to his true condition: Papageno, assistant to Tamino, will be one of Sarastro's initiates; Monostatos will return to the camp of the Queen of the Night. Thus the affinities of the Elements that they represent will be reestablished and the disorder that the Golden Age is to abolish will be undone. To a lesser degree, the same change will befall Tamino: we recall his admiration, at the opening of the first act, of the "star-shining" Queen.

In addition to their "elementary" significances, the protagonists of *Die Zauberflöte* are also charged with various symbolic missions.

SARASTRO

It has long since been observed that Sarastro is derived from Zoroaster (or Zarathustra), a semihistoric, semilegendary personage who inspired the muse of, among others, Rameau. The historic Zoroaster was a king of the Bactrians, an expert in astronomy, and was said to have invented magic. The most contradictory and marvelous legends were current about him. The eighteenth century made him fashionable, and various writers went so far as to identify him with the prophet Ezekiel, others with Nimrod, Moses, and Ham, son of Noah.[5] The Persian religion attributed to him one of its essential dogmas, the duality of the two principles of Good and Evil, Ormazd and Ahriman, and he thus finally became, in the likeness of a king-priest, the very incarnation of Good. Thence Sarastro.[6]

In the opera, Sarastro is a static personage, almost an abstraction. He knows nothing of passions or peripeties. A solar symbol, he is not married and he rules over a world of male initiates and is jealously on watch to maintain its supremacy over the adverse world of Women and the Night. We have already seen what is signified by the ascent, in view of its future succession, of the Initiate Couple and how it will put an end to that duality.

THE QUEEN OF THE NIGHT

She has no proper name, and we have seen what the personage signifies: a lunar symbol of rebellion against that supremacy of the "strong sex." We dealt with that in the preceding chapter.

TAMINO

Tamino and Pamina clearly are the Man and the Woman destined to form the Couple in the highest meaning of that term: Sarastro announces that to the assembly of the Initiates (No. 9A), and the choruses of priests vie in celebrating the *"Neue Paar"* that they are destined to form. Their names are revelatory. Tamino, Paul Nettl says,[7] signifies "man consecrated to Min," an Egyptian god; Pamina is the "woman consecrated to Min." The choice of names, then, announces the symbolic intention, and we should not be surprised that the two names begin with different consonants; unhappily, Schikaneder had no knowledge of Egyptian: he erred in forming the names, which, it seems, should have been Pamino and Tamina.* It matters little. Tamino, the superior Man, worthy to rise to wisdom, is a prince—a superior being in the eyes of the profane—but that distinction counts for nothing with the Masons. Several answers emphasize that: thus, Papageno, when introducing himself to Tamino (spoken scene): "Who

---

* Perhaps, also, Schikaneder let himself be confused by the analogy Tamino-Thamos because of the resemblance, already discussed, of the two Masonic librettos and by the memory that Mozart had preserved of his 1773–9 score. Naturally, it is impossible to entertain seriously Edward J. Dent's hypothesis (*Mozart's Operas: A Critical Study*, p. 220) that the difference of initials "may have been due to a clerical error or to a misprint in an early proof," though no doubt Mozart and Schikaneder had "realized that the identity of name would be a practical inconvenience."

am I? A man like you." At the beginning of Act II, the priests even doubt Tamino's ability to undergo the trials: "Imagine, he is a prince." Sarastro has to reassure them: "More important, he is a man" (*Mensch* this time, not *Mann*). We are in 1791, and perhaps closer to the Seine than to the Danube.

PAMINA

Pamina, the one whom the gods have destined for Tamino, is the daughter of the Queen of the Night because she is a woman. *Die Zauberflöte* is centered on the drama of Pamina's passage from one universe to the other as much as upon Tamino's initiation, and perhaps more. It is a sorrowful passage, which at first requires that she be kidnapped against her will and which causes tears and sufferings, but one that will end in the final apotheosis of the Couple. Here again it is essential to read the text closely. When Pamina was abducted, she was "seated alone, on a beautiful day in May, in her favorite retreat, the cypress grove." The funerary tree tells us of the somber destiny that would have been hers had she not been carried off by Sarastro; but the abduction is placed in the month of springtime blossoming, of the powerful renascence under the sign of Apollo, the solar god, and under the name of Maia (Cybele), goddess of creative nature.[8] She has tried to flee Sarastro's palace (Scene 5A), taking the water route of her sign: a canal (a mapped-out route) leading to a stand of palm trees (resurrection and new life), but her flight has been a failure: she has been caught by Monostatos (we shall see shortly what that signifies). She decides to rely upon Sarastro, whereupon everything changes. Brought into the presence of her beloved, she will be able to look upon his face and—little by little, by way of her trials—to reject all memory of her nocturnal origin, until she is even able to guide Tamino through the major trials: Fire and Water (the two sexes), after which they will be united as husband and wife in the final solar apotheosis (we shall return to that episode).

PAPAGENO*

His name obviously is derived from *Papagei*, the *papegeai* of Old French—that is, the parrot, which we see in its cage when we carefully examine the original design reproduced in Plate 15. In conformity with his sign, Air, he is a birdcatcher, a fact of which no one can remain unaware. So be it, but why a birdcatcher? The answer doubtless lies in the ritual of the Lodges of Adoption: in it, a live bird is used to represent the warning against feminine curiosity,[9] and the bird thus becomes the symbol of the futilities of the fair sex. In view of that, one understands why Papageno sells his birds to the Ladies, emissaries of the Queen of the Night, from whom he receives food and sustenance in exchange. The symbol, though not very pleasant, is nonetheless transparent.

Papageno—who is a man and sighs after a little Papagena—stands for "ordinary" humanity, full of good will certainly, but lacking courage and intelligence, and therefore unworthy of initiation: the attempt made despite him will end in defeat, and if everything turns out well for him in the end, that is less because of the symbolism in the action than because of the laws of the theater, which require a happy ending (as is said in almost those terms by the Speaker, Scene 19A). A comedic character answering to the generalized taste of the theater of the time for parallelism of couples—one noble and touching, the other popular and simple—the Birdcatcher was

* How should this name be pronounced—in the German way (Papagay′ no) or in the Italian (Papajay′ no)? Both are plausible, for we are dealing with a libretto in German in which the proper names are Italian. Today, usage tends toward the German pronunciation, but that is doubtless owing to prestige of singers of the Mozartean repertoire in that language. Following Dent (p. 220), I gladly agree that the most logical step is to adopt the Italian pronunciation of the Italian names. And that also applies to Sarastro (not the German Zarastro).

also valuable in furnishing a comic actor like Schikaneder with a role cut to his measure.

MONOSTATOS

He is involved in more subtle symbolism, and many mistakes have been made in attempts to explain him. His blackness, beyond being the symbol of Evil, has been seen as a forerunner of racism, an anticipation of his collusion with the Queen of the Night, and even an allusion to the black robe of the Jesuits, the foremost enemies of Masonry.[10] I believe that he too can be explained best through Masonic symbolism, upon which he depends, as does all the rest of the opera.

Isidore Lévy, in his *"Légende de Pythagore de Grèce en Palestine,"* mentions "an Egyptian story known as the *History of Siosiri* or *The Duel of the Magicians,"* in which "at long intervals there appeared at Memphis, at the court of the reigning Pharaoh, a black magician come from the South who, having launched a defi on the basis of sorceries . . . is on the point of triumphing when, at the last moment, one of the royal magicians . . . forces the demoniac sorcerer to disappear after promising never to return." [11]

Was that story known to the writers of the libretto? We cannot be sure, and Monostatos may well have been their invention—which would not mean that he has no significance. In Greek his name signifies "the isolated one" (he who stands alone), and in fact he, the Evil One, is very isolated in the kingdom of the Good. But, as with the Queen of the Night, to speak here of "Good" and "Evil" is to settle matters too quickly and too grossly. His monologue beside the sleeping Pamina (No. 12B), furnishes the explanation: he is the carnal man who despises woman (see the opening of his monologue) and desires her out of pure sexual appetite. Let Pamina fall back into the Kingdom of the Night and she will be his; without difficulty he will obtain what was

être incorruptible ; ce qui ſymboliſe le vrai Maçon, qui doit être vertueux pour le ſeul plaiſir de l'être , & ſe mettre au-deſſus des préjugés & de la calomnie.

D. Quelle forme avoient les planches ?

R. Elles étoient toutes égales & bien appla-nies ; ce qui nous démontre l'égalité par-faite qui doit régner entre nous , & qui doit être fondée ſur la ruine de l'amour-propre.

D. Comment l'Arche étoit elle éclairée ?

R. Par une ſeule croiſée pratiquée dans le haut du quatrième étage.

D. Quel oiſeau Noé fit-il ſortir pour ſavoir ſi les eaux étoient retirées ?

R. Le Corbeau , qui ne revint point , image de tous faux Frères , qui ſe parant des traits de la ſageſſe , négligent les innocens plaiſirs de la Maçonnerie , pour jouir en particulier des criminelles voluptés des ſens.

D. Quel fut l'oiſeau que Noé fit ſortir après le Corbeau ?

R. La Colombe , qui rapporta une branche d'Olivier , ſymbole de la paix qui doit régner entre les Maçons.

D. Donnez-moi le ſigne de Compagnone ?

R. Le voici.

(*On le fait.*)

D. Donnez-moi la parole.

R. Belba , qui ſignifie confuſion.

D. Donnez-moi le mot de paſſe.

E ij

The Raven and the Dove (Monostatos and Pamina).
Same source as page 88.

promised by her mother, the queen of this kingdom. But Pamina rebels against love of that sort, and that rebellion begins her ascension. Facing the sleeping Pamina, Monostatos represents, then, the degraded love of masculine desire, just as, when Tamino faints, the Three Ladies represent the degraded love of feminine flirtatiousness.

Monostatos's blackness as a Moor (the traditional civil state of guardians of slaves) is more than a theatrical convention. He evokes the darkness of the Earth, which is his sign; but that is further explained by the Masonic Legend recalled by one of the degrees of the rite of Adoption. When, after the Deluge, Noah sees the waters recede, Genesis says, he sends two winged messengers from the Ark. The first is a crow, the black bird, which flies about without alighting, and thus becomes the symbol of unhappiness; the second is the white dove, which returns with an olive branch in its beak, and thus becomes the symbol of peace. Evil was mixed with good in the world under those two symbols, and it has not ceased to spread. In this connection, we note the insistence with which Monostatos calls Pamina "my little dove," *Täubchen.* In recounting their history, the Freemasons take us as far back as Hiram, the architect of Solomon's temple, and to his companions, initiate brothers. Among the latter were hidden traitors, foreshadowed by Noah's crow, who yearned to steal the secret of the master word: Hiram perished at the hands of three of them, and his memory is piously preserved in the Masonic symbols. Just as the traitor Judas figured among the Twelve Apostles of Jesus, so it was entirely in conformity with tradition that among the servants of Sarastro there should figure the traitor Monostatos, whose name in itself tells us that he is an exception in this kingdom of virtue, and whose black color, apart from the significances already mentioned, allows us to foresee that in the end he will return to the Kingdom of the Night.

14

The
*Secondary
Characters*

We have seen that the six principal actors, who are grouped in dyads, allegorically represent, each according to his rank, the traditional cosmos, with its two suprastellar planets and its four Elements—those four Elements which will play a determining role in the trials during the second act.

The other protagonists who appear from time to time have not the same cosmic significance, but nonetheless are characterized according to the symbolic plan.

PAPAGENA

Although one part of this role is nothing but pure comedy, she is not outside the symbolic nature of the action as a whole, and the bizarreries of her behavior are only apparently such: in her way, she undergoes the same ritual tests as the other neophytes—but passively, like Papageno, without calling upon courage or will. Only when those trials have been passed can the Birdcatcher's dreamed-of companion be revealed to him in the freshness of her attractive appearance.

Thus one understands why up to that moment Papagena

appears to be a horrible old woman. In short, this is the counterpart of the interdiction laid upon Tamino in the same situation: not to look upon the features of his beloved except in effigy or through a veil.

Once Papageno's Papagena has become young and pretty, she is almost a copy of him: feathered like him, certainly she is not his superior in wisdom or intelligence. So that when, in their final duet, these two lovebirds outdo one another in singing, with significant musical description, that they are prepared to people the earth with little Papagenos and little Papagenas who will resemble them, it is easy to divine a very piquant satirical intention very distant from the morality of the foolish tales that commentators have confined themselves to discovering here.

Certain lines in the libretto even invite us to go farther, to ask ourselves if, in the minds of the authors, the ugliness of the old woman is not, fundamentally, the image of her true nature as a woman, the pretty appearance that she reveals at last an illusion of the man inflamed by wine and desire. We will come upon this question again when discussing the relevant scenes.

THE THREE LADIES

These are the only characters that seem to display some failure in the logic of a remarkably consistent play—if one examines it for what it is, and not according to the rules of the popular theater. In Act I, they encourage Tamino to place himself in the hands of Sarastro's Three Boys while describing Sarastro as an evil genius; thus they prepare Tamino's future initiation. In Act II, on the contrary, they are presented as fierce adversaries of the Freemasonry that the Boys represent. The contradiction is less glaring than it seems.

The Three Ladies are, first and foremost, messengers of the Queen of the Night. For that reason, they were originally intended to have been five, not three; necessities of casting doubtless justified this slight distortion. But after the rallying of Monostatos, the assault group led by the Queen will in fact include the five symbolic characters.

As representing the feminine world from which Pamina has come, and from which she just has been uprooted, the messengers of its Queen naturally are presented, as in the table on p. 100, as opposing to the masculine Masonry of Hiram (Sarastro's temple) the Order of Mopses, its symmetric feminine opposite. In Chapter 10, we saw how reluctantly entirely male traditional Masonry had welcomed the existence of that parallel order, susceptible, despite the obligatory presence of male officers, of placing in question traditional Masonry's monopoly and preeminence. Therefore one must ask a preliminary question: Are the Three Ladies initiates, and do they, as such, represent their Order in the conflict that places them in opposition to Sarastro's initiates?

What occurs in the first scenes of Act I appears to give an unequivocally affirmative answer. The entire beginning of the libretto bristles with allusions to the feminine ritual of the Lodges of Adoption. The serpent that the Ladies kill, the birds Papageno sells them, the padlock they place upon his mouth—all these figure in that ritual.[1]

Let us begin with the serpent. Its real symbolism will be elucidated later. Here let us recall that in the story of Genesis he appears as the essential instrument of the feminine Temptation in the Garden of Eden; thus, he is linked to the object of that temptation, represented by the apple. Genesis does not specify the botanical nature of the tree: for the Scripture (and here it is related to the symbolism of *Die Zauberflöte*), it was the Tree of the Knowledge of Good and Evil—and therefore of that deepened Knowledge which, according to the Masons, is attained through initiation, and to which their sisters, like Eve in the Garden of Paradise, also covet access.

The feminine initiation is full of allusions to the Biblical Temptation. In order to achieve the first degree—that of Apprentice—the future Sisters must hold the figure of a serpent in their hands. For the next degree, Companion, they relive the Edenic scene and must taste the Fruit of Knowledge, the apple that has been halved to reveal a five-pointed star at its core, five being, as we have seen, the number of femininity.[2]

The same is true of the episode of the padlock: to place the future Companion on guard against the perils of garrulity, the Inspectress applies the padlock to her mouth with the paste of the "Seal of Discretion," striking the five symbolic beats with a trowel.*[2] Note the gallant refinement of the libretto in describing the padlock of discretion as golden (gold, as opposed to silver, is masculine).

The same again applies to the birds, as we noted with regard to Papageno. This symbol of futility does not involve only the Birdcatcher: he traps birds on orders from, and for the account of, the Queen of the Night and her Ladies, who have need of them, and who, in exchange, nourish him, not upon the solid flesh of masculine game, but on the insipid sweetmeats that abounded in the feminine salons of the period: *Zuckerbrot und süsse Feigen* (Scene 2A). When we add that the Ladies, in announcing the arrival of the Three Boys (whose significance we shall examine shortly), behave as faithful precursors of the initiation that they later deplore, we must conclude that in fact they represent feminine Masonry, of which they are initiates.

But let us look at them more closely. Their faces are veiled,

---

* The facsimile on p. 112 reproduces a ritual very slightly different from the one published by Vat and Palou, to which our commentary refers, but the details do not affect it basically.

» cette nuit, la jarretière de l'Ordre, & de
» n'en point découvrir les myſtères aux Pro-
» fanes. Je promets touɩes ces choſes, aux
» riſques d'encourir l'indignation de mes
» Frères & Sœurs; c'eſt pourquoi je prie
» Dieu de m'être en aide. Ainſi ſoit-il ».

Le Vénérable relève la Récipiendaire, &
prenant ſa truelle, de laquelle il a trempé
le bout dans l'auge ſacrée, il la lui paſſe
cinq fois ſur les lévres, & lui dit : « C'eſt le
» ſceau de la diſcrétion que je vous appli-
» que; on vous apprendra bientôt la morale
» qu'il renferme. Reprenez ce fruit, il eſt,
» le ſymbole d'un grand Myſtère, & de
» notre Ordre & de notre Religion. Recevez
» auſſi notre Jarretière, comme étant l'em-
»blême d'une amitié parfaite ». Alors faiſant
paſſer la Sœur du côté de l'Afrique, il continue, en diſant : « Nous avons des ſignes & des
» paro'es pour nous reconnoître, en qualité
» de Compagnone, comme dans le Grade
» précédent. Le ſigne ſe fait, en portant le
» petit doigt de la main droite ſur l'œil droit
» fermé. On répond à ce ſigne, en mettant
» le petit doigt de la main droite ſous le nez,
» le pouce deſſus, l'index ſur le ſourcil, &
» les autres doigts ſur l'œil. La parole eſt
» Belba, qui ſignifie Confuſion ; le mot de
» paſſe eſt Lamaſabathani, qui veut dire,
» Seigneur, je n'ai péché que parce que vous
» m'avez abandonnée ».

The Seal of Discretion (Papageno's padlock).
Same source as page 88.

as is that of their mistress (as Papageno expressly says in Scene 2A). The reticences mentioned above are not the only reason. Even in their parallel Masonry, women never attain to Integral Knowledge; just as, in the Catholic clergy, they cannot achieve priesthood, so, in Masonry, their order includes only a limited number of degrees and initiate men constantly remain at their side. Papageno speaks a cruel, revealing phrase about the Three Ladies: "I don't believe that they are beautiful; if they were beautiful, they wouldn't hide their faces that way." As the Massins clearly saw, their benevolence is not flawless; above all, they dream of their own pleasures (to remain near the handsome young man) and limit their ambition to promising Tamino "happiness, honor, and fortune," whereas the complete initiates will speak of love and virtue, of wisdom and fraternity, and in return for the birds (futilities) with which Papageno furnishes them, they and their mistress promise him nothing but daily food and drink.

The "shift" in the second act is therefore less than it appeared to be. With the abduction of Pamina, the mission of Tamino, and, from the women's point of view, the treason represented by her decision to be initiated at his side, the war of the sexes is declared. It is declared on both the human and the Masonic level, the pride of the Queen of the Night driving her to use all means to usurp the masculine privilege of Knowledge, the Solar Circle that her husband left to Sarastro. Even the Order of these Ladies has ceased to be an ally: according to the very terms of the 1841 report cited above, "far from having them as auxiliaries," true Masonry found itself obliged to "struggle against them," and thereafter the battle became reciprocal. Here we would have to interrogate the historians of eighteenth-century Viennese Masonry; perhaps they could reveal curious rivalries between the traditional lodges and the Lodges of Adoption in Vienna around 1791. Thus they might give us the lost key to many allusions spread through *Die Zauberflöte,* principally with reference to the Three Ladies.

THE THREE BOYS

Sarastro's Three Boys (the symbol of the number is correct this time) correspond, in the camp of the adversary, to the Three Ladies of the Queen of the Night. That these Three Boys should often, for practical reasons, now be interpreted by women's voices, and that, in a recording conducted by Herbert von Karajan, such a substitution should have been calling them the "Three Genii," * the wording used in a book considered (rightly) to be one of the fundamental works of Mozartean learning—Alfred Einstein's *Mozart*[3]—this well illustrates the degree of misunderstanding into which the opera has fallen, for the Boys' role is specifically explained, above all, by the incapacity of the Ladies to fulfill the mission with which they are charged.

As we just have noted, in fact, the Three Ladies and their Queen are and remain veiled: women never attain to Perfect Knowledge. Therefore they cannot serve as Tamino's guides in Sarastro's kingdom, but for that very reason must be replaced by messengers capable of growing in knowledge. Therefore the Three Boys. In Masonry, age symbolizes the degree of knowledge: for example, an Apprentice is said to be "three years old." Young boys carrying the T-square, the ruler, and the compass were favorite themes of eighteenth-century Masonic iconography (*cf.* Plate 7).

According to the Ladies, who announce them, the Three Boys are "young, good-looking, gracious, and wise." We have seen why they are young. The triad "good-looking, gracious,

---

* This term does appear in the list of characters preceding the libretto in its original edition. But that list is incomplete and approximate in more than one detail. In the libretto itself, the indication *Die Knaben* (The Boys) is correct and consistent.

D.* Combien faut-il de temps pour faire un Apprentif ?

R. Trois ans.

D. Quel âge avez-vous ?

R. Trois ans.

D. Quelle heure eſt-il ?

R. Près de midi.

Le Vénérable : En confidération de l'heure & de l'âge, avertiſſez tous nos chers Freres, que la Loge d'Apprentif Maçon eſt ouverte, & que nous allons commencer nos travaux à la maniere accoutumée.

Le premier Surveillant : Mes chers Freres, ſur ma colonne, je vous avertis, de la part du Vénérable, que la Loge d'Apprentif Maçon eſt ouverte, & que nous allons commencer nos travaux à la maniere accoutumée.

Le ſecond Surveillant répete les paroles du premier ; &, dès qu'il a fini, le Vénérable, ainſi que tous les Freres, ſe levent, font le ſigne d'Apprentif, puis les applaudiſſemens, & crient trois fois *Vivat* ; enſuite chacun ſe raſſeoit ; & c'eſt alors que le Vénérable commence le Catéchiſme, ou s'il y a quelques Récipiendaires, on les reçoit avant, afin qu'ils profitent de l'inſtruction.

CATÉCHISME

The Masonic Age (the Three Boys) and the hour for beginning the labors ("*die Stunde schlägt*"). Same source as page 88.

and wise" remains. It is peculiarly eloquent for a Mason. Every Masonic temple is upheld inside by the three pillars denominated "Strength, Beauty, Wisdom." * These three virtues, furthermore, are the ones celebrated in the final chorus of *Die Zauberflöte*. The young boys lack only one of them: strength, which is replaced by grace; this is the logical consequence of their age, and the transmutation will occur by itself as an outcome of their growth.

The rubric states that when the Three Boys appear for the first time, leading Tamino to the base of the Temple of Wisdom (but, again, not themselves entering it), they are carrying silver palms. This attribute would seem to signify the transition from one world to another of which they are the liaison messengers: the palm is solar, but silver is lunar; the music itself seems to participate in the symbolism of this situation, mixing the feminine Five and the maculine Three, as we shall see when analyzing the music (No. 8). For the same reason, during the trial by Air, they can appear on a flying machine covered with the roses of the feminine initiation destined successively for Pamina and Papagena; they themselves are boys, but have not yet attained accomplishment of their sex.

THE TWO PRIESTS, THE SPEAKER

Little commentary is required here beyond an underlining of the fact that we are not dealing with fictional or symbolic roles, but with real functionaries of the Masonic hierarchy. As adapted to the Egyptian setting of the story, the word "priest" has merely been carried over; the Speaker (*Sprecher*), on the other hand, has kept his name and his function. Fur-

---

* Strength is a Doric column, Beauty Corinthian, Wisdom Ionic. The three are set about with "mosaic pavement." Nettl says that in eighteenth-century Austrian lodges they were replaced with three lights of the same names. But as the columns always support torches perhaps this is a mere difference of nomenclature.

thermore, he subsumes that of the "Expert," who perhaps was omitted so as to have one less cast-member to pay.

THE MEN IN ARMOR

These two episodic characters, who intervene at the moment when Tamino and Pamina are undergoing the two final trials, by Fire and Water, are perhaps the most mysterious in the story. The usual translation, "armed men," furthermore, is inexact: the text reads *geharnischte Männer*—that is, men wearing armor (not men bearing arms). The rubric specifies that their armor is black and fire burns on their helmets.*

The junction of these two indications gives us the key to this difficulty: guardians of Fire and Water, they must bear the corresponding attributes. That of Fire is explicit; that of Water, more difficult to realize on the stage, is represented by one of the two corresponding colors (see the table, pp. 99–100).

Their armor remains to be explained. Once again, the answer is to be found in the initiation ritual. The trial by Fire, as we shall see when discussing the second-act trials, corresponds to one of the precise actions of that ritual, and is accompanied by a clanking of armor, "the emblem," Jules Boucher says,[5] "of the battles that man is forced constantly to fight." The armor of the guardians of the Fire is thus an explicit reference to one of the aspects of the corresponding trial.

---

* Here one may recall that in *Le Bourgeois gentilhomme*, Molière, during the parody of initiation—doubtless borrowed from an authentic ceremony of some traditional confraternity or society—places lighted candles on the Mufti's turban (Act IV, Scene 8, second *entrée* of the ballet in the Turkish ceremony). Or should one evoke, as Dent does (p. 226), the "lamps which can be worn on the head like helmets" of Victorian chimney sweeps and masons? Sethos and his pupil Amedes, Dent explains, wear "similar headgear" during their first exploration of the Pyramids. But in the design for the first staging of this scene (Plate 20), the "flame" of the helmets resembles a cock's comb— that is, one of the usual symbolic representations of flame,[4] and not its material reproduction pure and simple, even though borrowed from a Victorian chimney sweep's hat.

We should not leave the Men in Armor without mentioning that their intervention is almost always described inexactly: "They sing a chorale." I remember a Paris Opéra staging in which these two guardians stood facing the audience, their legs apart, each on one side of the entrance gate, and appeared to sing a canticle for which no *raison d'être* was apparent. The rubric is altogether something else: they introduce Tamino and read him a luminous inscription inscribed on a pyramid placed high up in the center of the stage (Plate 29). We shall see what that inscription means. It was Mozart who, setting it to music, gave it the form and melody of a chorale—which I shall explain—thus adding symbolism of his own to that of his librettist.

To this review of the protagonists of the drama, we may add an examination of various objects or accessories that play a predetermined role in it, and which also may be considered as active elements. We shall take them in the order of their appearance.

15

Some Other Symbols

Now I shall consider, in the order of their appearance in the opera, various objects or accessories that play determined roles in the action and can be considered as active elements in it.

THE SERPENT

I have evoked its symbolism above in relation to the Three Ladies. The meaning of the scene in which it is central could not be isolated better than in the Massins' words: "A young, idle aristocrat is out hunting and finds himself disarmed by the sudden irruption of his blindest vital instinct (the symbolism of the serpent did not wait for Jung, but was established in that sense in all hieroglyphic traditions). The first awakening is of love. To the cries of alarm that he had emitted when alone and face to face with himself, the answer is the call to emerge from himself (the portrait aria)." [1]

The victory over the serpent was an episode in *Sethos* (Book III), but Sethos does not kill the serpent: he captures it alive and takes it back to Memphis. Dent does not take the thing seriously. This exploit is accomplished, he writes,[2] "after hav-

pomme, & lui perfuade qu'il faut qu'elle la mange pour être reçue, en ajoutant que c'eft cette marque d'obéiffance qu'on exige d'elle, & que, fans cela elle ne pourroit parvenir à la connoiffance des fublimes myftères de la Maçonnerie. On peut bien s'imaginer que l'Afpirante ne fait aucune difficulté d'y confentir ; mais à peine a-t-elle commencé à mordre la pomme, que l'on fait entendre le tonnerre & la grêle, puis on tire le rideau qui fépare cet Appartement de la Loge ; l'Inftigateur s'échappe adroitement, & l'Orateur, qui fe tient prêt, s'avance à pas précipités, arrête le bras de la Récipiendaire, lui détache fon bandeau, & lui dit, avec le ton de l'enthoufiafme : « Malheureufe ! qu'avez-vous fait ? Eft-ce » a'nfi que vous pratiquez les leçons de fa- » geffe que l'on vous a données ? Se pour- » roit-il que vous méconnoiffiez ces fenti- » mens d'honneur & de vertu, premier fon- » dement de notre Ordre ? Quoi ! au mépris » des promeffes que vous a fait le Grand- » Maître de récompenfer votre courage & » votre prudence, vous vous laiffez féduire » par ce monftre, (*Il lui montre le ferpent, » duquel on fait remuer la tête*) qui n'a d'autre » but que celui de corrompre votre inno- » cence ; quelle récompenfe devez-vous at- » tendre d'une pareille foibleffe » ?

Il eft aifé de penfer que la Récipiendaire, furprife & trompée elle même dans fes fen-

The Serpent in the Ritual of Adoption (Act I, Scene 1).
Same source as page 88.

ing first estimated its size exactly by means of trigonometrical observations. This, however, was perhaps ill-adapted to musical treatment, though it might have appealed to Mozart's youthful taste for mathematics." The irony is facile, but does not analyze the significance. In the Schaffers' design reproducing Schikaneder's staging (Plate 15), we see the serpent cut into three pieces. The rubric also describes it that way, but at the same time specifies that the Ladies' weapon is a silver javelin: it matters little that a javelin would not serve well for cutting up a serpent. Be that as it may, silver is a feminine symbol (see the table on pp. 98–9), and the three pieces of the serpent mark the first appearance of the masculine Three (the Three Ladies, as we have seen, are another matter). All that conforms perfectly to the proposed exegesis.

A curious coincidence: the seal of Cagliostro, one of the pioneers of feminine Masonry, represents a serpent with an apple in its mouth and pierced by an arrow (see p. 122).

The Padlock

We have already seen (p. 111) the explanation of the padlock. Golden (discretion being a masculine virtue), it nonetheless represents a rite of the feminine initiation of Companions, during which the mouth is sealed with a trowel to place the ladies on guard against the idle chatter native to their sex (*cf.* Plate 35 and p. 111). We recall that Papageno, though a man, is nevertheless in the service of the Kingdom of the Night.

The Portrait

It is, of course, by presenting Tamino, on the part of their mistress, with the portrait of her daughter that the Ladies instantly awaken his love for Pamina, thus setting the action in motion. The suddenness and violence of such emotion at the sight of a miniature may seem to us today as unbelievable

EMBLEME, CHIFFRE OU SCEAU
de Cagliostro

marquant apposé sur cire verte
au commencement et à la fin le manuscrit original
du RITUEL DE LA MAÇONNERIE EGYPTIENNE

Le comte de Cagliostro

Reproduction en fac simile de la signature de Cagliostro

Seal of Cagliostro (S-shaped serpent pierced by an arrow and
with an apple in its throat). Extract from Marc Haven, *Rituel
de la Maçonnerie égyptienne* (see Bibliography), Nice, 1947.

as it is arbitrary. It was not so for eighteenth-century spectators.

In fact, the *coup du portrait* was in a way a commonplace of the theater of that epoch, as "my mother's Crucifix" was at the dénouement; no one would have thought of being surprised by either. We have seen (*cf.* pp. 33–4) that Mozart himself had already treated it in *Zaide*. But here we are not dealing with a simple fictional story. Like everything else in the libretto, this action must be looked at from the symbolic point of view. Tamino, who has had his first, very imperfect revelation in the death of the serpent, must now come to true love. He will not be able really to look upon the features of his beloved except, first, by virtue of Sarastro's illumination and then, at last, when they both have passed the initiatory trials. Until that time he can know her only through her image, whence the portrait.

THE "MAGIC FLUTE"

Let us observe at once, as Cotte points out reasonably, that the traditional translation of *Die Zauberflöte* as *La Flûte enchantée* is faulty: the flute is "magic" in the sense that it *creates* enchantment; it is not "enchanted" in the sense that it has undergone enchantment.

That said, the flute itself plays a relatively modest role in the action. We saw in Chapter 5 the probable reasons for the disproportion between that modesty and the importance that might be foreseen from the title of the opera: the idea of making it the center of a magic-laden story doubtless was the point of departure. But thereafter, almost certainly under pressure from Mozart and Born, the story evolved in such a way that the flute became little more than an accessory. Moving farther and farther away from the model that had supplied the original idea, the story kept its title for commercial reasons. Once again I repeat that this in no way signifies a shift in the plan, but rather suggests a retouching of the entire libretto before it was set to music.

Between *Die Zauberflöte* and the models that Schikaneder first had envisaged using, there is a fundamental difference: in Wieland and his successors, the magic instrument is a supernatural object destined solely to smooth out the difficulties of the mission.* Here it is something altogether different: its role, the Three Ladies say, is "to transform the passions of men, to render the melancholy joyful, the misogynist amorous." Its symbolism is that of the music itself: to carry out his journey of purification, man needs aid from rites that give him the power to transform souls, and music is the most essential sign of them. Tamino will never employ the flute as it was employed in the models—to dissolve material objects magically—but only to find the courage to surmount them or to express feelings that he has not the right to express in words. We are far from Wieland's *Lulu* and *Oberon*. Does that explain why, in the original stage setting reproduced in Plate 16, what appears in answer to the flute's call is not, as the rubric asks, "animals," but "savages"?

One also notices how economical Mozart is of flute-sound in his orchestration: one might well have expected a concerto-like plethora of it. Quite the contrary, and the discretion is significant. Later (No. 21B), Pamina will reveal the origin of the magic instrument: it did not come, as had been believed, from the Queen of the Night, but from her husband, Sarastro's predecessor as master of the Solar Circle. In other words, music is not a proper pastime or hobby for women, as our official scholarly programs said until recently, because they have received it from earlier Wisdom. Furthermore, the

---

* Unless, as some writers seem inclined to think, esoteric backgrounds also played a part in the stories of that sort, an idea that would conform well to Wieland's personality, especially as he also was a Freemason. But that is another matter, and cannot be discussed here.

flute, a masculine symbol, is golden in color (not "of gold," one exact translation of *goldene*); the eighteenth-century flute was usually wooden, and the material of this one is specified: it was cut, Pamina says, from a millenary tree. That fact gives it a new symbolism: destined for use under the sign of Air (man's breath), it has been produced magically during a stormy night under a downpour (Water), to the noise of thunder (Earth) and the flash of lightning (Fire). It unites the four Elements, whence its perfection.

The Glockenspiel

One cannot say the same of the instrument given to Papageno in parallel. What exactly, for that matter, is this instrument? The original libretto calls it *hölzernes Gelächter*—"wooden amusement-piece" (literally, "wooden laughter")—but the score replaces that expression with *stromento d'acciajo* (steel instrument), with the significance that it retains today. Nevertheless, it seems that the notion of the "amusement-piece" was determinative, placing it in opposition to the magic flute, and that our keyed orchestral glockenspiels, too much perfected, take away some of the rusticity desired from an instrument meant to be played upon the stage and certainly not in the pit.*

But, "amusement-piece" or not, it is nonetheless as effec-

---

* Or, at least, to give the illusion of being played upon the stage. In the role of Papageno, Schikaneder played a sham instrument while the real one was played in the wings near him. One day, Mozart amused himself with one of those theatrical jokes which always delight comedians: without Papageno's knowledge, he took the place of the glockenspiel-player and, when the moment came, unexpectedly began to play something very different from what Schikaneder was expecting. Embarrassed and furious, Schikaneder glanced into the wings, recognized the composer, and adroitly recovered himself. He threw down the sham glockenspiel, pretended to stamp upon it, and shouted the equivalent of "Shut up." Whereupon, Mozart wrote to Constanze on October 8, 1791, "everyone laughed. I am inclined to think that this joke taught many of the audience for the first time that Papageno does not play the instrument himself."

tive as the flute in its symbolic action. Made of wood or of
steel, it is an instrument under the sign of Earth. In Act I,
it will have an irresistible effect upon Monostatos, who represents the same sign; in Act II, it is during Papageno's trial by
Earth that it will fulfill its purpose of summoning Papagena
so that she too may undergo that trial. Its use in the finale is
less easy to explain: perhaps, as so often in the libretto, the
explanation lies in parallelism with the preceding scene: just
as Tamino and Pamina underwent their trials by Fire and
Water together, so Papageno and Papagena too will be united
under the double sign of Air and Earth: the flute and the
glockenspiel.

16

The
Initiatory
Trials

The first act shows the preparatory labor that Tamino and Pamina must perform on the threshold of their initiation. The second act describes that initiation. As for Papageno and Papagena, they undergo the corresponding mini-trials, but in a tone of comedy.

I / THE INITIAL SWOON

Every cycle of trials presupposes a complete transformation of the personality: the future elect must first die in their former life if they are to be born into the new one later. That idea, which Masonry embraces at each advowson of degree (representing a new step toward Knowledge), is not its own. All religions, Christianity included, have known it in one form or another. "For ye are dead," St. Paul writes, "and your life is hid with Christ in God." [1] In the ceremony of ordination, the candidates lie full length upon the ground and remain there for long moments as though dead or in a swoon so that they may rise up later in their new condition.

An initiatory trial therefore appears as a sort of "rehearsal" of the final initiation, which will be physical death, and thus eases the passage leading from contemplation of that to the idea of a new resurgence into the future life. A universal idea, of which the Christian dogma of eternal life and the resurrection of the body is undoubtedly but one of the multiple aspects, and which esoteric societies have not neglected. The letters of Mozart and Schubert about death cited on pp. 68 and 69 (to speak only of musicians) are eloquent testimony. In vague but unmistakable terms, Sarastro preaches a doctrine of explicit survival. Should Tamino encounter a premature death during his trials, he says, "it will be given him to be received by Osiris and Isis before us, and to experience the divine joys."

It is by means of a swoon, the stage representation of that "symbolic death," that Tamino, Pamina, and even, belatedly, Papageno begin their "labors." On their first entrances upon the stage, Tamino faints on seeing the serpent, Pamina at the sight of Monostatos. As for Papageno, he falls to earth, felled by the thunder that drives the Three Ladies from the Temple. "Stand up," the priest then says to him, "and be a man" (*sei ein Mann*). That, hidden within an episode that is—perhaps incorrectly—thought comic, is the precise explanation of the trials as just outlined for the three characters.

Thus we see that the redemptive action begins for Tamino when the curtain first goes up. We know nothing of his past except that his father—he confides this to Papageno—often talked to him about the Queen of the Night, and that he feels unbounded admiration for her (which well corresponds to his pre-initiate condition). He appears, the rubric says, dressed as a Japanese* hunter. That may appear very strange at the outset of an Egyptian or pseudo-Egyptian drama—but it signifies that he comes from the East, where solar activity begins. He carries a bow, symbol of his potential strength,

* Some editions say "Javanese," but the sense is the same.

but he has no arrows, which is to say that he does not yet possess the means of using his bow. (Here one notes the nonsense of commentaries saying that he has "no more" arrows: the German text is *"ohne Pfeil."* *) The serpent of his first temptation will be killed by the feminine weapon, the silver javelin.

The presentation of Pamina is somewhat different. She too swoons upon her first entrance, but we have been informed of many things that have happened to her earlier: her abduction from her mother's Nocturnal Kingdom, her having been placed under the guardianship of the Moor, her attempted escape. All that has already been explained (p. 103), but now we can understand that her attempted escape could not succeed because she had not yet undergone the first essential metamorphosis.

When Tamino and Pamina awaken from their swoons, what they see before them is not at all what they expect: neither the Ladies for Tamino nor Monostatos for Pamina. The first person whom they see in their new life is none other than the futile, frivolous Papageno, incarnation of the phantasms of the evanescent Air. That first transformation has been only of the senses; they will not truly become themselves until they have answered the deeper summons to true love. It is still too early for them to contemplate the objects of that love in their true forms: Tamino will know his beloved only through a portrait, Pamina hers by the description given her by Papageno, Papageno his only under the hideous features of an old woman. In order really to see, they must undergo other trials, other transformations.

Among the partners in the two couples, only Papagena es-

---

* Roger Cotte recalls to me that in *Le Martyre de Saint-Sébastien*, Gabriele D'Annunzio, a readily esoteric writer, depicted the sexually ambiguous character that he gave the features of St. Sebastian as those of an *"archer inerme."* The word *inerme* (etymologically "without arms") is botanical: it signifies "without thorns"; whence the image of the archer "without arrows."

capes the pre-initiatory swoon, or at least does not swoon on stage. But that matters little, as, in the priest's words to Papageno, "the joys reserved to the initiate" will be forbidden to their future menage.

II / ADMISSION TO THE TRIALS

Not everyone who wishes to enter an initiatory society can do so. Admission presupposes a preliminary inquiry decided by a first vote and usually carried out by three brothers delegated for the purpose, who interview the candidate and then present a report. That report is read in the lodge, and leads to a second vote. If that one is favorable, the candidate is summoned and brought into the temple for an interrogation "under the blindfold"—that is, with his eyes covered, for he is not yet worthy to see the interior of the temple. After he has retired, the brothers deliberate, and a third vote decides whether he will be admitted to the trials.[2] These, which constitute the initiation itself, give place to still further deliberations, this time purely formal.

All of that will be found faithfully transposed in the first act of Die Zauberflöte. The Three Boys have the role of the three first investigators: their words clearly are the outcome of their earlier interviews. Tamino has been instructed sufficiently by them to know that what he has come here to seek is not Pamina herself, but "the goods of Love and of Virtue" which should lead him toward her. Like the role of the investigators, that of the Three Boys ends at the entrance to the temple: they lead Tamino there and then retire. The libretto dispenses with allusion to the second vote, but has us present at a transposition of the questioning carried out in the temple "under the blindfold." This, meant to make the postulant realize that he has not yet the right to see the interior of the temple, is replaced on the stage by the refusals to admit him. The old priest stands alone on the threshold: Tamino can

Mozart wearing the Masonic insignia
of the degree of Master

Masonic portrait of Ignaz von Born
with the attributes given Sarastro

See also Commentaries on the Plates, with Sources.

Masonic tarot of Etteilla
(c. 1790): Masonry of Hiram
and of the Order of the Mopses

Corresponding cards of
ordinary tarot

The Three Boys, engraving by
Boucher for a Masonic diploma

7

Master's apron bearing
several symbols used in *Die
Zauberflöte* (19th century)

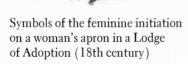

Master's apron with the
Flaming Star and super-
imposed G (18th century)

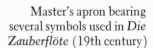

Symbols of the feminine initiation
on a woman's apron in a Lodge
of Adoption (18th century)

9

10

11

12

Above left and right:
Papageno in 1791 and 1794

13

DIE ZAUBERFLÖTE

eine

GROSSE OPER IN ZWEY AUFZÜGEN

fürs

CLAVIER oder PIANOFORTE

von

W. A. MOZART.

Chés J. J. HUMMEL, à Berlin avec Privilège du Roi.
à Amsterdam au grand Magazin de Musique et aux
Adresses ordinaires.

Scene 1 in a 19th-century
edition

The sword and the serpent,
Belgian Masonic medallion
(1838)

14

Schikaneder's mise-en-scène of 1794
Above: The Three Ladies in Act I
Below: Tamino charms the "savages"
(finale of Act I)

Schikaneder's mise-en-scène of 1794
Above: Entrance of Sarastro (finale of Act I)
Below: Pamina rejoins Tamino during the
Trial by Air (Act II)

Schikaneder's mise-en-scène of 1794
Above: The Priest takes Papagena from Papageno
after her transformation (Act II). *Below:* The
Trials by Fire and Water (finale of Act II)

Above: Backstage scene during the Weimar
performances of *Die Zauberflöte* in 1794
Below: Allegory of the birth of Freemasonry (1857)

Two portraits of Schikaneder (*left*) compared with Schaffer's 1794 drawings of Papageno (*right*)

Two 18th-century initiations. *Left:* In a regular lodge (partly symbolic engraving). *Right:* In a Lodge of Feminine Adoption

Lodge admittance medal representing the Trial by Fire

Opposite:
Upper left: The admonition to silence-statue of the J column, as represented on a diploma of the Grand Orient de France (beginning of 19th century). *Upper right:* French Masonic medal (1807), with Egyptian pyramid (figure 29) and transfixed serpent (figure 30). *Lower left:* Bronze "authentic solar circle" (Hittite period, c. 2500 B.C.). *Lower right:* Piece of Masonic jewelry showing the five pointed star, the rose on the T square, and the compass (19th century).

27

28

29

30

31

32

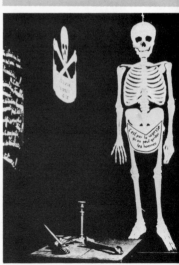

Symbolic engraving of the Cabinet of Reflection, frontispiece to the first edition of the libretto of *Die Zauberflöte*, 1791. (*See* Commentaries on the Plates.)

Upper right: The symbols of the Cabinet of Reflection, after Jules Boucher

Center right: Symbolic trowel of a Lodge of Adoption, used for sealing the postulant's mouth (Papageno's padlock)

Lower right: Inscriptions and writing desk from a Cabinet of Reflection

Prepared but unsigned Master's diploma
(the name was not inserted) of Mozart's lodge, 1792

The "Basin" of Mesmer, Freemason and apostle
of "animal magnetism," in whose home Mozart's
Bastien und Bastienne was first performed

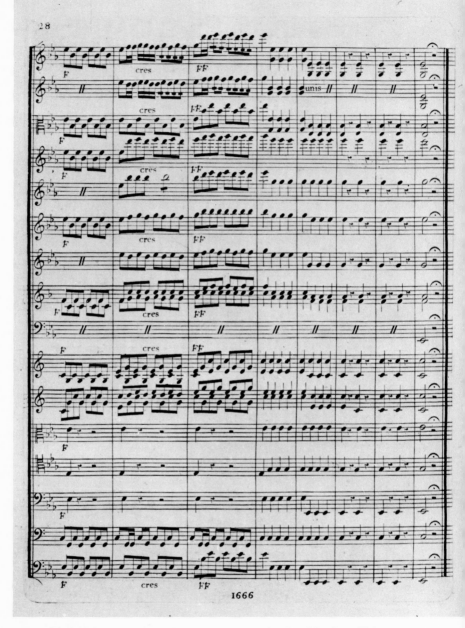

End of the Overture in the "revision" entitled *Les Mystères d'Isis*

The same passage (third measure on) in the authentic version

Entrance and waterfall of the Grotto of Aigen near Salzburg,
gathering place of Masons and "Illuminati"

advance no farther. "This interrogation," Ambelain says, "must always be clothed in the appearance of the greatest courtesy, and this will be related to having the profane filled with the tone of perfect tolerance which must reign in the bosom of a well-conducted Masonic lodge." [3] In fact, that is the direction given to the dialogue: the priest allows Tamino to criticize Sarastro and rectifies his judgments without harrying him or becoming indignant. Because the deliberation and the third vote take place only after the departure of the profane, Tamino is not informed of the result of his interview with the old priest: he learns only that he will be initiated "soon or never," which means that he will be summoned shortly if the decision is favorable, but that a rejection cannot be appealed. We are not present at that deliberation, but we learn its result from Sarastro's verdict: he orders that Tamino's head be veiled and that he be led to the temple of the trials. That is the sanction resulting from the third vote.

The veil in question is different from the one that prevents the light from reaching the Queen of the Night and her Ladies. Certainly it also symbolizes the ignorance of the profane, but its significance is defined by the rubric of No. 18A: it is "the veil that covers those vowed to consecration" (*Eingeweihten*). The present ritual requires a simple blindfold over the eyes. Sarastro adds that the strangers "*müssen erst gereinigt sein,*" customarily translated as "must first be purified." That is probably nonsense, for neither in the libretto nor in the ritual is there any place for a purification preliminary to the trials, which in themselves constitute that purification. Doubtless "*erst*" should be understood as "in the first place" or "above all." *

These, then, are the preliminary "examinations" from which Tamino emerges victorious. Nothing can be said of those of

---

* Unless it refers to the physical preparation, which in the ritual consists of partially disrobing the profane, as Plate 25 shows.

Papageno or *a fortiori* of Papagena. One even doubts that they take place: the authors would have had some difficulty in justifying their admission, and did not take the trouble. They happen without explanation.

Things occur differently for Pamina. There is no regular inquiry because no initiation in the full sense of the term is foreseen for women (we have seen that Adoption lodges held only a demi-initiation). Nor is there any mention of it in Sarastro's verdict regarding her. Pamina herself must win the right to accede to Knowledge, and that is one of the opera's most dramatic aspects.

III / OPENING OF THE LABORS AND THE DELIBERATION OF THE INITIATES

Every ceremony of reception begins with the "solemn opening of the labors." It starts with a processional entrance of the Brothers, which the Master of the ceremonies "leads slowly, in a regular, rhythmic march, quietly" [4]; that is precisely the nature of the March of the Priests which opens the second act. Among the actions that follow, of which the opera retains only a part, figures—at least in the "Egyptian" rite of Memphis-Misraïm—an invocation to Osiris and Isis, which is followed by a prayer to the "Great Architect" that corresponds to Sarastro's prayer (No. 10). [5]

The libretto gives a detailed description of the temple for this purpose. It was borrowed, Paul Nettl says, in part from *Sethos*, in part from Born, but not directly from the usage of the Lodge. We shall therefore explain it in Part Three.

The solemn march that opens the second act and the festive vestments in which the priests and Sarastro himself are robed tell us as the curtain rises that we are in the ceremonial domain and that the deliberation we are witnessing is a rite rather than a real discussion. In fact, the decision has been taken, as Sarastro has informed us at the end of Act I: no one would question his orders.

This corresponds to the ritual order, following upon what we just have expounded. Once the postulant has been summoned to the initiatory ceremony, he runs no further risk of being refused, but numerous repetitions in the rite symbolically recall the deliberations—the positive ones—that have determined his admission and the fact that he is free to turn back if he does not feel the courage to persevere.

The first phase of the initiation includes various rites, among which figures a symbolic demand for admission which Sarastro evokes when he announces that Tamino "has presented himself at the north portal of our Temple," that "a veil still covers his eyes," and that he "asks for admission into the sanctuary where the sublime light shines." The candidate, his eyes covered, is in fact led before the portal. In the true sense, there is no "north portal," but "north" is used symbolically: it is the side to which the light never reaches (*cf.* p. 238). Led by the "Brother Expert," he knocks on the portal, through which the dialogue is carried on. "Who knocks at the portal as a profane man?" the Venerable asks. The Expert replies that it is "a profane man who demands reception as a Mason." The Venerable questions the Expert as to whether this profane man possesses the requisite virtues.* The Expert gives the guarantee. A simulacrum of deliberation involving the Venerable and the Brothers follows, and they give final approval. Only then is the profane man, his eyes still covered, introduced into the Temple. The Venerable addresses a first allocution to him and places him in the hands of the Expert, whose mission it is to conduct him toward his first trial. Then they both leave.

---

* In the libretto, the profane man is called "virtuous, discreet, and charitable." In Ambelain's ritual, the formula is "free and of good morals." [6]

In the preceding, we recognize the exact unfolding of the first scene of Act II, except that the candidate does not appear (he is merely evoked) and that the Expert is replaced by the Speaker.* The prayer to Isis and Osiris takes place at the beginning of the labors in the ritual, but its transposition here to the end of the scene is easily justifiable for theatrical effect.†

The first trial to which the profane man is subjected is of a special nature: it includes a portion of the preliminary examination and of the initiatory trial properly speaking. We shall examine it later under the second aspect, but here let us concentrate on the first briefly.

IV / THE "CABINET OF REFLECTION"

The first trial, in addition to its symbolic character (it represents, as we shall see later, the trial by Earth in the set of the four Elements), constitutes a real test. Leaving the Temple with his eyes blindfolded, the profane man first is "stripped of his metals"—that is, all objects, silver included, that he is carrying (they will be returned to him later): the "metals" represent the impurities that the new initiate must never introduce into the Temple. After that, he is led to a narrow, dark place, the "Cabinet of Reaction," ‡ where his guide removes the blindfold and leaves him alone for a long time. Lighted only by a lantern or torch, the room is painted black and decorated with macabre symbols: skeletons, skulls, teardrops, inscriptions in white lettering inviting the profane man to renounce his purpose if his intention is sordid or selfish.

---

* The Speaker is also an officer of the Lodge. Perhaps Schikaneder wanted to economize by condensing the two offices into one. But as we do not have at hand the exact ritual of the Viennese lodges in 1791, we cannot exclude the possibility that in them the function was in fact filled by the Speaker rather than by the Expert.

† Same comment as in preceding footnote.

‡ The word "reflection" should be interpreted here in the sense of "return upon himself," not in that of "solitary thought." [7]

One often sees the word V.I.T.R.I.O.L., which is not an allusion to possible poisoning, but the abbreviation of a Latin clause which I shall discuss on pp. 138–9, and which relates the trial to the symbol of "Earth." A rooster also figures here, evoking the impending sunrise. The postulant is thus left alone in darkness. Before him he finds a table with writing materials and a questionnaire to which he is asked to reply in writing. It is called the "philosophic Testament." When the prescribed time has elapsed, the candidate is sought out, his eyes are again blindfolded, and he is once more led into the Temple. There, still blindfolded, he is present during a commentary on his "Testament," which is then burned. He is taken out once more, and a new vote (rarely negative this time) decides whether or not he is worthy to continue the trials.[8]

All of that is to be found, scarcely altered, in the subterranean scene that opens Tamino's trials (No. 10A). We are not present at the removal of the "metals," but that it occurs goes without saying, as later on (No. 16), Tamino and Papageno respectively are given back the flute and the glockenspiel that they had with them when admitted—which was when they were relieved of them. The décor of the Cabinet (sometimes also called that of the "Frightful Trials") is not copied, but suggested: the mortuary symbols are replaced by signs of abandonment and desolation: debris of pyramids, broken columns, thorny bushes,* whereas the written inscriptions, which would not be very effective theatrically, are omitted. The candidates are left alone in the darkness only a few instants. At least, that is suggested by the ensuing interrogation, which on stage takes place in the interior of the Cabinet it-

---

* This is the décor represented on the celebrated frontispiece of the original edition of the libretto (Plate 33). Unlike the other illustrations in the same libretto, it is more decoratively interpreted than theatrically faithful. See also p. 139.

self. One can consider the scene with the Three Ladies a true examination related to the philosophic Testament; it is related to the candidate's reactions in the face of accusations made against the Order. After the completion of this scene (we shall discuss its details later), the priests enter to announce to Tamino that he has passed his trial successfully; this is the transcription of the favorable vote. Thus he can approach the succeeding trials—the initiatory trials proper. Only after having undergone them will the profane man be called upon to take the oath and the blindfold be permanently removed from his eyes, whereupon the most blinding light will dazzle him.

Like Tamino, Pamina too will undergo the examination of her "Testament," which takes place regularly during her trial by Earth (the moonlight scene); the insinuations of the Queen of the Night against the initiates will be an exact repetition of the Ladies' diatribes against their Order, and her daughter's refusal to trust her will be equivalent to Tamino's refusal to debate with his accusers.

V / THE RITUAL TRIALS

I have already spoken of the first of the trials because of its "double" nature. At that place, I concentrated on its aspect as "examination." I return to it now, along with the others, with respect to its symbolic aspect.

Exactly as in the ritual of initiation into the Apprentice degree, the trials in Act II of *Die Zauberflöte* can be reduced to two essential themes: silence and the symbolic journey through the dangers of the four Elements.

(a) *Silence*

The trial by silence is clearly announced and the neophytes are frequently reminded of its terms. It corresponds to a ritual recommendation insistently made to future Apprentices (*cf.* Plate 28): silence about everything that they may see and hear in the Lodge, so that "secret society" may not be empty words. But in the framework of *Die Zauberflöte* this silence acquires a very special meaning corresponding to the general idea that we have discussed: it refers essentially to the discretion vis-à-vis women which a man should observe: "What can our talking together do, seeing that we are both men?" Papageno asks Tamino (Scene 15A). In the duet No. 11, the priests comment upon this trial explicitly as designed to harden man vis-à-vis woman, to teach him to despise her. That is doubtless why, paradoxically, Pamina will be the victim of the trial by silence, but will not herself be compelled to undergo it. It is also the reason why the trial is in two sections: Tamino is first confronted by woman in her social, frivolous aspect (Scene No. 12, with the Three Ladies), then in her emotional, amorous aspect (scene with Pamina). In the analysis we shall see the forms taken by that double test.

(b) *The Four Elements*

The trial by silence is explicitly announced, but that by the Elements is much more veiled, though at the foot of the mountain of Fire and that of Water (the only two trials of the series clearly presented), the luminous inscription on the pyramid, read out in the tone of a chorale, refers unequivocally to the presence of all of the four Elements (and not merely to the two represented there): "He who commits himself to this dangerous route will be purified by *Fire, Water, Air,* and *Earth*." The sentence refers not merely to this scene, but to almost the whole second act.

The trials by the four Elements are an important section of the initiation ceremony. This commentary appears in an authorized work:[9]

The most ancient Masonic rituals take into account purification by the four elements: probably what remains of a totemic symbolization of the development of Life with the help of, and through, these primordial, elementary entities. The first element is the Earth, the subterranean domain where germination and seeding develop. It is represented by the Cabinet of Reflection in which the Member-Elect is confined. The first journey is related to Air, the second to Water, the third to Fire. . . . The first journey is the emblem of human life, the tumult of the passions, the collision of diverse interests, the difficulty of undertakings, the obstacles that are multiplied in our path by rivals eager to harm us and always ready to thwart us—all that is represented by the irregularity of the route traveled by the Member-Elect and by the noise made all around him. . . . To give the Member-Elect assurance, he is made to undergo the purification by Water. It is a sort of philosophic baptism that washes him clean of all stain. . . . The deafening noise of the first journey has been followed by a clanking of arms, emblem of the combats that man is constantly forced to undergo. . . . In order to contemplate the Queen of Hell—that is, the truth hidden within himself—the Initiate must pass through a triple enclosure of flames. This is the trial by Fire. The Initiate remains amid the flames (circumambient passions) without being burned, but must allow himself to be penetrated by the beneficent warmth that they emit.

Not only Tamino, but also Pamina, Papageno, and even Papagena will in turn, each in his own way, pass through these trials. Very close to a literal evocation of the ritual in Tamino's case, they will be presented for the other characters in ways adapted to their roles in the opera.

A. Tamino

(a) Earth

As we just have seen, the trial by Earth is more or less intermingled with that in the Cabinet of Reflection. So it is for Tamino. Inside the place set aside for this purpose in the lodges an apparently arcane inscription appears: V.I.T.-R.I.O.L. It is made from the first letters of the words in this sentence: Visita Interiorem Terrae, Rectificando Invenies

Occultum Lapidem—Visit the Interior of the Earth by Following* the Right Road and You Will Find the Hidden Stone. On the frontispiece of the original (1791) edition of the libretto, which evokes this décor (Plate 33), we see, clearly evident alongside Egyptianizing designs and many of the usual symbols of the Cabinet of Reflection—such as the pitcher, the hourglass, and the decapitated statue that takes the place of the traditional skull [10]—a spade and a pickax that recall the "*Interiorem Terrae*" (*cf.* Plate 34).

"Tamino and Papageno," the rubric continues, "are brought in by the Speaker and another priest, who remove their veils and then retire. Night. Thunder rolls in the distance." This is easily recognizable. Thunder is not merely a well-known theatrical device connoting terror: it also represents the seismic shocks that speak of the forces of the Earth, and which for that reason recur throughout the trial.† As for the darkness, it is both a copy of that in the Cabinet of Reflection and the symbol of the ignorance from which the profane man now gradually must begin to emerge.

"Dreadful night!" Tamino says: clearly, the words used for all their meanings. On the other hand, the ensuing dialogue at once veers toward the superficially comic: now Papageno comes on stage. Two peals of thunder coming closer, punctuated by stage business showing the Birdcatcher's terror. The final exchange, however, should be noted again because it sums up the symbolism of the opera: "Get up," Tamino says. "Be a man," and Papageno replies piteously: "It's enough for me to be a girl." In the obvious sense, that means that he wants to be released from these accursed trials. But in a

---

* Rather than "in Rectifying," as Rectificando is translated by Hutin (p. 146) and Boucher (p. 30), which makes little sense.

‡ Sethos, in the novel, is frightened by the noise of thunder in the subterranean places, but this is, Dent says (p. 228), only "the reverberation through the subterranean passages of the noise of closing doors. . . ."

second sense it means: "I don't at all want to enter the service of masculine society—it will be enough for me to remain in that of the Queen of the Night."

The Speaker and the other priest enter bearing lanterns. The interrogation proceeds in a totally ritual manner. Equally ritual is the Speaker's warning: "Prince, there is still time to renounce your intention; one more step and it will be too late." "I shall succeed," Tamino answers, "for I wish to acquire knowledge of wisdom, and my reward is to be Pamina." That is—to remain within the perspective of the libretto—finally to acquire a love worthy of the name.

It is in this second sense that the rest of the dialogue is comprehensible, opposing Tamino's search to Papageno's very different conception: he too will be very happy if he can "finally get his hands on a pretty companion"—his aspirations are limited to that—but he has no wish to undergo dangerous trials in order to realize them.

The Masonic examination represented here by the "philosophic Testament" must still be represented upon the stage. This, as we have seen, is the chief purpose of the quintet, No. 12. The Three Ladies arise from under ground (always the Earth) and try to discredit the Order in Tamino's mind. But he is impervious to their arguments. Here the trial is threefold: it is amplified by the necessity to resist the Ladies' glibness, as the inserted duet of the priests (No. 11) just has recalled, and also by that of obeying the law of silence reiterated earlier by the Speaker.

Tamino having resisted these temptations victoriously (there is no preoccupation with Papageno here, he being only a supernumerary), when the Speaker (who is concerned only with Tamino) and the other priest return with lanterns, the Speaker can declare that the first trial has been passed successfully. The second priest does not say the same to the Birdcatcher, who still must undergo his trial by Earth. Both are led from the Cabinet of Reflection after being re-blindfolded, just as a real postulant is blindfolded again.

(b) Air

Continuing in the ritual order, Tamino next passes his trial by Air. It begins with the trio, No. 16: its nature is announced both by the *mise en scène* (the arrival of the Three Boys in a flying chariot) and by the orchestra, which in an extraordinary way translates into music that is, so to speak, suspended and without basses, the fluidity of the Element and the gliding flight of the machine that symbolizes it. From their flying chariot, the Boys lower a table set with appetizing dishes; then they disappear into the air. The trial consists partly in resisting the temptation of the good fare, partly in the continuation of the trial by silence, now on a higher level than before—for after not having spoken to women in general on a social level, Tamino must continue that strict observance even with the woman he deeply loves.

While Papageno throws himself gluttonously upon the victuals offered, Tamino resists and, instead of eating, plays the flute, the "wind" instrument just presented to him by the Boys—who have brought it in the flying chariot of the Air. Pamina runs in. Tamino refuses to speak to her, and she expresses her deep despair in a famous aria. The trial includes a seemingly irrelevant sequence: Papageno's imprudent boasting attracts Sarastro's lions, but Tamino's flute (the sign of the Air again) quickly puts them to flight, rendering them harmless. As this repeats the first-act episode of the animals without adding anything of value to the completed trial, the scene gives the impression of having been superadded to the original plan with a view to making the most of Schikaneder's cardboard lions and giving his role a supplementary comic effect. The chorus of priests (No. 18) announces that Tamino has come through his second trial (that by Air) successfully.

(c) Fire and Water

Only these two final trials are announced clearly. Further, they are linked together and the one follows the other without interruption, though uniquely in reverse order. The usual ritual order is Water-Fire; the reason for the change to Fire-Water will become clear shortly.

Because we are not told the nature of these trials, they remain a mystery. We merely see Tamino and Pamina (later on we shall see why they are together) set off toward them to the sound of the magic flute, and then return to announce that they have been passed successfully. Nothing even in the music describes the character of the trials: the rhythm of the flute does not change—and it continues its imperturbable march as they proceed.

The scene represents "two great mountains. On one of them, a cascade of water is heard roaring and seething; the other spits fire. Each mountain has an openwork grille through which the fire and the water can be seen. Where the fire is burning, the horizon should be of hellish red, and black clouds lie over the water. The stage is also scattered with large boulders, each closed with an iron door."

Such is the rubric. Its insistence on the red color of Fire (a masculine color) and the black of Water (a feminine color: cf. the table on p. 99) is notable. To the Société de Musicologie (December 1966), Carl de Nys presented the hypothesis that the décor had been suggested by the grotto in the park of Aigen, near Salzburg, represented in Plate 41. It belonged to a notable Freemason, Basil von Ammann, and in it he held reunions that probably were Masonic or Illuministic, and in which Mozart could have participated. From that grotto, one hears the sound of a neighboring cascade.[11] The connection is charming, but not certain, as Mozart's Masonic career at Salzburg remains very dubious, and in the rubric it is not a grotto, but mountains (*Berge*) and rocks (*Felsen*).

"Tamino," the stage direction continues, "dressed lightly and without sandals, is introduced under the guidance of the two men wearing black armor. Fire burns on their helmets. In loud voices, they read him the luminous transparent inscription on a pyramid. That pyramid is located very high up in the middle of the stage, near the grilles."

We already have given (pp. 117–18) the explanation of the Men in Armor and their uniforms. The lightness of Tamino's costume alludes to the ritual dress for the initiation (knee and chest uncovered, feet bare or practically so—see Plate 25), but it also supplies contrast with the dress of the two guardians: to endure life's struggles (symbolized in the ritual by the clanking of arms), the initiates are protected by strong armor; the profane must do without it. The inscription that the guardians read to Tamino is presented in an 1836 text as the inscription on Hiram's tomb.[12] It is taken, almost unchanged, from *Sethos* (see the facsimiles on pp. 145, 146). We have already cited its opening: here is the entire text as given in the libretto: "He who commits himself to this dangerous route will be purified by Fire, Water, Air, and Earth.* If he can surmount the terror of death, he will soar up from the earth toward the sky. Then he will be in a state to receive the light and to consecrate himself completely to the mysteries of Isis."

As all commentators know, the text is chanted to the melody of a Protestant chorale, *Ach, Gott, vom Himmel sieh' darein* (further, it is spelled out in the score). But why a

---

* Note that in *Sethos* the Earth is cited separately, as in the commentary upon the trials by the four Elements (p. ooo). The stage adaptation puts the Elements on a single level in the reverse of the order in which they appear in the ritual.

Original text of the "Chorale of the Men in Armor."
Das Erfurter Enchiridion, 1524 (facsimile reproduction
published by Bärenreiter Verlag, Kassel, 1929).

chorale—and why this one?* In another chapter (p. 277), I shall attempt to answer the first question, which will give me a chance to remark upon Mozart's extraordinary power of invention in the area of musical figuration. Here I shall confine myself to the second question.

): QUICONQUE FERA CETTE ROUTE SEUL, ET SANS REGARDER DERRIERE LUI, SERA PURIFIE PAR LE FEU, PAR L'EAU ET PAR L'AIR; ET S'IL PEUT VAINCRE LA FRAYEUR DE LA MORT, IL SORTIRA DU SEIN DE LA TERRE, IL

The Inscription of the Trials, in the novel
Sethos, edition of 1767. Collection Roger Cotte.

Evidently the choice of this chorale can have been dictated only by some detail of its text, which is by Luther himself (1524). It is a paraphrase of Psalm XI, *Salvum me fac* (not to be confused with Psalm LXVIII, which has the same incipit). Two passages in it attract our attention. First, the third verse of the first strophe—*Wie wenig sind die Heil'gen dein!*—which might suggest the idea of the small number of initiates. Even more, the first two verses of the fifth strophe, so easily understood as alluding to the trial by Fire (*cf.* the facsimile opposite):

* Some have wished to see here an allusion to the baptismal chorale *Christ unser Herr zum Jordan kam*. That the two chorales bear some melodic resemblance can be agreed to with great good will; but if Mozart had wanted to select that chorale and not the one that he adopted and *cited in a reference*, he would have done and said so.

Das Silber, durchs Feu'r siebenmal
Bewährt, wird lauter funden.

(Silver that has been tried seven times by Fire will be found
pure—an almost literal translation of the Psalmist's verse:
Argentum igne examinatum, probatum terrae, purgatum sep-
tuplum.) Silver being a feminine sign, the allusion is striking
here.

The Inscription of the Trials, in the novel
Sethos, edition of 1767. Collection Roger Cotte.

In fact, just when Tamino is about to pass through the
"gates of terror," he is rejoined by Pamina, who demands to
share the dangers of the "journey" with him. (I shall return
to this scene when discussing what concerns her.) She orders
him to play his magic flute and tells him its history, the
symbolism of which we already have seen: in the light of
these revelations, the significance of the flute given him by the
Ladies on the part of the Queen of the Night changes completely. From being the sign of Air which it was, it becomes
the bearer of the synthesis of the four Elements; the nocturnal
powers are no longer its only source, for it harks back to a
time before the Queen of the Night was crowned—to the
earlier age of Wisdom symbolized by her husband. It signifies
the magic power of music in the sense in which it was understood in the primitive cosmology, in which it was borrowed
from the language of the gods.[13]

The presence of the magic flute gives a new dimension to the trial as not only the carrying-out of a fixed program, but also a résumé and a synthesis. Not only does the flute condense the four Elements in itself, but it is also when animating it by his breath (Air) that Tamino (Fire), accompanied by Pamina (Water), penetrates to the bosom of the Earth, there to confront the two elements of their own symbol, Man and Woman.

And it is perhaps because of that symbolism that, contrary to the ritual, the trial by Fire is placed before that by Water: Tamino must be a Complete Man by precedence before the Woman can be joined to him and, thus magnified, form with him the Perfect Couple.

Be that as it may, when Tamino and Pamina, hand in hand, leave the mountains for the second time, having passed their quadruple trial, everything is accomplished, and the chorus can celebrate their final victory.

B. PAMINA

Pamina's trials display a remarkable gradation. Whereas she undergoes the first of them passively, almost unwillingly, in the succeeding ones she takes a more and more considerable part, and in the two final ones ends up not only identifying herself with the Man, but also guiding and counseling him. Thus a sequence is followed of which the preliminary trials of Act I have already provided a rough sketch, and it often has been remarked that the musical style of her role itself reflects this.

(a) Earth

This is, as for Tamino, and in the ritual order, the first of her initiatory trials, those of the first act having been only preliminary.

The scene devoted to it (12B–13) has always been considered strange and incomprehensible when it has not actually aroused ridicule or irony. It corresponds, in the ritual order, to the first appearance of Pamina in Act II, after Tamino has undergone the parallel trial.

The stage represents an agreeable garden, with trees cut in horseshoe shape (stamped upon the Earth). In the middle is a bed of roses and other flowers upon which Pamina is stretched out. The rose is a symbol of initiation,[14] and more particularly of feminine initiation: the Grande Maîtresse of the Lodges of Adoption used to carry a bag decorated with roses, and in the past century the Children of Mary often appeared crowned with roses (*cf.* Plate 9).

It is night: the subterranean darkness of the Cabinet of Reflection is also the kingdom of Pamina's mother. Pamina is sleeping with her face in the moonlight, the moon being a feminine star. Monostatos (incarnation of the Earth) enters and seats himself on a grassy bank in the foreground (that is, near the Earth). After a silence: "There she is, then," he says, "that proud beauty, that insignificant creature for whom I have been at the point of leaving this life and have let the soles of my feet be bruised. In short, of what was I found blameworthy? I was infatuated with that strange flower transplanted here. But what man would remain insensible to such charms? I ask the stars to be witnesses." (Note again the allusion to the Kingdom of the Night, emphasized by the nocturnal décor and the lighting of Pamina's face by the moon). Monostatos assures himself that no one is watching him, and then announces that he cannot resist the temptation to steal "a kiss, one little kiss."

We commented upon this scene in relation to Monostatos. What it signifies in relation to Pamina is more troublesome. Faced by Monostatos, whose attentions repel her, Pamina has experienced her pre-initiatory swoon. During the first phase of her initiation, and without her participation or consent, she must endure the assault of the elementary, instinctive forces represented by the Earth. All this takes place in the domain of the Night, and Monostatos's monologue multiplies the allusions, insistently contrasting Pamina's whiteness with his own blackness—black and white being, we should remember, the two colors of femininity. "Whiteness is beautiful; I must embrace it. Pardon me, dear, good Moon, hide yourself, and if that would displease you, well, then, you have only to close your eyes."

At this juncture, the Queen of the Night materializes suddenly from below (always the Earth), like the Three Ladies for Tamino. Then, after having driven off Monostatos, she gives her daughter, who awakens at her call, the confidences that I have analyzed. They are the pendant to the reflections on Masonry submitted to Tamino by the Ladies in the form of the philosophic Testament of the regular ceremony. The Ladies subjected Tamino to the temptation of doubt; the Queen subjects her daughter to a much more serious temptation: she hands her a dagger (weapon of terrestrial metal) and orders her to kill Sarastro.

That order conceals an easily understandable symbol: by the union of the sexes which Woman introduces into the kingdom of men, she finds herself possessed of a redoubtable arm that can, if she wishes it, kill the element in them which is their own. The young girl's love for Tamino leads her to refuse that role and to make herself worthy of the new society into which she enters; she must, by her refusal, be repudiated by the one that she is leaving.

Pamina, left alone with the dagger in her hand, ponders the order just given her. Kill Sarastro? She could never do that. And while she continues to meditate, Monostatos returns.

Now he knows that Sarastro's Solar Circle possesses magical virtues and that the young princess must commit a murder in order to appropriate it: "Here," he says, "is something that serves my plans marvelously": he is going to blackmail Pamina. Either she will give herself to him or he will reveal everything to Sarastro, in which case her mother will be thrown "into the underground waters destined, it seems, for the purification· of the Initiates." That is not a simple image: we know that Water represents the feminine element.

When Pamina refuses in horror, Monostatos takes the dagger from her and threatens her. "You refuse," he says. "And why? Is it because my face is black?" And he would strike Pamina if Sarastro did not appear at that moment. His arrival ends the trial by Earth as that of the priests ends each of Tamino's trials.

(b) Air

At the outset, Pamina finds herself associated with Tamino: the initial trial is a shared one. But she still does not know that, and here plays only a passive role. She is only asked, without explanation, to understand that at times her beloved must be able to remain silent with her. She will not, furthermore, understand this until later, and until then will suffer cruelly.

That Pamina is to be included in Tamino's trial by Air is indicated without circumlocution by the stage direction, which specifies that the flying chariot of the Three Boys is covered with roses (No. 16), which are, as I have said, the sign of feminine initiation. Nonetheless, her trial is not completed here, and she must submit to another also. It must be admitted that this breaks all records for obscurity, but the symmetry of the plan leaves no room for doubt. One must look for it at the beginning of the finale (No. 21), in the scene in which she wanders onto the stage like a madwoman, dagger in hand, ready to kill herself. The relationship to Air may seem remote, but it doubtless is suggested by the commentary cited above: "The first journey (that of Air) is the emblem of human life . . . represented by the irregularity of the route that the candidate has followed" and which is marked by obstacles and threats. Perhaps a better explanation could be found. But the significance of the scene is not in doubt: when Pamina appears, she, like Tamino—and just after him—has undergone her trial by Earth, just as in Act I she underwent her swoon just after his. There was a strong prejudice in favor of symmetry in the theatrical world of the epoch. Tamino has now experienced his trial by Air, and as the two following trials will explicitly be, for both of them, those by Fire and Water, it is clear that after Tamino's by Air, the scene for Pamina alone can only be her trial by the same Element.

(c) Fire and Water

Here again, Pamina and Tamino will go through the trials together. But we note the progression: not only does Pamina know that she is facing the trial, but also in a sense she assumes its direction: "I shall be at your side everywhere. I myself shall lead you, and love will guide me. Roses [always roses] will be scattered along our path, for roses are never far from thorns." And she takes Tamino's hand to lead him toward the "gates of terror."

The gesture, associated with the combined trials by Fire and Water—that is, with the very representation of the wedded couple—probably was inspired by the ceremony called "Conjugal Avowal," sometimes referred to pejoratively as "Masonic marriage." It is a "white dress" ceremony—that is, open to everyone, including the profane, and has as its object, when a Brother comes to marry, that of "acknowledging" his wife in the bosom of the fraternity of the Order—without her being really initiated. The Brothers form a chain broken by a vacant place, that of the husband, who is "kept close to his wife." The Venerable then expresses the wish to see the Brother retake his place and reconstitute the chain, and begs the wife herself to lead him there. "She thus will learn that the wife of a Freemason always must encourage her husband to fulfill his Masonic obligations regularly."

We note that the Woman as such has been officially authorized for the first time to undergo initiatory trials. The morality trio, which precedes the movement toward the Fire, merits careful attention in that regard: "A woman who fears neither night nor death is worthy of being consecrated." Officially, she will be consecrated only by Fire and Water— that is, by the two Elements of the Couple—and perhaps it was for that reason that the authors took care to introduce the complementary signs of the two other Elements into the trial. But in fact we have seen that Pamina already has traversed the two absent Elements, even though unwittingly, without being ordered or permitted to do so.

In this trio, for the first time since the beginning of the action, the Woman as such is relieved of her indignity. Thenceforward, she merits being one with the Man who is going to behave as a man, *als Mann zu handeln,* and that is why, upon entering, she will fall into his arms and will remain linked to him, hand in hand, through the decisive trials. From that instant onward, Pamina is no longer the inferior woman of the Kingdom of the Night. She has been declared worthy of being initiated; she has been embraced by Tamino, who thus has communicated the influx of his masculine nature. She has not trembled in the face of dangers. Now she is the complementary element of the Couple. Not only will she follow the Man in his trials and in his ascent to final apotheosis, in which she will be associated, but also she will go so far as to counsel and guide him, exactly as the Masonic ceremonial of Conjugal Avowal prescribes.

Thus we see that *Die Zauberflöte* is an antifeminist work only in appearance. Certainly it passes severe judgments on the adepts of the Kingdom of the Night, and in doing so merely reflects the general attitude of the *"galant"* eighteenth century, for which woman too often was nothing but a toy or a pet bird. But it stands out from that century precisely in that it proclaims her rehabilitation and her rise above frivolous appearances. In that, this "naïve" and "stupid" libretto seems singularly in advance of the concepts of its time.

C. PAPAGENO

Here the style changes. What is more, perhaps the authors change equally. Like Tamino and Pamina, the Birdcatcher undergoes the four trials, but the symbolism often is summary, the presentation being determined by the "comic effects" in which one seeks for the juxtaposition along the traditional lines of parallelism and contrast.

Papageno is present at the first two of Tamino's trials, but he takes no part in them, being limited to dotting them with clowning and, at every moment, to supplying contrast to his master's behavior. It matters little that the same exhortations are addressed to him simultaneously because of symmetry— or at times are frankly forgotten. His personal trials are presented separately, in very disorderly fashion.

(a) Water

Papageno's preparatory swoon, or what takes its place, occurs belatedly, when Tamino has just undergone his first trial. I spoke of this on p. 128.

Next comes his trial by Water, which is inserted into the

background of Tamino's trial by Air and precedes it (No. 15A). Papageno complains of thirst. An old woman enters bearing a jug of water and a goblet. Papageno *does not drink* (so the stage direction informs us), but, exasperated by the old woman's simpering, throws the water in her face.

What does that act mean? In the form of the traditional bacchic jest, before the first of the four Elementary trials, Papageno has demonstrated his craven nature: he, who loves only wine, has, despite his thirst, refused to absorb the despised beverage. But Water is also the feminine symbol. Refusing to be marked by it, the Birdcatcher has defaulted on the synthesis of the Couple. He has poured the water back over his future companion—who thus in a sense has been baptized by him: only Papagena, and not Papageno at all, will be marked by the feminine sign.

(b) Fire

The episode is without ambiguity (and also without great imagination). It is Scene 19A: Papageno wants to leave, but flames bar his way. Frightened, the poor fellow comically breaks into tears.

(c) Earth

The episode is tied to the preceding one. The Speaker comes on stage and reproaches the Birdcatcher for his pusillanimity: "You deserve to finish your life in a dark abyss in the bowels of the Earth"—a roundabout way of announcing the trial. Nevertheless, the gods grant him grace, though it is now established that he will never experience the joys of the Initiates. "That's all the same to me," Papageno answers. "I'll be satisfied with enjoying a good glass of wine." "You shall have it," the Speaker says. And an immense glass of wine arises from the earth (note its origin). Ecstatically, Papageno drinks.

It is impossible to doubt that this is the beginning of his trial by Earth. Wine has for a long time been the symbol of the products of "our Mother, the Earth," and here the "Egyptian mysteries" agree with the Greek—which, moreover, stemmed from them.[15] Dionysus, god of wine, belongs with Persephone to the cycle of the chthonic mysteries of Eleusis.

Perhaps the wine here also has a precise function, which will be recalled (*Seit ich gekostet diesen Wein* . . .) in the finale: water having brought on the appearance of an old woman lacking any attraction, wine with its illusion will adorn her with the deceitful seductions of youth and beauty.

Here the symbol is linked to theatrical conventions, in accord with which, just as Tamino's trials finally will win him Pamina, so those of his companion normally should lead to a pretty Papagena. The trial by Water has set the matter in motion. It proceeds with a new appeal from Papageno, who, inflamed by the wine, seizes his glockenspiel and demands his portion of love: this is the famous aria *"Ein Mädchen oder Weibchen."* The glockenspiel (a terrestrial instrument, as was said earlier) summons at a run—dancing and striking the earth with her cane (a gesture essential to the significance of the trial)—the little old woman who will become the jolly, airy Papagena (Earth and Air being complementary, as Fire and Water are). He wants to embrace her at once, but the Speaker separates them because, he says, the trials have not been completed (this is in fact only the third of the four trials by the Elements: that by Air remains to be undergone).

In despair, Papageno cries out in complete innocence: "I shall follow her even if the Earth swallows me up." Immediately the earth yawns beneath his feet, thus completing "his" trial for the unhappy plumed man.

(d) Air

This, as a simple tally tells us, is the last of the trials awaiting Papageno. It takes place during the finale and forms a violent contrast with the preceding scene, that of the final trials of Tamino and Pamina.

They have just surmounted those trials with the help of their magic flute. It would have been usual, for the sake of symmetry, for Papageno in his way to use the glockenspiel for the same purpose. But because it is not a wind instrument, it cannot serve to determine the sign of the trial, for which reason Papageno returns to his earlier fluting. As in Act I, he uses his five-note run to call the woman. Then, obtaining no response, he comically climbs a hillock (Air = ascent) in order to hang himself. The Three Boys, arriving in the flying chariot of the trials by Air, stop him in time, and it is from the chariot that Papagena descends, finally summoned by the terrestrial glockenspiel, feathered like her husband and therefore marked like him by the sign of Air.

Thus the imperfect couple will be marked by the sign of the Air-Earth dyad just as the perfect couple is marked by the Fire-Water dyad. Whence the famous comic duet *"Papapa . . . papapa,"* the sense of which, as we have noted, is much less naïve than it appears to be.

D. PAPAGENA

Although, as we just have seen, her trials are more or less mixed with those of her vis-à-vis, they have a character of their own nonetheless.

Only one trial remains foreign to her: that of Fire, in which she does not participate at all. We have explained this symbolism: Fire is a masculine sign, the necessary complement of the feminine sign of Water in the constitution of the Perfect Couple. Tamino and Pamina have passed those two trials together. Papageno has refused the trial by Water. Papagena has not passed the trial by Fire any more than she has experienced the preliminary swoon. Their couple will never attain perfection.

On the other hand, we have seen that Papagena, hidden under the features of the old woman, received the "baptism" of *Water* from Papageno; and that, summoned by the terrestrial glockenspiel, she entered dancing and striking the *Earth* with her cane; and that, finally, the Three Boys led her to Papageno in their flying chariot during the course of his terminal trial by *Air*. We have also seen the meaning of her transformation from a sordid old woman into a resplendent young damsel.

Recapitulating at this point what we just have analyzed, we see that—except for a few details—we have gone through the entire second act, and therefore that its "mysterious" action is in reality perfectly coherent and rigorously ordered.

17

From Libretto to Score

In a famous passage customarily denatured of its meaning by being quoted only in part, Igor Stravinsky declared, not, as often is said, that "music cannot express anything," but that "If, as is almost always the case, music appears to express something . . . it is simply an additional attribute which, by tacit and inveterate agreement, we have lent it, thrust upon it as a label, a convention—in short, an aspect which, unconsciously or by force of habit, we have come to confuse with its essential being." Only thus can we understand what the author meant by the famous passage, which must be cited without omitting this clause: "I consider that music is powerless to express anything whatever *by means of its essence* . . ." * [1]

If "Stravinsky's axiom," even when cited exactly, leaves us with some reservations,† it nonetheless defines the way in

* [Translator's note.] The standard English version of this clause is quite meaningless: "For I consider that music is, by its very nature, essentially powerless to *express* anything at all. . . ."

† That declaration has had considerable weight because of its author's prestige. Nonetheless, it was almost a simple paraphrase of a remark made by the

which, according to a tradition as old as the music itself, Mozart collaborated with his librettists so as to add his commentary to theirs.

In an introductory chapter such as this, I cannot undertake to deal with the innumerable intentions that, in this respect, crowd a score that is extraordinarily worked out; that undertaking will appear throughout the analysis. Here the citation of some examples will suffice. We already have seen how the very plan of the Overture expounds the fundamental idea of the opera. In Part Three, we shall see how it describes for us—by means of elements that are none the less effective because they perhaps are "additional"—the opposed characters of the two confronted worlds, even telling us "in music" Mozart's feelings about the problems then agitating Viennese Masonry with respect to woman's role in the Order. Examples of that sort will be numerous.

As with J. S. Bach, in supplying these "additional elements" numbers play a role that is all the more effective because they figure importantly in Masonic symbolism, which did not forget that it went back in part to Pythagorean traditions.* It has become commonplace to emphasize the constant presence of the number Three in the libretto: not only 3 Ladies, 3 Boys, etc., but also 3 temples, 3 virtues praised 3 times by the 3 Boys, etc. But that is only a crude approach.

We have been informed by the first notes that the action is going to develop through the conflict between the Five and the Three: those two numbers play truly important roles

---

philosopher Alain ten years earlier (1926) in his *Système des beaux-arts*, IV, p. 10. I attempted a serious examination of it in the *Journal de psychologie*, No. 4, October–December 1963, pp. 407–20, under the title *"L'Axiome de Stravinsky."* My conclusion was that Stravinsky was mistaken and that his error lay in "hasty generalization of entirely correct remarks."

* On this question, see the works of Jansen, Smend, Geiringer, and—in France —that of J.-J. Duparcq. See also Jacques Chailley, *Les Passions de J. S. Bach,* P. U. F., 1963.

throughout the score. Everything in the course of the drama which touches upon inconstancy, futility, or the nocturnal world of Booz as opposed to the solar world of Jakin will be shot through with quinary allusions: the Birdcatcher's fluting runs through its five notes; the Three Ladies join Papageno and the still-uninstructed Tamino to form the quintet of the first morality. A lightweight motive of five notes, comparable to the "five little beats" of the ritual of Adoption, appears first in the trio of the Ladies in G major, and recurs, almost unchanged, under all appropriate circumstances. Cadences on 3 or 5, according to the situation, most often punctuate the terminal formulas: exceptionally, we find one on the 7 of Wisdom in Sarastro's aria.

By the play of key-signatures, this numerical symbolism involves the symbolism of tonalities. The reflex is visual and speculative much more often than auditive, as tonalities heard as identical are employed in different senses according to whether they are written in sharps or in flats,* and variations in pitch do not affect the psychological motives. These latter are no less powerful. At the center is C major, central point of reference for all the other tonalities, and therefore the paradigm tonality, sign of factuality, of sincerity, of light: Charles Gounod would say: "God speaks in C major." † It is in C major that the revelation in Mozart's "Dissonant" Quartet arrives, that the "Es ward Licht" bursts forth in Haydn's Die Schöpfung, that the fanfares salute the arrival of Sarastro. On the two sides of C major, the key-signatures lo-

---

* I had the experience of giving students for comment the chorus of César Franck's Sixième Béatitude, which Vincent d'Indy praised for the "scintillating clarity of the key of F-sharp major"—but after I had copied it out in G-flat major (which is exactly the same thing to the ear). All of them, without exception, then spoke of the veiled, inward, slightly gray sweetness. . . .

† Monostatos also, it may be objected (No. 13). But there we are dealing with the special matter of "Turkish music," the tradition of which is to avoid key-signatures.

cate the two opposed worlds. On one side, the solemn flats of Wisdom; on the other, the fluttering sharps of profane lightness (at least, that is the significance, not generalized, which they are given in *Die Zauberflöte*). From the mixture of that symbolism with the significance of the Number is born the hieratic preeminence of E-flat major, which brings together the Three of perfection, the major of serenity, and the flats of solemnity.* This tonality, which encloses the entire opera (Overture and final chorus), will be not only that of the grand initiatory scenes, but also that of most of the pieces, and even phrases, having solemn or didactic meaning.[2] The relative C minor will indicate incomplete or tortuous advance. Its curtailed signature, two flats, will give us the B-flat major of the Queen of the Night (No. 4), which, openly at war with the Initiates in Act II, will decline to a single flat (F major). At the opposite pole, the smart G major will be the profane tonality par excellence. Around these three principal supports—C, E-flat, and G major—the other tonalities will be organized according to relationships to them, thus creating a sort of code that will be respected throughout the opera, as is demonstrated by this tally:

C major: 1 C, 8 ACE (1st finale), 11 (morality duet), 13 (Monostatos), 21 C (march to the trials). *E-flat major:* Overture, 3 (portrait aria), 7 (morality duet), 21 A (the Men in Armor), 21 F (2nd finale). *G major:* 1 B (the Ladies) and most of the scenes in which Papageno plays a leading role: 2, 6, 8 B, 12, 21 D.

Forming the progression between *C major* and *E-flat major,* *F major:* 8 D (Pamina, then Monostatos before Sarastro), 9 and 10 (march and prayer of the priests), 14 (the Queen of the Night's malediction), 20 (the glockenspiel), 21 B (Pamina rejoins Tamino for their trials). *B-flat major:* 4 (the Queen of the Night gives

---

* In the same spirit—though naturally with Christian rather than Masonic perspective—Bach employs the tonality of E-flat major in homage to the number Three of the Holy Trinity at the beginning and end of his collection called "Dogma Chorales," framed by a ternary prelude and a triple fugue, both in that key.

Tamino his mission), 5 (morality quintet), 19 (trio for Sarastro, Tamino, and Pamina), and its relative G *minor:* 17 (Pamina's sorrowing). Inverted reflection of *E-flat major,* its relative *C minor:* 1 A (the serpent) and 21 E (assault by the Night).

Beyond G *major* the sharps alter the meaning and progressively approach clarity: *D major* 18 (chorus of priests), A *major* 16 (trio of Boys), E *major* 15 (the realm of peace described by Sarastro).

I have cited only the principal tonalities emphasized by their signatures. The same symbolism is pursued minutely, often from phrase to phrase, throughout the developments and modulations. In the analyses these will be referred to in small type.

A single exception: Sarastro's aria, in which the accumulated sharps (*E major*) break out of that symbolism and carry the nearby pieces with them. The reason is doubtless this: *E major* is the most sharped tonality ever employed by Mozart, and it parsimoniously: in the catalogue of all his instrumental works by tonalities, it occurs only three times up to 1780, twice from 1780 to 1791, almost always in minuet trios.* It was especially apt for describing the idyllic serenity of the happy sojourn evoked by this piece— even though when using it, Mozart disregarded the rather different conventions of the other tonalities of the score.

One among many possibilities will show us the point to which these relationships among tonalities were worked out in the score. In the introduction (Scene 1), Tamino is tempted in C *minor,* the imperfect relative of the perfect *E-flat major.* But the serpent is killed in *E-flat major,* its death referring to the initiation. Their *Heldenthat* accomplished, the Three Ladies move far from the opening *E-flat major* to chatter in G *major,* thus displaying their very profane interest in the young prince's beauty. When Tamino arrives at the portal of the Temples, he immediately speaks in D *major.* That profane sharped tonality is cleanly cut off by the *B-flat major* of the first "*Zurück!*" Overwhelmed, Tamino drops to the relative minor of *B-flat,* G *minor.* The second "*Zurück!*" sounds in *E-flat major.* Tamino tries to stay in that tonality,

* See Table No. 4 in the appendix of the Massins' book.

but cannot sustain it: in one measure he falls to *C minor.* So as to be able to deserve *E-flat major,* he must pronounce the words of Love and Virtue: *"Der Lieb' und Tugend Eigenthum."* Still in *E-flat major,* the priest says: "You have spoken well. But . . ." And that "but" suffices to dissolve the *E-flat major.* And so on.

To be sure, tonality is not alone in evoking the culminating phases of sacred feeling. Like all the classical composers, Mozart knows that the "ordinary" harmonic language of his time always included successions of tonics and dominants, more or less ornamented and more or less modulatory. It is rare to find them evaded without the background's outlining some special significance. The III and VI chords notably (which the treatises on harmony call "modal" without knowing clearly what that adjective means*) evoked in the ears of that epoch the accompaniment of Church plain chant, being summoned up by association of ideas with religious music, and later with feelings of the same nature. One might propound as a general rule that *until about 1880, every chord on the third or sixth degree given some prominence is linked to an idea of prayer or religious allusion,* or, again, to a sentiment related to meditation and catharsis—for example, with Beethoven or Berlioz, the serenity of nature. *Die Zauberflöte* is rich in allusions of this genre: as early as its second chord, for example, we know by the use of the sixth degree on beats 2 and 3 of the five percussion beats that this has a religious sense: it refers not merely to the Ladies' number, but also to their Masonic Order as such. The same is true of the series of thirds and sixths in parallel chords, descended from the medieval *faux-bourdon* as preserved in certain churches and ab-

* They gladly believe that because these degrees are different in major and minor, they therefore are according to the "mode." In reality, it is a survival of plain chant accompaniment according to the usage of the seventeenth and eighteenth centuries, because, with their eight "modes," it was almost the only place then employing that class of chords.

sorbed into the "canticle style": the entrance of the Three Boys and the march of the priests furnish examples. This canticle style, used in the lodges, as in the churches, possessed, furthermore, other characteristics—for example, a special manner of beginning feminine cadences (*Die Zauberflöte* offers many examples, each possessing allusive value).

Developing this particularism of musical situations to the maximum, Mozart came, one might say, to create a sort of "stylistic Leitmotiv" of his own. Tamino, Pamina, Sarastro, Papageno, the Queen of the Night—each has a distinct musical color throughout the action. Better, the partial motives, the melodic or rhythmic cells respond and recur from one piece to another, evoking related situations. Tamino exclaims *"Dies Bildnis ist bezaubernd schön!"* as he contemplates the picture of Pamina's features; Pamina will exclaim *"Tamino mein!"* when she finally sees Tamino's features in reality—and the two phrases, at the two extremities of the score, have the same melodic design. Again, the same design underlies the *"Vielleicht sah er Paminen schon"* that expresses a closely related idea. Another example: the Three Ladies will ask *"Ich sollte fort?"* when they discover the very beautiful young man in a swoon; Papageno will sigh *"Schön Mädchen, jung und fein"* when contemplating the beauty of the unconscious Pamina. The same situation, the same music. In our analysis, observations of this nature will be numerous. If one wants to look for the remote origins of the Wagnerian Leitmotiv, one should go, not to Weber, as is customary, but to Mozart.

Many other aspects of this inexhaustible score could be remarked: for example, the very personal way in which Mozart here enlarges the notion of the *aria da capo*. But I fear that if I were to pursue that route, I should take leave of readers who reject pure technical discussion. Here it must suffice to assert that Mozart yielded nothing to his librettists with respect to the amplitude and complexity of the ideas suggested.

Mozart is said to be, of all the classic composers, the one least inclined toward the much-decried "figuralism" that nevertheless is revealed by all the acts and gestures of, for example, Bach; but *Die Zauberflöte* can be cited above all his other scores to prove the statement false. The fashion in which the orchestra visually describes the undulations of the serpent, which alternately slithers forward, becomes rigid, and collapses; or, again, Tamino's quickly deflated impetus toward the closed, hostile gate of the Temple; or the "hand of friendship" sweetly but firmly sustaining the weak uninitiate by the unison in which its cellos lead the voice—all of these, and many other passages, oblige us to take our stand: after Bach, after Schubert, after so many other composers, Mozart must be expunged from the list of those "pure musicians" who have been congratulated for not having "compromised" with the torrent of the poor "signifiers." Who, then, God, remains outside that torrent in which the greatest are drowned?

Part Three

ANALYSIS OF THE OPERA

NOTE: In the course of the following analysis, I have thought it best to sidestep observations about musical technique which are essential to a thorough study: I have presented them in smaller type in such a way as to facilitate their being skipped by readers unfamiliar with such ideas.

The usual abbreviations: T-tonic, TP-principal tonality, D-dominant, SD-subdominant, I-first degree, M-major, m-minor, R-relative, RM-relative major, Rm-relative minor. For fugue: S-subject, R-response, CS-countersubject.

The numbering of the scenes is that of the traditional division of the score. The spoken scenes are numbered with added letters (2A, for example).

18

Overall View

At the beginning of this book, I gave the reader the sort of
analysis of *Die Zauberflöte* which most of the so-called "appreciation" works and programs provide with a few variations. It
leads up to the question: "What can this be trying to say?"—
and gives no answer.

Now we are in a position to propose a very different analysis
of the same opera.

Act I

Intended to illustrate the individual preparation that precedes
actual initiation, it can be divided into three episodes showing
how that preparation is carried out: first Tamino; then Pamina; and finally the conclusion—admission to the trials.

(a) Preparation of Tamino
Faced with the serpent of the first awakening of the senses,
Tamino, who still lacks the "arrows" of experience, undergoes

his first transformation by swooning. The serpent is killed by the Three Ladies, servants of the nocturnal kingdom of feminine frivolity, who much wish to "flirt" with the handsome young man. When he reawakens ready for love, he wants to set out, but is stopped by the Birdcatcher, Papageno, the Ladies' purveyor of useless gewgaws, symbol of the emptiness of the sign of Air (complementary to Fire, represented by Tamino), who lies to him about the nature of this first, false love.

The Ladies return, punish Papageno by placing upon him the "seal of discretion" that forms part of their own initiation, and, abandoning their "flirtation," point out to Tamino the road to true love, that of Pamina, daughter of the queen of the feminine kingdom. Pamina has been carried off, against her will and to her mother's great fury, by the master of the enemy kingdom, Sarastro, master of the solar kingdom of the Wisdom of Men, to which Tamino must go to win her. He may not yet know her except through an image of her, a portrait that the Ladies give him on behalf of their Queen, who thereupon herself comes to confirm Tamino's mission. Papageno will accompany him during his journey: as he too eagerly desires to find a woman to his liking, one can well foresee how he will acquit himself in the adventure, which terrifies him.

(b) Preparation of Pamina

Since her abduction, Pamina has known cruel disappointments in the Kingdom of Men: her first master is a vile, lecherous traitor, the Moor Monostatos (a sign of Earth complementing Pamina's sign of Water), who desires to force his love upon her and enslave her. She has tried to flee by means of her Water sign, but, still not prepared, has failed in the attempt. Recaptured by Monostatos, she swoons, as Tamino did, and thus undergoes her first transformation.

Like Tamino, Pamina awakens to find Papageno before her:

the Birdcatcher, as light as air and playing his five-tone flute—
five being the number of the feminine Kingdom that he serves
—has been able to reach her unopposed. Like Tamino by
means of the portrait, Pamina discovers through Papageno's
account her true love for the man whom she still may not look
upon in reality, and whom, for the time being, she seeks in
vain; the call of Papageno's flute is deceptive, and the two
young people fail to find one another.

(c) Request for Initiation

The first, superficial initiation by means of the serpent and the
Three Ladies does not qualify Tamino to find the road of
true love. So that it may be pointed out to him, the Three
Ladies must be replaced by Three Boys, symbols of the start
of true initiation because they are capable of growing in
knowledge and of themselves becoming wise Men later on.
They lead Tamino to the portal of the Temple of Wisdom, to
which he must gain entrance in order to win Pamina. In terms
very closely resembling the first sections of Masonic initiation,
Tamino requests admission and receives the first teachings.
Then he attempts to call Pamina, but the magic flute given
him by the Queen of the Night is impotent to bring him anyone but Papageno, who is related to its sign as a wind instrument.

For their part, Pamina and Papageno escape from Monostatos, thanks to the glockenspiel with which Papageno has been
furnished, and which, as a metal instrument, and therefore of
the Earth, acts magically upon the Moor, who is related to the
same sign. Pamina decides to take refuge under the protection
of Sarastro and confide herself to him, an action that for her
is symmetrical to Tamino's; Papageno merely trembles in
terror.

Appearing in all his puissance, Sarastro pronounces his judgment: Pamina shall not be returned to her mother, but shall

be freed from the unhealthy love of Monostatos; Tamino will be admitted to ritual initiation. Papageno is scarcely mentioned: he will follow Tamino as a matter of course.

Act II

The second act is occupied entirely by the initiatory trials. Modeled very closely upon the "journeys" of Masonic initiation to the first, Apprentice, degree, they successively evoke the four Elements: Earth, Air, Water, and Fire. Further, they are accompanied by a strict injunction to silence and discretion on the part of the two men, principally vis-à-vis the opposite sex.

(a) Introduction—Deliberation of the Initiates

Convened in solemn session, the Initiates discuss the admission of Tamino proposed by Sarastro, and decide to admit him to the trials.

(b) Ritual Trials

1. *Tamino, Trial by Earth.* The scene changes from the ritual hall to a dark place, the "Cabinet of Reflection," where the postulant must be tested for his knowledge and for his feeling toward the Order into which he is asking admission. That is why the Three Ladies, here representing the social aspect of the feminine world, rise up from under the stage (the Earth), trying to discredit the Initiates in Tamino's eyes. This gives rise to a scene full of then-contemporary allusions and permits the authors to protest publicly against the accusations then being leveled at Freemasonry. By refusing to believe them or to discuss them with the Ladies, Tamino passes the test of the Earth.

At the end of this scene, a malediction against women drives the Ladies from the Temple. Frightened, Papageno swoons, unaware that he is thus beginning the cycle of his own initiation, in which he will fail pitifully.

2. *Pamina, Trial by Earth.* Asleep in a symbolic setting, Pamina suffers a final assault by the forces of the Earth represented by Monostatos, who attempts to embrace her without her knowing. Then her mother, the Queen of the Night, rises from the Earth and also tries to discredit the Initiates in Pamina's mind: by refusing to believe her mother, Pamina, like Tamino, passes the test of the Cabinet of Reflection. It is during this scene that the Queen explains to her daughter the profound meaning of the libretto and the significance of the antagonism between the Kingdom of the Day and the Kingdom of the Night, between Sarastro's kingdom and her own. Furious at her daughter's resistance, she hands the girl a dagger (metal, a terrestrial material), orders her to kill Sarastro, and, in a famous aria, curses her if she should disobey.

Monostatos, who has overheard everything, snatches the dagger (of his own sign) from Pamina and threatens to kill her if she does not satisfy his desires. Sarastro arrives just in time and chases away Monostatos—but refuses to take revenge upon him, singing instead of the idyllic peace of the abode of the Wise, where transgressions are forgiven.

3. *Papageno and Papagena, Trial by Water.* In an interlude, we are present at the trial of Papageno and Papagena by Water. A little old woman appears and offers Water to the Birdcatcher. He refuses with disgust and throws the Water at her. He is unaware that he thus has failed his test by Water and has baptized by that sign his future wife, who, in their state of non-initiation, can appear to him again only in the graceless features of her true nature.

4. *Tamino, Trial by Air.* Appearing on a rose-covered flying platform (sign of feminine initiation, a fact that informs us

that the trial is also Pamina's), the Three Boys hand Tamino and Papageno the "metals" that were taken from them according to the Masonic rite—the flute and the glockenspiel—and at the same time cause to be lowered from their machine a table garnished with appetizing tidbits. Whereas Papageno rushes gluttonously upon the repast, Tamino divines that he must choose between the flesh and the spirit. Foregoing the food, he takes up his flute and plays. Thus he also passes the test by Air.

Pamina appears, radiant with joy at finding her prince again. Bound by the rule of silence, Tamino refuses to talk to her and sadly but firmly starts off to the sound of his flute. He thus has fulfilled his duty of firmness toward women both in their social aspect (the Ladies) and in their emotional aspect (Pamina). Not understanding the apparent coldness of her lover, Pamina sings of her sorrow. Surrounded by his priests, Sarastro salutes the success of the first two trials and announces the two final ones.

5. *Pamina, Trial by Air.* Veiled, Pamina is brought into the presence of Sarastro and the priests, who preserve a hostile silence. This shows that, having passed the test of the philosophic Testament, she is to be allowed, despite her sex, to undertake the three "journeys" (which explains her "farewells" to Tamino). The hour sounds, Sarastro says, while the orchestra "sounds" the twelve strokes of noon of the Opening of the Labors, signal for the initiation itself. Her trial will be interrupted midway by the following Papageno episode, but will resume later with an evocation of the distracted "irregular march" that the candidate must undertake during this trial: Pamina wanders about as though mad, threatening to kill herself. The Three Boys restrain her.

6. *Papageno and Papagena, Trials by Fire and Earth.* This double scene interrupts Pamina's action by an interlude without music. It begins by showing us Papageno very wretchedly

undergoing his trials by Fire and Water: in the face of the *flames* that bar his way, he crumples up, whining. Then, from the *Earth*, a huge goblet of wine arises, produced by the terrestrial forces of Dionysiac renewal: the bird-brained Birdcatcher rushes to drink and then, slightly befuddled, seizes his glockenspiel of terrestrial metal to bring back the *Mädchen* of his dreams. She appears: it is the little old lady seen shortly before, dancing and striking the ground with her cane—for she too is undergoing her second trial, that by Earth. Befuddled by the wine fumes, Papageno sees her adorned with all the graces: she is transformed, appearing in his dazzled eyes as a young, ravishing Papagena. The Birdcatcher rushes to embrace her, but she is taken from him: the trials have not been completed. As the result of Papageno's bragging, the Earth opens and the Birdcatcher disappears comically into the hole: he has failed his trial by Earth. The trial by Fire is the only one that Papagena does not undergo: a sign of masculinity, it is foreign to the role that she will play in the imperfect couple.

7. *Tamino and Pamina, Trials by Fire and Water.* Now we return to Pamina's trial by Air, begun before the Papageno interlude. It runs into the admirable scene of Fire and Water, the only trials clearly presented, trials that Tamino and Pamina pass together, of their own free will. In front of the cascade and the flaming mountain, two men in black armor, fire gleaming on their helmets (Water and Fire), lead Tamino in and read him the sacred inscription, legendarily the epitaph on the tomb of Hiram, the revered ancestor of Freemasonry. This reading is done above a chorale melody of which the text, which Luther adapted from Psalm XI, proclaims the purification of silver by Fire, silver being a symbol of Woman— and thus proclaims that Pamina, recently an impure princess of the Kingdom of the Night, will be "worthy of being consecrated." Pamina rejoins Tamino, who plays on his magic

176 /   THE MAGIC FLUTE, MASONIC OPERA

flute (the magical power of music); then, hand in hand, the two courageously face the terrible trials from which they will emerge victorious.

8. *Papageno and Papagena, Trial by Air.* Papageno decides to hang himself, and for that purpose climbs a hillock, thus unintentionally carrying out the ritual gesture of the trial by Air. The Three Boys stop him and have Papagena descend from their rose-covered machine. Thus she is marked, like her future husband, by the sign of Air. The two are delighted, and vow to people the world with a multitude of Papagenos and Papagenas—which, given the mediocrity that they represent, is not without cruel satirical irony. They will never know the joys of the initiate, but they will be happy as they are. In their eyes, at least, everything will end well.

(c) Epilogue: Defeat of the Night, Triumph of the Couple

From underground, led by Monostatos, the Queen of the Night and her Ladies prepare an assault upon the Temple. Monostatos extracts the promise that if their plan succeeds, he will be given Pamina as his recompense: thus we are told what awaits Woman in the event of victory by the Kingdom of the Night. That victory will not occur: a thunderclap, and the Queen and her suite are swallowed up.

Conquerors, Tamino and Pamina are consecrated beside Sarastro. Thus, in the holy couple, Woman is relieved of her indignity; like Tamino, she wears priestly vestments (*beide in priestlicher Kleidung*), the Boys present them with the flowers of their achieved initiation, and the chorus chants the victory of the Sun and the advent of the Golden Age of sacred legend.

19

The Overture

Like the March of the Priests that introduces Act II, the
Overture was composed at the end of Mozart's work on *Die
Zauberflöte*—according to Seyfried, it reached the musicians'
stands on the day of the dress rehearsal "with the ink still wet."
It offers us (to use a cliché rarely as justified as it is here) a
complete "résumé of the action." A slow, purposefully vague
introduction, reflecting the traditional description of Chaos,
follows the sounding of the five chords of feminine initiation,
domain of the Queen of the Night. This is abruptly succeeded
by a straightforward rhythmic fugue, placed in its surroundings
by the three chords of masculine initiation, which describes
the active, ordered society of the rival kingdom of Light. The
first section of the fugue, modulating very little (exposition and
first development, tonic to dominant), emphasizes that struc-
tural precision and is punctuated by sforzandos resembling
the blows of the Venerable's mallet during the trials. Then,
after the middle section, comes a very different episode, modulating frequently and abounding in minors and chromaticisms.
This seems to allude, in its "tonal journey," to the protago-

nists' "journeys" during their trials. After the stretto and re-exposition, a final episode reverts to openness of sound and clarity of writing, which now lead to the terminal fanfares signifying the victory of the Sun, in the initiatory E-flat major that dominates the piece (and the opera), the symbolic significance of which is also recalled by the three punctuated chords of the final cadence.

We examined the meaning of the five initial chords in Chapter 11 and need not return to it here. But one may note further that not only the "initiatory tonality" of E-flat major, but also the "modal" accents which, from the second of the beats, mark the chords on the sixth degree immediately announce the religious nature of the opera.

The "chaos" of the Nocturnal World is depicted by the means characteristic of that type of picture,* but with a singular wealth of means: halfhearted statements of aborted themes, shambling syncopations, tonal instability, abrupt silences, absence of clear timbres, slithering by an insidious bassoon. One observes the interior pedal of repeated notes (a common feature in depictions of chaos), enhanced by a special dynamic (a crescendo that only this pedal introduces amid the lack of nuances in the other parts).

The succeeding allegro provides a sudden burst of light by asserting inverse characteristics: a steadily maintained rhythm, squareness, straightforwardness, and neatness of theme, rigorous construction, and an unambiguous tonal layout. The fugued form that it borrows is significant in itself: in the progressive spacing out of the voice entrances, the fugue represents the ideal figuration for the building of an edifice (Arthur Honegger will use the same symbol in *Amphion* to represent the raising of the walls of Thebes at the sound of the lyre). Here one re-encounters the architectural symbols inherited

---

* *Cf.* the "Dissonant" Quartet and, later, the introduction to Haydn's *Die Schöpfung*. See p. 84.

from Operative Masonry (old-time working masons) through
Speculative Masonry, and one remembers that Mozart, who
once had studied counterpoint and fugue at Bologna with
Padre Martini, had discovered, while studying Bach in about
1782 at the instigation of Baron van Swieten, that this way of
writing could "also" have artistic value. . . . We know how
much his composing was enriched from then on by that revelation.

The *theme* (fuguists say the "subject") of the fugue is borrowed from a sonata by Muzio Clementi.* It is remarkable
for the enthusiastic élan of a leap of a fifth prepared by a dash-
ing *grupetto*, and also for its syncopated accents, which have
given rise to considerable exegesis. Appearing in every fourth
measure, and then—by the play of the countersubjects—in
every second, they mark out the exposition of an almost regular series of accents on weak beats, more and more concise,
reminiscent of the noise made by hammers breaking stone—a
little like Siegfried's forge *avant la lettre*—or, to put it other-
wise, masons at work, either in reality or symbolically. If
Mozart intended something of the sort (which is very possible), one would think, rather, of the gavel with which, at
more or less regular intervals, the Venerable pounds on his
lectern to punctuate the changing phases of the ritual. The

---

* Opus 43, No. 2, in B-flat major (opening allegro). In a second edition
published in the year of *Die Zauberflöte*, Clementi had this note engraved:
"This sonata, with the toccata that follows it, was played by the composer
before His Imperial Majesty Joseph II in 1781." That was a roundabout way
of asserting his priority and of accusing Mozart of plagiarism without naming
him.[1] In truth, we know that when Clementi played before the emperor on
Christmas Eve, 1781, it was in the presence of Mozart, with whom he had
been invited to one of the musical tournaments then in vogue. Mozart
appears to have kept a lively memory of this theme, which one also finds,
though less textually, in the "Prague" Symphony, K.504. Clementi's theme
is not treated fugally. It is accompanied by a *basso continuo* and lacks the
syncopated accents that Mozart gave it. A certain relationship also has been
remarked between the *Zauberflöte* Overture and that of Ignaz Holzbauer's
Günther von Schwarzburg, which Mozart had admired greatly at Mannheim
in 1777.

two images flow together, as the second is only a symbolic figuration of the first. In this group of four quarter-notes, which the sforzandos emphasize so dynamically, is it fortuitous that they prefigure the little five-note rhythmic motive (4 quarter-notes and an introductory note) which, as we have seen, recurs throughout the opera with the evident purpose of alluding to the "five little equal strokes" of the feminine ceremonies of Adoption? And in that case, what is it doing in this tableau of masculine activity unless signifying male domination over the feminine Five, which complete initiates include in the fullness of their wisdom? This exegesis may be daring, but in any case it is perfectly in tune with the teachings of the opera, for we must not forget that in Sarastro's realm, Isis is worshiped along with Osiris—for the reason given earlier.

As already observed, the *plan* of the fugue is very simple: after a regular *exposition, a first development that modulates little* leads to the tonality of the dominant. Then the fugue is interrupted, and one hears, in the special orchestration of the "Masonic winds," the *ritual call* of 3 x 3 which defines the meaning of the fugue and opposes it to the 5 of the introduction.

The theme resumes for a *second development,* which is of a very different nature: by its tormented harmony and by the incessant modulations of its "tonal journey," this part evokes the trials of the symbolic "journey" of initiation, the subject of the opera's second act. The happy success of that journey brings a return to the same tonality: *stretto** and *re-exposition,* after which a victorious *coda* represents the triumph and final glorification of the two protagonists.

THE EXPOSITION is regular: 2 x SR, with mutation the first time,

---

* *Stretto* (from the Italian for "tightened") is the term for a traditional section of a fugue in which the thematic work is "tightened," in which the successive entries of the subject follow one another rapidly.

without mutation the second; countersubject (CS) formed of three successive elements of unequal importance: a descending scale CS1, an ascending scale CS2, a syncopated cell CS3. CS1 is merely a sketch in its first presentation, at the entry of R measure 20. It takes on its full form in measure 26, where it serves as a bridge before the 3rd entrance. CS2 will be encountered again in the development, but will remain secondary. On the contrary, CS3 will take on more and more importance. For the rest, the CS is not treated scholastically and is not found again automatically at each entrance of S or R. A new element CS4 is even introduced in the viola, measure 29, and this too will be found again later (measure 35); one may consider it as the result of an abbreviation of the *grupetto* in the subject, going back to its anterior form in the "Prague" Symphony.

FIRST DEVELOPMENT, modulating little (fuguists say "divertissement"), first in E-flat major (39–49), then, after a transition (50–52), in B-flat major, key of the dominant, which concludes it. Here one finds the S, whether in its true form or close to the fifth-less form of CS4, CS1 (40, etc.), CS2 (59, etc.), CS3 (69, etc.). Coda from 84 to 96, ending in the dominant tonality.

A supple transitional melodic pattern, markedly rhythmic in character (59), will take on such importance later that some see a second sonata theme in its continuation accompanying the subject in the dominant (64); but such an analysis is clearly untenable.

The 3 x 3 anapestic strokes of the MASCULINE BEATS then are heard in the middle of the structure on an unchanging chord, in the wind orchestration characteristic of the Lodge.

SECOND DEVELOPMENT. After that unmistakable allusion, the fugue continues, this time for a "tonal journey" through rapid modulations (symbolic "journey" of the initiatory trials): B-flat m, C m, E-flat M, G m, B-flat M, G m, whereupon the sequence is cut off abruptly after cadence by a measure of silence (trial by silence?). This entire section, with compact thematic development on the subject + CS1, presents a minor, chromatic aspect that well fits the symbolic exegesis; the pattern of measure 105, which proceeds through the entire section, can be considered a chromatic transformation of CS3. The succeeding section (128–43), in less compact counterpoint, presents a descending harmonic march from C m to TP E-flat M—where a derivative of S alternates with a pattern derived from CS1. *Stretto* in the keytone (144–54), the first notes of F accompanied by CS1, leading to the RE-EXPOSITION. This leads, not to the exposition of the fugue, but to the section that follows (154 = 39), which is justified by the fact that the latter begins with an artifice that, in the present case, constitutes an "artful" compromise between fugue, the procedure chosen here, and sonata form, the usual procedure of the overture. In fact, re-exposition in sonata form is characterized by transposition of the second theme, which, having already been set forth in the dominant, is now restated in the tonic. Here that principle is applied to the fugue: the answer to S (accompanied by CS1), rather than R, is the same subject put into T (154–57 = 39–42). Several episodes follow, borrowed in condensed form from the 1st section and likewise transposed into T (158–67), a divertissement on CS3 and the tail-end of the subject, taking up textually the development of the first section (43–52). What then follows refers less literally to the end of the first section as transposed to the tonic. A CODA (203–end) uses formulas from standard cadences, with the crescendo that Rossini later would systematize and render banal; it ends in the traditional triumph of the hero with the usual final restatement of the essential theme and three chords in the tonic (E-flat), which are not three accidentally. It is entertaining to compare these final measures with the "correction" inflicted upon them by poor Lachnith when he made *Les Mystères d'Isis* out of *Die Zauberflöte*. A whole "history of musical taste" emerges from that picturesque confrontation (see Plates 39, 40).

The First Act

First Scene

THE DOMAIN OF THE QUEEN OF THE NIGHT

The stage represents a desert of wild rocks, chaotic symbol of Nature still virgin and uncultivated, with here and there isolated trees in bud. Huge mountains rise on either side of a round temple. This savage landscape is that of the kingdom of the Queen of the Night; the temple, conforming to the regular symbol of her sex, is hers.

No. 1 / INTRODUCTION:
The Serpent and the Three Ladies

Unarmed, Prince Tamino is unable to defend himself against a serpent that is pursuing him. He swoons. Three veiled ladies enter, kill the serpent, and are captivated by the beauty of the young man. They leave him regretfully to report to their mistress, the Queen of the Night.

The symbolism of this scene has already been examined. Tamino's costume (Japanese hunter = Orient; bow without arrows = potentialities not yet available), pursuit by the serpent (still-obscure first temptations), swoon (first transformation, through "symbolic death"); then the Three Ladies, messengers of the Night (representing female society in its frivolous and superficial aspect), death of the serpent trisected by a silver javelin (the Ladies engender the first intimations of virility), and the Ladies' excited reactions to the beauty of the unconscious young prince.

The action of this scene is related to the Overture in the relative relationship. This is a "sectional scene," including two uninterrupted but distinct episodes; that of the serpent, then the Ladies' amorous simperings.

First Episode: The Serpent

A. Pursuit and Swoon
(C minor)

The tonality of C minor (with three flats, as in the Overture, but minor: no initiation has yet taken place) again calls attention to the Masonic symbolism of the opera now beginning. The agitated introduction is longish (the length necessitated by the accompanying *mise en scène*); it describes first the undulation of the serpent (it rears up and falls back), then Tamino's alarmed flight, interrupted by stops and backward glances. Orchestral restatement below Tamino's singing, stressing the principal notes as he calls out for help.

After eight measures, bifurcation: a harmonically ascending march, then a chromatic creeping of the repeated basses, translating the *"Schon nahet sie sich"* (It is upon me already), and a sharply avoided cadence marking the prince's swoon and coinciding with the arrival of the Ladies.

B. The Three Ladies Appear and Kill the Serpent (A-flat major)

Tamino just has swooned when the gate of the temple opens. Three Ladies emerge veiled (light cannot reach them), each one carrying a silver javelin (metal of femininity).

Tonal break (C minor to A-flat major) of notable brusqueness which (a very rare occurrence) marks the intentional "harmonic error" of two consecutive octaves and fifths in the leading chords. The Ladies' appearance and the killing occur very rapidly in three measures: *"Stirb, Ungeheur! durch unsre Macht!"* (Die, monster! by our power)—this in an arpeggio and an equally imperious octave leap; an organ point accomplishes the modulation to E flat, and the monster is dead. Does this symbolize the suddenness and superficiality of the initiation thus represented, which is a far cry from the genuine love that demands many sacrifices?

C. Song of Triumph (E-flat major)

The Ladies' victory trio: *"Triumph! Triumph! Sie ist vollbracht, die Heldenthat!"* (Triumph! triumph! the heroic deed is done!), in the style of a fanfare hymn in the initiatory tonality of E-flat major, relative of the preceding key. This is the first Masonic victory (the unique feminine victory, the only one allowed the Kingdom of the Night). The "heroic deed" consists, for the Queen's followers, of annexing the man. In the second-act aria in which the Queen will threaten to curse her daughter if, on the contrary, she should permit herself to be annexed by the adverse kingdom, she will employ the same musical phrase: *"So bist du mein."*

Second Episode: Simperings of the Three Ladies over the Unconscious Tamino (A-flat major, then C major)

No interruption in the music: only a modulation to the SD, A flat (inflection of pity in the lower fifths), accompanied by a swift change in style, indicates that we are turning the page. The Ladies discuss Tamino's beauty seriatim and conclude in trio that if they should ever love anyone, it would be this young man.

This is all expressed in flatted tonalities, which is to say in the region dominated by the initiatory E-flat major. We are soon to leave them, to approach the "profane" and futile region of G major. The way in which the Ladies reduce the revelation of Love to mere "flirtatiousness" is only the sad evolution of a feeling that could be noble: its first appearance remains solemn and dignified, almost ritual, until it bifurcates toward a wholly different atmosphere.

The construction, as in the preceding section, constantly emphasizes the number Three, which underlines the fact that the center of the action is Tamino, not the Ladies. Three elements ABC, each of them in turn articulated in ternary form.

A. Section in A-flat major

Tripartite interior construction:

1. *"Ein holder Jüngling, sanft und schön"* (A noble youth, gentle and beautiful). Ravishing Mozartean arcs with delightful tendentious inflections (E natural toward F, D natural toward E flat). The cadence by a fourth (D flat—A flat) symbolizes the quasi-ritual aspect of the episode.

2. *"Lasst uns zu unsrer Fürstin eilen,/ Ihr diese Nachricht zu erteilen"* (Let us hasten to our mistress to tell her this news). A different motif, formed of staccato notes with accent

on the fourth beat, as in the fugue in the Overture. *"Vielleicht, dass dieser schöne Mann/ Die vor'ge Ruhe ihr geben kann"* (Perhaps this beautiful man can restore her former peace). One may see a subtle allusion in the return of *a*, it being a question of the young man's calming the Queen: (the Three Ladies amorous of Tamino): the emotion is the same, the superficial, impure love of the domain of the Night.

3. Each of the Three Ladies invites the other two to carry out the mission, so that she herself may remain near the beautiful young man and watch over him. The close of the section, through C minor, modulated to A-flat major, the flatted tonality of more serious scenes, to G major, sharped tonality of the light scenes. The passions of the fair sex are merely comedy.

B. Trio in G major

The next section (G major) is in fact treated allegretto as a comedy trio forming an interlude: asides by each of the Three Ladies, explaining at length—just in case the spectator has not understood—the selfish reason for her invitation to the other two. Symmetrical ternary construction a a b, c c d, c c d + formulary restatements of d as a coda. We must remember

the casual little motif of five grace-notes which

persists through this sequence (measure 2, etc.), for we shall encounter it again several times later on.

C. Trio in C major

In the homophonic tonality of the initial C minor, this trio includes three elements, allegro, a b a'. The same idea as in the preceding section (happily, the music is much lighter than the text). Significant alteration of descending scales—*"Ich schütze ihn allein!"* (I'll watch over him by myself)—and ascending scales—*"Doch keine geht; es kann nicht sein!"* (Neither of the others, then, shall leave). Middle section, *"Du trauter Jüngling, lebe wohl"* (You, darling youth, farewell), recalling the tender episode of A; the final blackout, *"Bis ich dich wieder seh'"* (Until I see you again) including a modified restatement, or at least a reminder, of the first section, with its descending scales. The Three Ladies leave the scene by reentering the Temple of the Night, the gate of which opens and closes unaided at their approach (this symbolism is clear). Final formulary cadences in C major end the scene on an affirmation of the number Three by the brasses and timpani.

We shall recall the apparently secondary little motive that runs through the G-major allegretto of this trio: its five-note rhythm, which seems to resemble the "five equal little knocks" spoken of in the ritual of Adoption, will be encountered from the beginning to the end of the score, and always when there is a reference, in one form or another, to the futilities or the cabals of the Nocturnal Kingdom.

No. 1a / SPOKEN SCENE:
Tamino's Awakening and Papageno's Entrance

Tamino regains consciousness and wonders what has happened. The muted orchestra plays the ritornello of the succeeding aria, which describes the arrival of someone playing a syrinx. During this ritornello, Tamino speaks, asking himself who is approaching, and then hides. Papageno enters.

As everywhere, this has a precise significance: after his first experience with the simulacrum of love, the reawakening man is disappointed to find before him nothing but vacuity: the plumed Birdcatcher, dedicated to the sign of Air, with the five notes (the feminine Five) of his fluting.

No. 2 / PAPAGENO'S ARIA

In the key of futility (G major) Papageno introduces himself in the pleasant style of a popular song in couplets. He is, he says, the Birdcatcher, known to everyone, young or old, near or far. The pity is that his net catches birds rather than young girls. He would like to be able to carry off all the young girls and then choose the prettiest, embrace her, wheedle her, and marry her.

We saw (p. 104) the Birdcatcher's somewhat ambiguous role. For the moment, he limits himself to displaying his insouciance, blowing on the five-note syrinx (the significance of which has just been noted), which serves to decoy the feathered folk, and with which he periodically interrupts his singing. We note, further, that the characteristic rhythm of the symbolic 1–2–3–4–5 does not occur solely in his fluting: it also appears in his song, and is curiously linked with the 1–2–3 figure in the horns:

Because of the joyful candor of its symmetrical breadth, the striking melodic vein of its quick-witted inflections, the saltiness knowingly introduced into it by the amusing call of the syrinx, and its popular aspect as confirmed by the traditional *"hopsasa"* (analogue of the "tralala" of our childhood repertoire), Papageno's aria quickly became famous. It is found "recorded" on a bird-organ* almost contemporary with the opera, a "recording" that is a precious document because it brings us a living example of the *"fioriture"* used at the time

---

* A bird-organ (*serinette*) was a small barrel-organ that played repetitious series of notes intended to teach canaries to sing.

to embellish every musical text of this genre during perform-ance.[1] It begins like this:

Three identical couplets TDT, preceded by a prelude-ri-tornello resembling them and intended to accompany the stage busines of Scene 1a.

No. 2a / *SPOKEN SCENE*

A. Papageno's Lie and His Punishment

Tamino emerges and interrogates Papageno, who does not understand what he means when he says that he is a prince. The bumpkin does not know who his own parents were or who rules the country; he is not even aware that other coun-tries and other men exist. He has, however, been told that his mother once served the "*sternflammende Königin*" (star-flam-ing queen); thus his mother is pictured as a mistress of ig-norance, not having taught him anything during his child-hood. As for himself, he lives by eating and drinking "*wie alle Menschen*" (like all men) and by trapping birds for the Queen and her Ladies, who in exchange assure him his drink and his food (women support those who furnish useless trifles).

At the words "*sternflammende Königin*," which appear in the ritual [2] (= false lights providing no illumination), Ta-mino divines that they refer to the Queen of the Night and burns with a desire to see her (not yet initiate, he can still admire the false light of women). Papageno mocks him. Tamino expresses doubt that Papageno is a man, having judged by his plumage that he is a bird.

Papageno notices the dead serpent and begins to tremble.

But when he brags of his gigantic strength, Tamino believes that it was he who strangled the serpent. Delighted, Papageno is careful not to disillusion him (false bragging about amorous prowess as symbolized by the death of the serpent).

The Three Ladies return, and Tamino asks Papageno: "*Sind sie vermutlich sehr schön?*" (Are they really very beautiful?); Papageno replies: "*Ich denke nicht. Denn wenn sie schön wären, würden sie ihre Gesichter nicht bedecken*" (I don't think so. If they really were beautiful, they wouldn't cover up their faces). Papageno, as usual, offers them his birds. But instead of wine they give him plain water in a "beautiful bottle," instead of cakes, a stone, and close his mouth with a golden padlock (gold = masculine) to prevent him from lying (a reminder, as we have seen, of the feminine initiation). Then they reveal to Tamino that it was they who saved him: they have no intention of being deprived of a return gift in gratitude. The conclusion of this episode is deferred: we shall find it at the beginning of the quintet, No. 5.

B. Beginning of the Second Episode:
   Tamino's Mission

Having undeceived Tamino about the death of the serpent, the Ladies hand him "on behalf of their powerful Queen" the portrait of her daughter and repeat her words to him: "*Findest du, sagt sie, das diese Züge dir nicht gleichgültig sind, dann ist Glück, Ehr' und Ruhm dein Los!*" (She says that if your reaction to these features is not indifferent, then joy, honor, and glory will be your reward); see p. 113 for comment on this passage. They depart mocking Papageno.

No. 3 / TAMINO'S ARIA: The Portrait

Tamino gazes at the portrait with violent emotion and immediately expresses his love for the girl it pictures (commentary, pp. 121–3). The initiatory tonality of E-flat major alerts us to the symbolic value of the episode.

Here, as in other arias of his final period (*cf.* also Pamina's aria, No. 17), Mozart thus remarkably enlarged the rather stereotyped form of the *aria da capo*, abandoning literal repetition and replacing it with a single reminder of the relationship. The boundary between recitative style and that of the aria is often vague. No longer a "theme to develop," but instead easily recognizable characteristic inflections appearing throughout the piece, assuring its unity. They even go beyond the individual piece to take on a sort of Leitmotiv value *avant la lettre* (*cf.* the exclamation of love, *"Tamino mein!"* in the finale, 21B).

a) (measures 1–16) *Tamino gazes at the portrait in ecstasy* (tonic). Larghetto, with long leaps of a sixth or a seventh into the upper vocal regions, particularly emphasizing his enthusiasm on the word *"Götterbild"* (heavenly picture).

b) (measures 16–35) dominant key, B-flat. *He questions the nature of his emotion and discovers that it is love.* Now the orchestra dialogues with him: clarinets, then violins. The second question (in the dominant): *"Soll die Empfindung Liebe sein?"* already has a Schumannesque atmosphere.

c) (measure 35–end: return to the tonic) *Passionate call to the girl whose picture is before his eyes.* Here the access of enthusiasm is not, as in *a*, a sudden burst followed by descents, but a long, linear ascent, first on the violin, frantic twistings followed by silences interrupted by emotion, then for the voice alone (the two sorts even coexist in measures 37–9), the one leading into the other without interruption, with a measure of meditative silence after *"Was würde ich?"* Even the cadential repetitions and amplifications, often mere empty formulas, take on meaning here because of the stammering, distracted statement of love which they convey.

I have said that this aria suggests the ABA form in some ways, but does not employ it literally: that resemblance, though not exact—of the vocal elements of the first and third sections—is easy to detect: upward leap, cropped phrases, a characteristic cell (measure 10, restatement measure 40, then measures 46–47); the tonal plan T-D-T emphasizes this symmetry. Nevertheless, the impression left is not that of a "formal aria," but of an uninterrupted, free, generous melodic flow and of extraordinarily warm lyricism. In Pamina's aria, No. 17, one finds an identical enlargement of the concept of the *aria da capo*.

No. 3a / SPOKEN SCENE: *Recounting of the Abduction*

At the end of his aria, Tamino is ready to depart. The Three Ladies reappear and detain him (flirtation as opposed to real love). The Queen, they say, has understood everything and has resolved to make Tamino "the happiest of mortals" because her daughter will be saved if he is as brave as he has showed himself to be responsive. And they describe the abduction of Pamina by an evil genius one May day when she was seated in a cypress wood, her favorite retreat (symbol: woman lives in a cemetery). The tyrant—that is, the fully developed man—lives in a charming and agreeable valley; his castle is superb and well guarded (one notes the contrast). Tamino at once asserts impulsively that he wants to kill the tyrant and deliver Pamina. Immediately, the rubric says, a tremolo chord is heard, music not notated in the score. Thunder. The mountains open, revealing the Queen of the Night seated upon a star-spangled throne.

No. 4 / ARIA OF THE QUEEN OF THE NIGHT: *Tamino's Mission*

The Queen tells Tamino of her daughter's abduction by the evil Sarastro (largo) and imperiously orders him to set out to deliver her. If the young man will obey and bring Pamina back to the maternal kingdom, she will be his forever. We notice that in this stage of his development, Tamino accepts orders from the Queen of the Night without replying. Furthermore, he is implicitly considered one of her vassals, if not of her subjects (Scene 2A): the Queen calls him *"mein lieber Sohn."*

This is the first of the two great arias that have made this difficult role famous among "coloratura" sopranos. Mozart composed it for his sister-in-law, Josefa Hofer, who was then a member of Schikaneder's troupe. Their formal vocalises (soaring to high F) nevertheless are not mere displays of virtuosity, as was so often the case in operas of the period. To say, as the Massins tried to say, that they evoke "the artificial nature of the character" is not convincing: at that time, such vocal prowess was not at all scorned by esthetes, as it is now. Quite the contrary. Here they transmit, on the word *"ewig"* (forever), the promise that Pamina will belong to Tamino forever if he rescues her. The conventions of the era normally gave that word and the idea that it represents an emphasizing artifice (a held note or a vocalise). When Mozart adapted it to this role, he was merely following tradition.

Unquestionably, however, the music of this aria leaves an impression of the Queen's complete insincerity. The description of her motherly sorrow is remarkably arid,* impossible to confuse with the genuine sorrow of Pamina in No. 17. She is not sincere until she spits out her hatred against the *"Bösewicht"* (scoundrel) Sarastro, her enemy. The description of Pamina's terror during her abduction is extravagantly theatrical, and the intentional artificiality is brought out in a significant detail: "Help," the text says, "is all that she said." And the contrast between the theatrical cry *"Ach helft!"* and

---

* The Massins, who studied this character well, give a curious explanation: they say that the first ritornello was taken from *Thamos*, in which it emphasized the disloyalty of the traitor Pheron, and that it thus alerts us at once to the Queen's maliciousness, not yet revealed in the text. One may, it is true, object that this relationship is incommunicable to anyone unacquainted with *Thamos* because it does not rely upon any particular musical element except, perhaps, an insidious chromaticism in the inner parts which often is a sign of sly hypocrisy in the vocabulary of the Mozartean opera.

the neutral, strictly noncommittal *"war alles was sie sprach"* tells us a lot about her psychology. The impression left is comparable to that made during a rehearsal by a tragedienne interrupting a dramatic tirade to ask a stagehand to bring her a chair.

Kufferath said that this aria contained resemblances to an aria in Wranitzky's *Oberon*, which Schikaneder constantly pointed out to Mozart as a model because of its success in the same theater. It contains two (non-modulating) sections: the first, characterized by wide, imperious intervals (the order to leave: *"Du, du, du,"* on an ascending arpeggio), which recurs throughout the score with a sense of recall (*cf.* the Ladies' song of triumph); and the second (the promise that he may have Pamina forever), characterized by the long, formidable vocalises of great virtuosity emphasizing the word *"ewig."*

Introduction (recitative) and two-part aria: largo and allegro in the key of B-flat major, which perhaps evokes the imperfect initiation of the great nocturnal priestess (only two flats, whereas Sarastro is given three).

1st   *Recitativo stromentato*, "noble" form of narration almost invariably used for gods, kings, etc. Also, the Singspiel made little use of *recitativo secco*.

Orchestral introduction agitated by syncopation, perhaps motivated by the first words: *"O zitt're nicht"* (Do not tremble). The Queen reassures and flatters Tamino: he is wise, just, and good, and he will be able to assuage her maternal sorrow. Unlike Bach's narrations, Mozart's seldom are meant to be symbolically descriptive. Only one figurative touch is encountered here: the flatted darkening of the Neapolitan sixth on the word *"tief"* (deep) describing her grief. Up to that point, particularly in the spaces between her phrases, the orchestra continues the rhythmic motion of the preamble, the syncopes of which continue to reflect the opening *"O zitt're nicht."*

2nd   Two-part aria: a largo in G minor (Rm) and an allegro in B-flat major (TP). The largo describes the sorrow of the mother whose child has been abducted, and is divided into three sections, roughly ABA', taking G minor for the TP.

A (T G minor to RM B-flat major). The mother's sorrow, deliberately expressed with a certain aridity. The Queen's real character shows itself when, modulating to the relative major, she furiously spits out the word *"Bösewicht."*

B (RM to T, *"Noch seh' ich"*). The girl's terror during her abduction, marked by the gasping rhythm of the orchestra and the piecemeal phrases interrupted by the voice and set against the continuous inner line emphasized by the unusual viola-bassoon doubling.

A' (T G minor, *"Ich musste sie"*). The abducted girl's calls for help. Echo of musical elements used in A, but reused here without rigor. The cry *"Ach Helft!"* is dramatic, but the succeeding passage—*"sie sprach"*—suddenly collapses back into a neuter tone that breaks the atmosphere: the Queen is a comedienne. Tamino must lend his assistance because, she says, *"meine Hilfe war zu schwach"* (my help was too weak). We note the significant rejoinder.

A swift chord of brutal modulation, and we change to TP: B-flat major, for the allegro. Tamino is ordered to set out on the quest to free the girl. As a reward, she will be his forever.

No. 4a / SPOKEN SCENE

The Queen and her entourage vanish; we have returned to the preceding setting. Tamino wonders if he was dreaming, and wants to depart. Papageno bars his way (futility comes between the man and the woman when he wants to set out to win her).

No. 5 / QUINTET:
Tamino, Papageno, and the Three Ladies

A long scene in juxtaposed sections. The Three Ladies remove the padlock from Papageno and give Tamino the magic flute that is to protect him. Papageno is terrified by the Ladies' order that he follow Tamino; they hand him the glockenspiel, which will be, for him, the equivalent of Tamino's flute. Then they announce that as they approach Sarastro's castle they will be replaced by *"Drei Knäbchen, jung, schön, hold und*

weise" (three boys, young, good-looking, charming, and wise).
Farewells.

This scene concludes the introductory episode and the transition to the principal scene of the act (the arrival at Sarastro's stronghold and the request for initiation). We have already explained the padlock (p. 121), the flute (pp.123–5), and the glockenspiel (pp. 125–6), as well as the Three Ladies' announcement that they will be replaced by Three Boys (p. 114).

A. Tamino-Papageno Duet

The padlocked Birdcatcher expresses himself in onomatopoeias and makes signs that he wants to talk: *"Ich kann nichts tun, als dich beklagen,/Weil ich zu schwach zu helfen bin"* (I can't do anything but lament for you because I am too weak to help you), Tamino replies (= not yet armed with the powers of the initiate; *cf.* the words just spoken by the Queen: *"Denn meine Hilfe war zu schwach"*).

The scene is amusing, and the idea for it can be found in various earlier Singspiels. For example, in *Der Stein der Weisen*, Schikaneder himself had introduced a similar situation, in which the character Lubanara spoke, at certain junctions, only in mewings.[3] But is this really nothing but comedy? The key of B-flat major tells us the contrary, and Tamino's phrase *"Ich kann nichts tun"* is too much like certain other initiatory responses to permit that interpretation. Further, is it coincidental that this exact phrase markedly resembles words in the portrait aria: *"dies Etwas kann ich zwar nicht nennen"* (this something, it's true, I cannot name)? We have touched upon the significance of the padlock: Tamino by means of the serpent and Papageno by means of that padlock have received the beginning of initiation, but initiation into the feminine world. Tamino's answer underlines that world's insufficiency.

The style, though light and popular, is nonetheless different for the two characters. Papageno's murmurings and staccato notes in the form of a refrain are comically followed by a bassoon that clarifies the melody (the actor can only murmur it), whereas Tamino's singing, legato melody is supported by expressive chords. When they finally join in duet, the contrast is striking. We also notice the description, in the two measures of prelude, of Papageno's gesturing as he points to his padlocked mouth and then spreads his hands in an impotent gesture.

B. Papageno's Release and the Conclusion of
the Episode of the Serpent (F major, D of TP)

The Ladies return, remove the padlock, and make Papageno swear to lie no more. This follows the feminine initiation, in which the candidate's mouth is uncovered as she is made to promise to learn how to remain intelligently silent. Further, this moral is drawn: "If every liar had a padlock of this sort on his mouth, instead of evil, lying, and black hatred [evocative eighth-notes on these words], love and brotherhood would reign."

Like all the moralizings in the opera, this one is sung *sotto voce** by all those present on the stage, who "depersonalize" themselves, like characters in a modern revue addressing the audience after stepping out of their roles. One can, then, dispense once and for all with the perplexed or sarcastic comments that, after Oulibichev, became traditional with regard to the often evident disparity between the singers' roles and the maxims that they are asked to sing in this way. In the present case, the object being to evoke "Masonry of Adoption," the number of which is 5, it is not accidental that the

* The expression means "in an undertone," but its literal meaning gives an idea of mysterious confidence; it is used almost systematically during the morals that dot the opera. Would there not be here a sort of play on words regarding the esoterism of the teaching thus imparted?

singers are united in a quintet. Naturally, they express themselves strictly in homorhythm, so that the meaning of the
words that they address to the spectators can be understood
plainly.

Modulating bridge supplying the return to TP B flat.

C. The Return of the Magic Flute (B flat, TP)

Tamino and Papageno having in turn undergone a significant
trial of the ritual of Adoption, the Ladies now busy themselves
about Tamino. He must now pass beyond the provisional
stage; the Ladies will set him upon the path that will lead
him to full knowledge. The flute, symbolizing the power that
an initiate has over the spirit and of which the sign is music,
will be the leading instrument.

One observes the care with which Mozart here eschews all material literalism: not only is there not a single scale from the flute—
which certainly would have been played if we were dealing with
a simple talisman from a fairy tale, as in *Lulu*—but also the flute
is absent from the orchestration. More, we have forgotten its
timbre almost completely, as it has not been heard since the
Ladies' farewell at the end of No. 1, after which it disappeared
from the score, not to return until the trio following No. 6.

The First Lady returns the flute (its history will be revealed
in Act II). Her melodic phrase will be reheard later (*sind zu
eurem Schutz*) and again in No. 10, Sarastro's prayer to Isis
and Osiris. Then the Three Ladies, in homorhythmic trio,
relate its virtues (number 3: then we know from the final explanation that the flute came, not from the Queen of the
Night, but from her husband). The two men then join the
Ladies to re-form the preceding quintet and to give the audience the moral of the "flute episode": "*O so eine Flöte ist
mehr als Gold und Kronen wert; Denn durch sie wird Mensch-
englück und Zufriedenheit vermehrt*" (A flute like this is

worth more than gold and wealth; by means of it, human woe could be changed to happiness and contentment).

Modulating bridge to the relative.

D. Papageno's Bells (relative G minor to TP B-flat major)

This comic scene balances the "serious" sequence just completed: Tamino has received his magic instrument, and one is needed for the comic character. It cannot be one of the "noble" instruments of the orchestra: the glockenspiel fits the requirements:* its symbolism was pointed out on pp. 125–6. We do not hear it at this point any more than we hear the flute—not for the same reasons, but because one circumstance leads to the other.

Papageno, who has had enough, asks for permission to leave (interrogative cadence). The Ladies in trio, parodying his style (all three belong to the same kingdom), refuse and tell him that their mistress will send him to Sarastro's castle. Here again (and throughout the entire sequence) we hear the five-note formula already discussed (p. 188): it is repeated several times during interventions by the Three Ladies. Terrified, the poor man reminds the Ladies that they have pictured that lord as a savage tiger (augmented sixth) and that he therefore sees himself plucked, carved up, and roasted (rapid comic-scene declamation). The Ladies reply: *"Dich schützt der Prinz, trau ihm allein. Dafür sollst du sein Diener sein"* (The Prince will watch over you, trust only him. You in return shall be his servant); the chromatic phrase here recalls the "Hungarian" episode in the finale of Mozart's Violin Concerto in A. *"Dass doch der Prinz beim Teufel wäre"* (May the

---

* Gluck and Mozart had not disdained to compose for a related instrument, the glass harmonica, consisting of tuned glass cups that were either struck or rubbed.

Prince go to the Devil [again the augmented sixth]). *"Mein Leben ist mir lieb"* (My life is dear to me).

On a passing E-flat modulation, partially repeating the phrase that accompanied their presentation of the flute, the Ladies then give Papageno the glockenspiel that will protect him; they assure him that he will have no difficulty in playing it.

Concluding quintet (return to B flat): *"Silberglöckchen, Zauberflöten sind zu eurem Schutz vonnöten. Lebet wohl! wir wollen gehn. Lebet wohl, auf Wiedersehn!"* (Silver bells and magic flutes [= music charged with magic feeling] are there to protect you. Go—until we meet again!). Is it coincidence that the phrase *"sind zu eurem Schutz,"* used to recall the presentation of the flute, so closely resembles the second-act invocation *"O Isis und Osiris"*?

Transition: Tamino and Papageno, having left anxiously after that farewell, now retrace their steps. *"Wie man die Burg wohl finden kann?"* (But how can the castle be found? —interrogation on the dominant).

E. Announcement of the Three Boys and
   Final Farewell (TP B flat)

After a fermata, the Ladies' reply is heralded by a contrastingly solemn andante prelude. The woodwind sonority (clarinets and bassoons supported very lightly by violin pizzicati) bespeaks a Masonic reference. In its opening rhythm, this somewhat foreshadows the march of the priests that will open Act II and foretells, in the rhythm of its clausula, the canticle that will soon begin the finale; the sixth degree of its second chord and the abundance of consecutive fifths which follows set the religious character, suggesting the *sotto voce* of mysterious revelations. This canticle is heard thrice, first in the prelude (first "open" section only); then doubled by the Ladies' reply, their tripping diction in contrast to the sustained style maintained by the orchestra: "Three boys, young, good-looking, charming, and wise, will guide you: follow well all of their advice." A third time, finally: Papageno and Tamino repeat the beginning of the instruction, the Ladies its end.

We already have seen (pp. 114–16) the meaning of the Three Boys as announced here: they represent the beginning of the real initiation (in Masonry, age signifies the degree of knowledge); a beginning perfectible as they mature, whereas that wisdom is refused to women, who remain inexorably veiled even when initiated. That is why the Three Ladies conduct Tamino and Papageno no farther: they may not enter Sarastro's stronghold. They will approach it in Act II only by a rebellion that will be punished severely.

The ravishing farewell scene follows, taking up as a coda the final part of the canticle and ending on three chords punctuated by a triple formal bow by the strings—exceptionally discreet when one considers the usual insistence of Mozart's cadences.

Second Scene

A SUMPTUOUS EGYPTIAN-STYLE CHAMBER IN SARASTRO'S CASTLE

What naturally follows is the counterpart for Pamina of what just has been told us about Tamino. The same swoon on seeing an unworthy simulacrum of love, the same awakening encounter with the fantastic Papageno, the same emotion when faced with an image still remote from the person whom the gods have destined for her (Papageno's narration here replacing the portrait).

Here one may observe that a hierarchy of four categories of

amorous relationship are symbolized in the opera: the basest
lechery (Monostatos); flirtation, less abject certainly, but
superficial and frivolous (the Three Ladies); the "bourgeois"
couple, honest, but without ideals (Papageno-Papagena); and
finally the Perfect Couple, whose vindication is the principal
aim of the work (Tamino-Pamina).

As for the serpent and the padlock (the symmetry is complete), the conclusion will be reported during the next episode (finale, No. 8): Monostatos will lead the fugitive before
Sarastro, expecting a reward. To his astonishment, he will find
himself condemned to receive bastinado strokes, and Sarastro
will reveal to Pamina that he is holding her prisoner for her
own good; he tells her that she will understand later.

No. 5a / SPOKEN SCENE

The slaves assisting Monostatos rejoice at the prospect that
the hated Moor surely will be punished because, having been
detailed to guard Pamina, he has let her escape. That "pomp-
ous fellow full of lechery" believed himself at the point of
achieving his end when his victim uttered Sarastro's name.
That name troubled the bully, who, then, is fully aware that he
is acting against his master's wishes (now Sarastro's name appears as an element of liberation). Profiting by his hesitation,
Pamina has run to the canal, jumped into a gondola, and disappeared among the palm trees.

The "local color" of the Egyptian gondola need not be
emphasized: we commented upon the symbolism of this
episode on p. 103. Pamina has acted under her sign, that of
Water: she has taken a predetermined route (canal) when
trying to reach the palms, plants associated with the solar sign
of Sarastro's kingdom.[4] We soon learn that her premature attempt has failed.

In fact, one hears the voice of Monostatos offstage. He has
caught Pamina, and in the grip of the *idée fixe* that testifies

to his terrestrial symbolism, he orders irons brought to fetter her. These are the irons (Plate 26) placed upon the uninitiate female until she is freed by the feminine initiation. They are also an image of slavery to the senses as long as the sensual urge is not sustained by true love. Moved by pity, the slaves run away so as not to have to obey Monostatos.

No. 6 / TRIO

This is not really a trio, but a sectional scene made up of two successive duets: Monostatos-Pamina first, then Papageno-Monostatos.

A. Pamina's Swoon (Pamina-Monostatos duet)

Key of G major, which sets the action in the climate of comedy which belongs to the second section, if not to the first. Perhaps also a warning not to take Monostatos too seriously: he will be the buffoon of Sarastro's entourage as Papageno was that of the Queen of the Night's—and, like Papageno, he will later switch his loyalty. Both will thus reveal their true natures, for Monostatos is as basically evil as Papageno is basically good. Also, as we have seen (diagram, p. 100), this change is ordained by the very nature of their basic symbols.

Agitated music, as at the opening of the act: the musical similarity of the two scenes is striking: Pamina is pursued by Monostatos as Tamino was pursued by the serpent (the man by his instincts, the other by a man who has yielded to those instincts). *"Du feines Täubchen, nur herein!"* (You fine little dove, come with me!), the black man says. (Is this meant to recall the symbolism of the crow and the dove mentioned earlier?) Pamina cries out: *"O welche Marter, welche Pein!"* (O what torture, what pain!) while calmly taking up the (curiously) major melody begun by her adversary. Should we see anomaly or negligence in that? Throughout the score, the conscious intentions are carried out too much in detail to allow us to believe in negligence here. Perhaps, as suggested earlier, Mozart simply did not want to dramatize the scenes of sensual love. *"Der Tod macht mich nicht beben"* (Death does not frighten me), Pamina says, *"Nur meine Mutter dauert mich"* (But I cannot bear my mother's grief—syncopated rhythm of the emotion). *"Sie stirbt vor Gram ganz sicherlich!"* (She will surely die of grief—minor inflection on *"stirbt"*). Imperiously, with the orchestra underlining the gesture, Monostatos orders the irons to be brought (general rise in pitch, signifying action). *"Lass mich lieber sterben . . . Barbar"* (Let me die instead . . . barbarian), Pamina says (syncopations by the orchestra, flatted inflection on the word *"sterben,"* urgent climb toward the word *"Barbar"*). *"Weil nichts . . . dich rühren kann"* (As nothing can touch you); on these words, her voice falls back, not supported by the orchestra, which is silenced to prepare for the arrival of the tonic: Pamina has swooned.

Transition: Terrified, Monostatos calls out for help; then, contradicting himself, he orders that he be left alone with the princess: doubtless he wants to take advantage of the situation. We observe the similarity of the rising chords to those which, at the beginning of the act, emphasized Tamino's call for help when he first saw the serpent.

B. Papageno Face to Face with Monostatos

The music becomes frankly comedic. Papageno enters, asks where he is, and sees Pamina. He exclaims: *"Schön Mädchen, jung und fein,/ Viel weisser noch als Kreide"* (Pretty girl, young and dainty, much whiter than chalk).

Throughout, there is considerable insistence upon Pamina's whiteness, which is contrasted with the blackness of her jailer. White and black are both lunar and feminine colors (see table, pp. 98–9), but they represent two differing aspects, positive and negative qualities. The Queen and her Ladies are black; Pamina is white. The true nature of this daughter of the Night is as foreign to her milieu as that of the black Monostatos to the kingdom of the sun into which he has made his way.

A happy rhythm runs through this passage, with exquisitely simple orchestration (flute in the high octave of the violin alternating with the bassoon in its low octave); at first, it is only a light new motive of the sort that occurs constantly to Mozart. But note that when Papageno sees Pamina, a slight transformation of this motive suffices to give it a new form. In the latter, we shall find, scarcely altered, the elements of the trio (also in G major) which the Three Ladies sang when Tamino likewise swooned; it will be heard again in the melody of the glockenspiel. Further, it does not lack the five-note motive that accompanies allusions to female society; the words have the same meaning (Papageno says that Pamina is as beautiful as she is white).

Observing further that the trilled rhythm accompanying Monostatos's order to the slaves was also found in Scene 1, where it persisted through the beginning of the final section in C major, one must agree that Mozart could not have showed us more clearly the symbolic parallelism of the two scenes.

This scene is completed with a very amusing buffo duet, with Papageno and Monostatos, the two opposing elements of the Air-Earth dyad, face to face. Each believing the other to be the Devil, each saves himself in his own way while the orchestra comments by recalling Papageno's entrance theme in brief, light, silence-starred touches.

One also notes the lightness of the final measure, which ends on a weak beat so as to describe better the stealthy departure of the two frightened men—a procedure of description by counter-usage which such a composer as Pascal de L'Estocart had employed in the sixteenth century to describe the disappearance of melting ice, or which one might compare to the *dimisit inanes* in Bach's *Magnificat*. Nonetheless, this remains exceptional, if not unique, justified by its descriptive purpose. Stravinsky will take it up, without intending any allusive reason, at the end of Part I of *Le Sacre du printemps*, and Berg will borrow it from Stravinsky at the end of *Wozzeck*.

No. 6a / SPOKEN SCENE

Pamina regains consciousness and calls for her mother. Like the awakening Tamino, she finds Papageno instead: when she awakens, the purely sensual nature of her initiation allows her to see nothing but the Birdcatcher's futilities.

Papageno starts off by talking about Monostatos: *"Bin ich nicht ein Narr, dass ich mich schrecken liess? Es gibt ja schwarze Vögel in der Welt, warum denn nicht auch schwarze Menschen?"* (Wasn't I a stupid fool to be afraid? There are black birds in the world, so why not black men too?—an allusion to the crow of the legend after the allusion to the dove). Then he notices Pamina, recognizes her from her portrait, and presents himself as the messenger of the Queen of the Night. He tells the story of the portrait presented to Tamino and reveals to Pamina that this unknown prince immediately fell in love with her and is coming to set her free. *"Wohl denn, es sei gewagt!"* (Well, then, let us get started), Pamina says, indicating that she already reciprocates Tamino's love. And Papageno laments that he has no Papagena to love.

One exchange of dialogue deserves special attention. Pamina

asks: *"Wie hoch mag wohl die Sonne sein?"* (What time is
it by the Sun?)—and Papageno answers *"Bald gegen Mittag"*
(It is nearly noon). This is a precise allusion, one of those
"details in the text" to which Mozart said that he had drawn
a companion's attention when trying to make him understand
the interest of the libretto—and about which he became so
irritated when the man did not understand. Noon is the symbolic time for beginning the labors, and before declaring them
begun, the Venerable must ask what time it is by the Sun.
Not until he has received the answer "It is noon, Venerable
Master" can he declare the session open. All initiate Masons
must understand the meaning of Papageno's reply: the hour
for Pamina's initiation has not yet arrived, but will do so
shortly (*cf.* the facsimile of the ritual, p. 115).

Another question asked by Pamina deserves mention: will
the prince free her from her fetters? We recall that the gesture
of removing the chains from the candidate's arms is one part
of the feminine initiation.

No. 7 / MORALIZING DUET

In the tradition of *opéra-comique,* the spoken dialogue about
love will perforce lead into a passage of lyric comment. Like
all the moralizings in *Die Zauberflöte,* this one is sententious
and general in character. It is not a love duet for Papageno
and Pamina, but a morality about love by the two characters
who happen to be on stage at the moment. That fact renders
footless the charges of lack of verisimilitude which often have
been leveled against this libretto.

The scene is essential to the economy of the action: despite
the platitudinousness of their phraseology, its words contain
the high fundamental morality of the opera (true love, and
not that inferior love which has just been symbolized to each
of them). *"Die süssen Triebe mitzufühlen,/ Ist dann der
Weiber erste Pflicht"* (To share man's sweet urges with

him is a woman's first duty)—these words, spoken by Papageno, are the essential key to the work. Once the two have been united and have recognized one another, *"Mann und Weib, und Weib und Mann/ Reichen an die Gottheit an"* (Man and wife, and wife and man, attain to godliness).

Mozart was so conscious of the importance of this duet that at first he had worked out a much more highly developed and "noble" version of it than the one we know. For theatrical reasons, Schikaneder, who played the role of Papageno, had him redo it (doubtless also because of his own limitations as a singer) in a more popular style related to the character. What we have is that second version.

In E-flat major—tonality of Masonic high moralities—first Pamina, then Papagena, then the two of them in duet (aa'b) sing two similar verses of pretty melodic flow, the second ornamented; after that, they join in the usual *sotto voce* unison in which the moralities in the opera generally are sung, reaching the conclusion: *"Mann und Weib."* We notice that the winds leading to the *sotto voce* mount in thirds, evoking the simultaneous ascent of the man and the woman toward the announced condition of divinity.

Here Pamina's vocalises take on an emphasizing value, opposing harmonious legato to her mother's imperious staccato style. Three chords at the close.

A change of scene.

Third Scene

BEFORE THE TEMPLE
OF WISDOM

The first scene has showed Tamino's preparation, the second Pamina's. Now, for both of them, comes the development—duly stylized, but nonetheless faithful—that has been led up to: the ceremonial request for admission.

The scene represents a woods (the "sacred wood" of the

Ancients). At the rear of the stage is a handsome temple decorated with the words *Temple of Wisdom*. Colonnades link it to two other temples: at the right, the *Temple of Reason*, at the left, the *Temple of Nature*.*

No. 8 / FINALE

This long, sectional musical scene appears to be a break only to those exegetes who have not understood the preceding scenes. It can be divided into two large sections, I and II, and they in turn subdivided (ABC, etc.). The first shows Tamino arriving outside the Temple of Wisdom, followed by Papageno. The second announces Sarastro's verdict. He condemns Monostatos and orders the initiation of the strangers, whereas Pamina, who has glimpsed her destiny, must await the hour when her suitor will have achieved initiation through his own moral suffering, and thus will have qualified them both for the sublime love celebrated in the preceding duet, which will make them "equal to the gods."

I / ARRIVAL OF TAMINO AT THE TEMPLE OF WISDOM

A. The Three Boys

(a) *Trio of the Boys and Their Dialogue with Tamino*

The Three Boys, announced by the Ladies, come in leading Tamino. Each of them is holding a silver palm frond (symbol of the passage from the lunar—silver—world to the solar world

---

* The column is so important an element of Masonic symbolism that the musical ensembles heard in the Lodge are called "columns of harmony." Wisdom, the essential object of Tamino's conquest, is linked to the two elements from which it stems. Reason, on the right, has supremacy over Nature, which latter, however, must be understood in the sense given to it by the eighteenth-century *philosophes* under the influence of Jean-Jacques Rousseau. The triad Nature-Reason-Wisdom does not seem to figure among the numerous Masonic triads we have encountered (it is known that the motto of the French Republic —*Liberté, Égalité, Fraternité*—is one of them, but it is not certain whether

—palm, image of the "triumph over death by resurrection"—
cf. pp. 116 and 233).

We are made aware of the quasi-religious atmosphere of this
scene by its first notes. At the same time, the music represents
the aforementioned symbol in the most ingenious manner: in
the solemn key of C major, the "Masonic winds"—trombones
and bassoons—give out in a meditative larghetto the Five
rhythm of the Overture, and at the same time other brasses,
(deep trumpets with mutes and bass trombones), punctuated
by the timpani, transform it into a Three rhythm by emphasizing the uneven beats.

Here one might have expected the initiatory E-flat major (it
will appear at essential moments), but the sequence is doubtless
defective: no spoken interval follows the preceding number in
E-flat major.

The "paradigm" key of C major also is in its place (*cf.* p. 160).
To the sonority of the "Masonic winds," that of the cellos is
sometimes added, but "it does not count." This is doubtless a
holdover from the slightly earlier period of the *basso continuo*.

The timpani are "muted"—*timpani coperti*—a novelty in orchestration which Berlioz would recall. But perhaps it also has a
simultaneous intention, as in the *sotto voce* of the moralities.
When Sarastro appears, the score specifies *timpani senza coperta*.
All of the orchestration of this passage is remarkable and deserves
close study, including its relationship to the context, which it
highlights by contrast.

The symbolic mixture of the Three and the Five in the orchestration may have been traditional: it is already to be seen in 1779,
at the beginning of the Overture to Philidor's *Carmen Seculare*
(*cf.* p. 90).

After the third of the five beats, the strings intone, piano,
a melody supported by parallel thirds and sixths in a definite
canticle style:

Masonry suggested it or adopted it); in any case, it well reflects the order's
spirit, and we cannot be certain that it was not used by Viennese Masonry in
1790.

Of contemplative character at first, this canticle soon tends toward march rhythm: it accompanies the entrance of Tamino led by the Boys, whose significance we have seen (pp. 122–5). Now the limited role of the nocturnal initiation is over and we approach the first periods of true knowledge.

The words of the Boys demonstrate again how everything in the libretto is symbolic. They do not talk like either infants or fairy-tale guides; they make no mention of the goal of the journey of Pamina's lover. They speak like initiates, to the canticle music already presented in the introduction (or, at least, to its first phrase, which develops differently, but in the same style); their advice is the moral instruction for the initiation. *"Zum Ziele führt dich diese Bahn,/ Doch musst du, Jüngling, männlich siegen./ Drum höre unsre Lehre an"* (This road will take you to your goal, but you must comport yourself like a man. Therefore you must heed our precepts). These instructions include a new triad, extracted from the ritual of initiation,[5] each term of which, announced first with the firm support of the muted timpani, is followed by the emphasis of a held half-note for the Masonic winds: *"Sei standhaft*" (Be steadfast), held note; "*duldsam*" (patient), held note; "*und verschwiegen*" (and silent), held note.

Tamino has not yet reached that level. Still incapable of raising himself above the symbol, he merely asks if he will find Pamina again. The music underlines the difference: after the Boys' religious verse, Tamino's reply brusquely changes character, falling back, under the banal strokes of the second violins, into the style of opera which had been abandoned. That style disappears as soon as the Boys speak again. Not replying, they reiterate their triple commandment followed by triple emphasis, and then prolong it in a conclusion in which the ending of the prelude returns: "*Bedenke dies; kurz, sei ein Mann,/ Dann, Jüngling, wirst du männlich siegen*" (Think of this; in short, be a man, and you will conquer in a manly way). Here "man" is "*Mann*," not *Mensch*: that is, man as opposed to woman, the basic element of this duality, and we have already noted the importance of that concept in the libretto. For the rest, are not the three virtues advocated the antithesis of the "feminine" qualities in the perspective of the libretto?

The Three Boys take their leave to a postlude recalling the opening of the canticle, and Tamino remains alone upon the stage.

(b) Tamino's Aria

The element of Air framed between two recitatives of action. Or, if one prefers, recitative bisected by a morality in the style of Air.

Recitative: Tamino has understood the lesson: "*Die Weisheitslehre dieser Knaben/ Sei ewig mir ins Herz gegraben*" (May the wise counsel of these Boys remain forever engraved upon [literally, dug into] my heart—whence the descent on the word "*gegraben*," with its rhyming echo of "*begraben*"—

buried). *"Ist dies der Sitz der Götter hier?"* (Is this place the seat of the gods?)—the questioning tone of the augmented sixth. *"Es zeigen die Pforten, es zeigen die Säulen,/ Dass Klugheit und Arbeit und Künste hier weilen"* (These portals and columns show that sagacity, labor, and art reign here)—a new triad, this time not emphasized.

Aria: very short, presenting the morality of the fragment: *"Wo Tätigkeit thronet und Müssiggang weicht,/ Erhält seine Herrschaft das Laster nicht leicht"* (Where action is enthroned and idleness gives way, vice cannot hold its dominion). This is a very distinct reference to the portrait aria, a fact that retroactively but clearly underlines its symbolic content.

Recitative: Tamino is resolving to knock on the portals (rising scale of action), for his *"Absicht ist edel und lauter und rein"* (his purpose is noble and elevated and pure). Then the recitative orchestra becomes animated with syncopations: *"Erzitt're, feiger Bösewicht!"* (Tremble, dastardly scoundrel) —with Tamino docilely repeating the word *"Bösewicht"* used by the Queen of the Night. *"Pamina retten ist mir Pflicht"* (To rescue Pamina is my duty). Final cadence in D major (sharpened key of non-wisdom: Tamino still imagines that he is to deliver a persecuted captive).

B. Tamino Requests Admission into the Temple

(a) *He Is Driven Back from the Two Lateral Temples*

Not having undergone the necessary initiation, in fact, Tamino cannot penetrate the secrets of Nature, which, fathomed thanks to Reason, lead to Wisdom. Approaching successively the portals of the right-hand temple (Reason) and the left-hand one (Nature), he is driven back both times by a voice from inside which calls out: *"Zurück!"* (Go back!). We remember that at the beginning of every initiatory ceremony the candidate's request for admission is made from outside and answered from within. We are, then, at the prolegomena to the final initiation.

In the actual ceremony, the postulant never is rejected (if undesirable, he would not have been allowed to present himself), but the ritual nonetheless provides for a simulacrum of inquiry and deliberation before authorization to enter is given. We shall find that deliberation at the beginning of Act II as analyzed in Chapter 16 (p. 127).

This whole sequence (G minor to C minor) is traversed by a motive that precisely represents Tamino's actions: an ascending impetus toward the portals (trilled group) followed, when he meets with rejection, by a retreat closely resembling the opening of the quintet No. 5.

Three times this motive shows Tamino bounding up the temple steps: the first time full of confidence and not fearing any setback: D major. The refusal descends like a knife: *"Zurück!"* on an unexpected B flat that sounds forth like a true break in tonality.

In fact, the break is only apparent: this B flat is merely the third degree of G minor; the first of the preceding D major very quickly becomes a fifth of G minor. Apropos of the opening chords of the Overture, we said that the "modal" degrees 3 and 4 always are used evocatively, most often in a religious sense—and with this exact repetition we are entering the very heart of the religious mystery. Note also that the oblivious postulant moves forward in a sharpened tonality (which in *Die Zauberflöte*, a few exceptions aside, is the mark of ignorance), and that the mysterious reply reintroduces the flats of the initiatory scenes.

Rejected by the Temple of Reason, which he has had the presumption to claim before having been prepared, Tamino attempts to penetrate the Temple of Nature; but his first setback has weakened his confidence: this time the motive is in a minor key (G minor, a less "profane" tonality than D major). The same cadence with the third degree: another *"Zurück!"* that leads to E-flat major, the perfect Masonic tonality.

Tamino cannot maintain himself in that tonality: he regresses to C minor for his third attempt, on the Temple of Wisdom (note the symbolic progression of the tonalities). This time, he behaves appropriately, with wisdom, asking for initiation. The stage direction, in fact, specifies *"Er klopft"* (He knocks), whereas twice earlier he rushed forward with presumption rather than knocking submissively. No further *"Zurück!"*; instead, always by transition through modal degrees (A-flat major, sixth of C minor), a slow, majestic ascending arpeggio that describes—adagio—the emergence of an old priest from the temple. He will be the postulant's first instructor.

(b) Tamino, at the Third Temple, Receives the First Teachings

It is toward the perfect tonality of E-flat major that, by way of a cadence IV-V-I, the old priest directs his questioning: *"Wo willst du, kühner Fremdling hin?"* (What do you wish, bold stranger?).

To a spectator who has believed that he is witnessing a simple "story," Tamino's answer may seem to be of astonishing theatrical inconsequence; in reality, it shows once more that the apparently anecdotal is of little importance as compared with the real, hidden action (this will also, a century later, be the esthetic of *Pelléas et Mélisande*). Tamino seems to have forgotten completely that he has come to his enemy's stronghold to carry off the woman he loves. His answer is not "Pamina," but "Love and Virtue." He is responding ritually to a ritual question: we are not at the theater, but in a temple.

Further, the music tells us so. It accompanies his answer,

in E-flat major this time, with a choral phrase for the winds
(clarinets and bassoons, cello doubling without CB) which
will be the point of departure for the religious march in Act
II and which also recalls, by its descent in thirds, the reply of
the Three Boys. The progression by modal degrees (VI, then
II) emphasizes the sacred character.

The priest expresses approval in E flat, but we immediately
leave that significant tonality for the minor—on the word
"*Allein*": the priest places the sincerity of Tamino's answer in
doubt (the reproving diminished seventh) because, he says,
the applicant is motivated by death and vengeance. All modal
inflection disappears, and we are back in the idiom of the
opera, with, perhaps, the darkening of the Neapolitan sixth
(A flat) to emphasize the blackness of the design. (This passage might be understood as in either C or G.)

Tamino agrees, but asserts that his vengeance is directed
only toward a tyrant (docilely, he repeats the word "*Bösewicht*," which the Queen of the Night has used; an octave
leap displays his immature wrath, as does the swiftness of his
replies, in contrast to the old priest's *langsam*). "*Den wirst
du wohl bei uns nicht finden*" (Him you will not find among
us), the priest says. Diminished 7th: "*Sarastro herrscht in
diesen Gründen?*" (Doesn't Sarastro reign here?). The diminished 7th opens out into a perfect cadence. "*Ja, ja! Sarastro
herrschet hier*" (Yes, yes! Sarastro reigns here). "*Doch in dem
Weisheitstempel nicht?*" (But surely not in Wisdom's Temple?). "*Er herrscht im Weisheitstempel hier*" (He reigns in
Wisdom's Temple here)—conclusion in E-flat major. "*So ist
denn alles Heuchelei!*" (Then all is hypocrisy), Tamino cries
out, desiring to leave (tremolo diminished 7th).

A short phrase syncopated with insistent appoggiaturas, and
repeated three times, marks that decision, for which the priest
asks the reasons. In operatic recitative, Tamino repeats his
hatred of the inhuman tyrant Sarastro. Pressed to explain

further, he reveals the sources of his information and expresses pity for the Queen, the *"unglücklich' Weib"* (unhappy woman) who is Sarastro's victim (diminished 7th).

The priest's reaction is important to the pervasive meaning of the opera: he literally shrugs his shoulders at the notion that a woman's words can be taken seriously, and in a peremptory "arpeggio of majesty" supported on a fine C-major chord (tonality of affirmation and certainty), pronounces in the name of Wisdom the sentence against which there is no appeal: *"Ein Weib tut wenig, plaudert viel./ Du, Jüngling, glaubst dem Zungenspiel* [a word-by-word translation of "tongue-play"]/ *O legte doch Sarastro dir/ Die Absicht seiner Handlung für!"* (Women don't do much, though they chatter a lot. Young man, do you believe such talk? Oh, if you could only learn the reason for Sarastro's actions!). (Here a not very clearly motivated diminished 7th occurs: perhaps because the purposes have not yet been revealed.) Tamino says, fairly enough: *"Die Absicht is nur allzu klar!"* (The purpose [which he does not know] is all too clear): *"Riss nicht der Räuber ohn' Erbarmen,/ Pamina aus der Mutter Armen?"* (Didn't the thief ruthlessly tear Pamina from her mother's arms?). *"Ja, Jüngling, was du sagst, ist wahr"* (Yes, young man, what you say is true). *"Wo ist sie, die er uns geraubt?/ Man opferte vielleicht sie schon?"* (Where is she, who was stolen from us?/ Has she, perhaps, already been sacrificed?). Here there is a melodic line that the Queen of the Night will take up in her second-act aria, *"Der hölle Rache kocht,"* and which leads to something rarely found in Mozart, a dominant 9th.

"Dir dies zu sagen, teurer Sohn,/ Ist jetzt und mir noch nicht erlaubt" (I am not allowed to answer you yet, my dear son). *"Wann also wird die Decke schwinden?"* (But when can this veil be lifted?). Characteristic interrogation on the dominant.

One notes that in all this it is not Pamina, but her mother, that Tamino sorrows for and the priest accuses: it deals with the trial of feminine society, incarnated by its Queen.

The priest's answer has oracular solemnity thrown into relief by a remarkable orchestral idea: doubling of the uncovered voice by the cello in an expressive register (a discovery so effective that the naturalism of the nineteenth century will vulgarize it into a veritable method, even aggravating it at times by moving it to the deep octave of the voice): *"Sobald dich führt der Freundschaft Hand / Ins Heiligtum zum ew'gen Band"* (As soon as the hand of friendship shall have led you into the holiness of our Order). As Paul Nettl observed, the unusual doubling doubtless was meant to depict that affectionate induction. The same idea is expressed in the same way in Sarastro's aria (No. 15).

Harmonically we again find here the descent by thirds with modal degrees (here, VI) of all the initiatory phrases of the scene, whereas the priest's voice descends with the habitual "hollowness" of Mozart's oracular sentences. The affirmative aspect of the phrase again is reinforced by the orchestra in two or more syncopated cadences, a procedure that solemnly triples the affirmation.

To that prediction, Tamino reacts by a pathetic invocation, in which, by means of a few notes, the recitative (which recalls the opening of the Queen of the Night's aria: *cf.* the word *"Nacht"*) achieves the most intense beauty: *"O ew'ge Nacht! Wann wirst du schwinden? Wann wird das Licht mein Auge finden?"* (O everlasting night! When will you end? When will my eyes find the light?). The meaning of the reply is quite clear: we know that the essential moment in Masonic initiation is the removal of the blindfold that has masked the postulant's eyes since the beginning of the ceremony.

Musically, the anguished tension of this question is produced by intensive alteration of the 6th (introduced in the interrogative formula) to the dominant already used without alteration in Tamino's earlier question. Thus reinforced, the questioning takes on an almost Wagnerian coloration.

This time the answer comes *sotto voce* from inside, from an invisible male chorus: *"Bald, bald, Jüngling, oder nie!"* (Soon, soon, young man, or never!). Further, a new, impressive voice is heard in the orchestra: that of trombones, the traditional instrument of grand oracular scenes,* which has not been heard since the Overture except in the canticle of the Three Boys.

"Lebt denn Pamina noch?" (Is Pamina still alive?). To that third question, the oracle replies with a third answer identical with the second: *"Pamina, Pamina lebet noch!"* (Pamina, Pamina is still alive). Thus the oracular phrase is heard thrice. And Tamino closes the recitative scene by letting his gratitude shine forth, through the medium of his flute (expressive wide interval of the terminal cadence).

(c) In Gratitude, Tamino Plays on His Magic Flute

We already have noted how remote the magic flute is from the talisman of fairy stories. In such a story, Tamino would have played it as soon as he encountered the obstacle offered by the closed doors of the temples, which would have opened immediately, allowing him free passage toward his Pamina. Not only did he not do that, but also when he unexpectedly turns to the magic instrument, the object of his quest cer-

---

* We recall that such hoarse timbres as those of regals, cornets, and the deep brasses were habitually used in the Monteverdian orchestra as the color for infernal scenes. That led to the introduction of the trombone, not then commonly included in the opera orchestra, into scenes of that type, and especially those of oracular nature (Gluck's *Orphée et Eurydice*, the oracle in *Idomeneo*, the Commendatore in *Don Giovanni*, etc.). To recall this is useful in the face of the delirious comments that these examples, above all the last, sometimes have aroused.

tainly does not appear before him. That is because Tamino has not yet been admitted to initiation, and therefore is aware only of the appearance of things. The only answer he receives is the five notes of Papageno's fluting, and by the time the Birdcatcher comes on stage with Pamina, Tamino will have disappeared.

The song of the flute relieves the tension of the preceding scenes. Carefully held in reserve in the orchestra (where it has not appeared since No. 1), the flute presents a light, symmetrically outlined ritornello that Tamino repeats in variations somewhat in the manner of a piece in verses or the prelude to an aria. A sort of preliminary sketch for this can be found in Mozart's 1778 Paris ballet, *Les Petits Riens*. Here, as the flute sounds, all sorts of beasts come up to listen; birds chirp as long as it continues. This somewhat childish business is intended to show the power of music and the analogy to Orpheus' lyre; above all, Schikaneder seems to have wanted it so that he could make use of his menagerie. But the design of the original *mise en scène* (Plate 16) has a surprise for us: the "animals" announced by the rubric are just a few flying birds, and the main part of their role is being performed by wild *men*, who perhaps are the slaves of Monostatos, among whom Giesecke appeared. That underlines the symbolism. At Weimar, on the other hand, in 1794 (Plate 21) there were "real" cardboard animals.

One detail of the scoring deserves the attention of specialists: in some editions (others have been corrected), the initial anacrusis is annotated differently for the flute (dotted eighth-note, sixteenth-note) than for the voice (eighth-notes), though their performance is clearly the same. This was clearly a survival of the rule about "unequal notes" which had been followed slightly earlier.

Suddenly, in a measure that one would have expected to be the first of a cadence, Tamino interrupts himself. He suddenly has realized that even if it is very seemly to manifest his joy on the magic flute, it could render him more useful service than that of summoning the cardboard menagerie onto the stage of the Theater auf der Wieden. The style changes abruptly: Tamino goes back to the grand vocal outbursts of the portrait aria, and in spaced-out appeals, playing short, imperious phrases on his flute, he finally calls for his beloved.

In reply to the rising scale on the magic instrument, the five notes of Papageno's fluting are heard offstage; we have already discussed the symbolic significance of that. Still not free of appearances, Tamino is satisfied, and himself repeats the five notes, which thus alternate prettily between orchestra pit and wings.

"*Vielleicht sah er Pamina schon*" (Perhaps he has already seen Pamina), the prince says with unchanged enthusiasm (the same "intervallic" leaps). "*Vielleicht führt mich der Ton zu ihr*" (Perhaps his melody will lead me to her)—and he goes off in one direction as Pamina and Papageno enter from the other! Here again the libretto would be incoherent if this were nothing but a fairy tale. On the contrary, we already have seen its perfect logic in the symbolic sequence, which is what really matters here. The notes of the fluting are deceptive: in the search for love, one sets off in the wrong direction.

C. Pamina and Papageno Escape from Monostatos

(a) Entrance of Pamina and Papageno

The rubric specifies that both Pamina and Papageno are "free of bonds," meaning that Pamina, by foiling Monostatos's plans, has avoided the fleshly subjection to which the lascivious Moor has had the fixed idea of subjecting her, but also that she has passed the first tests of the feminine initiation before facing the more serious tests that will make her Tamino's equal.

She is still far from that condition, which is why, when she arrives with the Birdcatcher, a rapid modulation takes us back to the superficial tonality of G major and to the comedic style of the light duets.

From the seventeenth century on, voices in parallel thirds have been musical symbols for harmony and shared feelings (whence their frequent, often excessive employment in love duets). Here the usage has a precise meaning: Pamina's harmonious relationship with the futile Papageno well indicates that she is only just about to begin her ascent, in which her style itself will undergo evolution. Another musical detail confirms that idea: the "five equal little knocks" already heard so often in light and frivolous scenes, and which recur throughout this scene, as earlier—in the same G major—they recurred in the scenes of the Three Ladies.

By means of a paradox that alone explains the hidden meaning of the libretto, it is in almost offhand manner that the duettists evoke the dangers that they have escaped, the courage that they have needed, and their haste finally to re-encounter Tamino. The explanation of that unexpected offhandedness: Papageno sounds five notes on his syrinx and Tamino answers him from the wings with the same five notes in the symbolic rhythm.

In the first part of the duet in thirds, Pamina sang in Papageno's buffo style. But her own personality reasserts itself in a phrase of very different melodic nature when she thinks of Tamino: "*Holder Jüngling!*" (Noble young man!) "*Stille, stille, ich kann's besser!*" (Quiet, quiet, I can do it [*i.e.*, call Tamino] better!), the Birdcatcher answers (very quickly returning to his own style and playing comically on the sonority of the word "*Stille*"). What he can do is to sound the five notes of his fluting without noticing that they repeat the futile rhythm just sounded by the second violin. Tamino answers on his magic flute: this is the exact inversion of the preceding scene.

Duet in thirds which harmonizes Pamina with Papageno,

duet of five notes on the two flutes illustrating the harmony of Tamino with the same Papageno. Now one understands why, despite the power of the *Zauberflöte*, it is impotent to bring the two young people together: it still commands only the imperfect circle of the quinary initiation. Neither Pamina, who has not yet renounced the feminine world of her mother's kingdom, nor Tamino, whom Sarastro has not yet declared prepared to face the real tests that will make him *"ein Mann,"* is yet ready to face the other. They are desperately searching for one another, but can communicate only through that ludicrous interpreter, the Birdcatcher to the Queen of the Night and her twittering ladies. Sarastro's presence itself is needed so that they can finally see one another in its illumination, though even then they still will not be able to remain together.

After the calling episode, the duet in thirds starts again, with rejoicing over the result. A short episode in the dominant and a reprise of the refrain, in which we again find "unequal notes" (group notated with dotting the first time, without dotting the second, but no reason to vary the interpretation). A third verse, still in thirds, prescribes diligence, and the repetition of the words *"Nur geschwinde"* (Only hurry) plays amusingly on the sonority of the words while recalling the conclusion of the refrain.

(b) Irruption of Monostatos

Suddenly, just as Pamina and Papageno are about to leave, the sneering Moor rises up before them. His entrance is a *chef-d'oeuvre* of musical farce, recalling some of Osmin's scenes in *Die Entführung aus dem Serail*. He begins by chanting with his victims *"Nur geschwinde"*; then, as the strings and winds reverse their roles (a simple change of octave by the strings), the phrase begun by the fugitives is completed ironically by their persecutor.

Monostatos, still in the grip of his fixed idea, again wants to load them with chains (of which we know the symbolism), and his call to the slaves is reminiscent of Leporello's celebrated aria. At the same time, the beginning of his allegro strongly resembles that of *Eine kleine Nachtmusik*, whereas in the driveling phrase with which he says that he will teach them good manners—and they would try to deceive Monostatos!—Mozart in his way tells us what in fact Monostatos is: the phrase is that of one of his most incisive canons: "O *du eselhafter Martin*," * the words of which are nothing but a series of more or less coarse insults.

This time, Papageno shows himself more resourceful than under other circumstances. In an amusing phrase (which this time recalls an aria of Osmin also heard in a Mozart flute concerto) which is accompanied by pizzicati that punctuate the phrases of the glockenspiel without covering them, he calls upon his magic instrument. Unlike the flute, it is treated like a talisman in a fairy tale, and the theatrical law of the era requires that, as we have seen one at work, we shall not wait long to see the other; furthermore, whereas Tamino's flute (sign of Air) brought Papageno (same sign), Papageno's glockenspiel (sign of Earth) will act upon Monostatos (same sign).

At the pizzicato-punctuated sound of the glockenspiel, Monostatos and his slaves begin to dance (he stamps on the Earth with his foot, as Papagena will strike it with hers during her lover's trial by Earth). Thus rendered harmless, they exit singing and dancing. One notes that their song, "*Das klinget so herrlich*," based upon the preluding by the glockenspiel, begins with the reversal of the preceding Pamina-Papageno duet, "*Schnelle Füsse*."

The scene is borrowed from *Oberon*, in which the enchanted

---

* Usually known in France in its adaptation as "*Oh Martin qui bat Martine!*" (Jacques Chailley, *48 Canons*, published by Salabert).

horn turns Almanzor to stone and involves his slaves in a
dance that leads them away (Weber kept this episode in
Scene 3 of Act III of his *Oberon*).

(c) Moralizing Conclusion

When Monostatos and his slaves have disappeared, the characters left on stage (Pamina and Papageno) turn to the audience, and again stepping out of their roles, draw the moral:
*"Könnte jeder brave Mann/ Solche Glöckchen finden!/ Seine
Feinde würden dann/ Ohne Mühe schwinden,/ Und er lebte
ohne sie/ In der besten Harmonie!/ Nur der Freundschaft
Harmonie/ Mildert die Beschwerden;/ Ohne diese Sympa-
thie/ Ist kein Glück auf Erden!"* (Oh, if every honest man
could find bells like these, then his enemies would vanish and
he would live in the greatest tranquillity without them. Only
friendship's harmony can banish grief; without such sympathy,
there is no joy on earth).

Exceptionally, this duet is not marked *sotto voce* and includes, in the B section of its ABA, a brief canonic element
that breaks the syllabism, though without interfering with
comprehensibility. One will note its religious style (particularly the feminine ending) and the resemblance of its first
phrase to a famous Schubert song composed twenty years
later, *Heidenröslein*.

II / SARASTRO'S JUDGMENT (8D)

(a) Transition: Announcement of the Master's Arrival

Trumpets and unmuted timpani (it will be recalled that they
had been muted for the temple oracles) sound a fanfare.
Chorus (C major): *"Es lebe Sarastro!"* In comic staccato
notes, Papageno asks himself what is happening, and trembles
(evocative trill for the violins). Pamina continues Sarastro's
phrase, but legato, thus immediately altering its character. As

soon as the Master of Wisdom is announced, she begins to separate herself from the clown; during the rest of the opera, she will elevate herself above the style of the Birdcatcher's world and identify herself with that of the initiate Man. Nevertheless, she continues to see Sarastro as an enemy: *"O Freund, nun ist's um uns getan,/ Dies kündigt den Sarastro an!"* (O friend, this is the end for us. The voices announce the arrival of Sarastro).

Papageno comically outdoes her: he would like to become a mouse and disappear into a hole, a snail and crawl back into its shell (amusing contraction of diminished seconds). He asks his companion: *"Mein Kind, was werden wir nun sprechen?"* (My child, what shall we say to him now?). Pamina's noble, unequivocal answer (arpeggio of majesty, grand cadence of affirmation in the C major of certainty), sharply raises the tone: *"Die Wahrheit, wär sie auch Verbrechen!"* (The truth, even if it were a crime!).

Chorus (in conventional theatrical style) announcing the Master's arrival. A rubric ("This chorus is to be sung until Sarastro shall have descended from his chariot") reminds us, moreover, that this is the simple indication of a scene to be prolonged *ad libitum*. It is the finale in full theatrical panoply: the chariot drawn by six lions ($6 = 2 \times 3$; lions = associates of the sun[6]), deployment of supernumeraries, brilliant illumination, etc. The theme of this chorus is borrowed from the opening chorus of *Thamos*, a hymn to the sun: the similarity of meaning is evident.

(b) Judgment of Pamina

The scene opens, larghetto like the beginning of the finale, with the five chords of the feminine initiation, with five notes in the strings and three in the winds—including for the first time the basset horn (alto clarinet) often used in the Viennese "columns of harmony," but reserved in *Die Zauberflöte* for initiatory scenes.

The tonality of F major, following C major, does not attain the perfection of E-flat major, but nonetheless marks a movement toward the "serious" flatted keys: this will be the first true meeting of the Man and the Woman.

Pamina throws herself at Sarastro's feet: "*Herr, ich bin zwar Verbrecherin,/ Ich wollte deiner Macht entfliehn!/ Allein, die Schuld ist nicht an mir;/ Der böse Mohr verlangte Liebe;/ Darum, o Herr, entfloh ich dir*" (My Lord, I have broken your laws! I wanted to escape from your power. But the guilt is not mine. The cruel Moor desired my love; therefore, my Lord, I ran away from you).

The appeal is significant: Pamina has told us that she will be sincere: "*die Wahrheit.*" She will accept Sarastro without Monostatos: what she cannot admit in love is its degraded aspect. Must ugliness thus intrude into that beautiful feeling? Because of that ugliness, the well-born woman will sometimes want to leave the kingdom of Love itself. Will Sarastro "cover" Monostatos? Or did the *guignol* Black introduce himself into the kingdom of illumination by false means?

Sarastro will answer that question in still-veiled terms: a man of his rank is not required to divulge his secrets to an outsider, much less to a woman. What he really thinks, he will say to his priests at the beginning of Act II. Now he says only: "*Denn ohne erst in dich zu dringen Weiss ich von deinem Herzen mehr:/ Du liebest einen Andern sehr./ Zur Liebe will ich dich nicht zwingen,/ Doch geb' ich dir die Freiheit nicht*" (I need not question you further, for I already know what is in your heart. You love another deeply. I will not dictate whom you must love. But [and here his voice descends] I cannot set you free now).

Pamina insists, saying that filial devotion calls her to her mother (the phrase somewhat resembles one of Tamino's

phrases in the portrait aria). Sarastro cuts her short and reveals a little more: *"Steht in meiner Macht./ Du würdest um
dein Glück gebracht,/ Wenn ich dich ihren Händen liesse"*
([Your mother] is in my power. Were I to give you back into
her hands, you would lose all chance of happiness [imperious
dotted rhythm, to be explained by the following answer evoking the Queen's pride]). Pamina protests that she loves her
mother. Then Sarastro loses patience, and to close the discussion states the fundamental moral of the opera: *"Und ein
stolzes Weib! Ein Mann muss eure Herzen leiten,/ denn ohne
ihn pflegt jedes Weib/ Aus ihrem Wirkungskreis zu schreiten"*
(She is an arrogant woman! A man must lead your heart, for
without such guidance every woman roves beyond her assigned
position). His statement ends on an affirmative cadence, to
which there is no reply; it is of the first importance to any
explanation of the libretto.

(c) Judgment of Monostatos

A light, tripping comedic motive runs throughout this sequence, showing that Mozart, contrary to the appearance of
the libretto, did not take seriously the black-faced "traitor."
In a sense, he makes him into Sarastro's Papageno. While
dealing with Monostatos, even Sarastro abandons his grave
demeanor for a moment and takes part in an unexpected comic
passage not entirely in tune with the solemnity of his character.

In the meantime, Monostatos has captured Tamino, and
he now comes on stage to display his captive to his master.
To everyone's amazement, Tamino pays no attention to the
dreaded great man: he sees Pamina and she recognizes him.
Then, not thinking about anyone else, in a halting emotional
exchange accompanied by an ascending phrase reflecting their
aspirations, the two young people—who have never seen each
other before—fall into each other's arms.

Scandalized, Monostatos separates them and then starts to

tell Sarastro, with full emphasis on his own zeal, how he captured the two strangers who had come to steal Pamina from him. *"Verdient, dass man ihr Lorbeer streut!/ He, gebt dem Ehrenmann sogleich—"* (This man deserves laurels! Ho, give this worthy fellow—), the Master begins. The Moor protests like a courtier expecting a fine reward: *"Schon deine Gnade macht mich reich!"* (Your graciousness already makes me rich!). But Sarastro continues right on: *"Nur siebenundsiebenzig Sohlenstreich!"* (Only seventy-seven lashes on his feet). In a minor key, the stupefied jailer exclaims: *"Ach, Herr, den Lohn verhofft' ich nicht!"* (Ah, my Lord, that reward I did not expect!), to which Sarastro replies affably in a pleasant major: *"Nicht Dank, es ist ja meine Pflicht!"* (Don't thank me, it is only my duty!). *"Es lebe Sarastro"* (Long live Sarastro), the ever-satisfied chorus concludes, *"der göttliche Weise! Er lohnet und strafet in ähnlichem Kreise"* (the godlike sage! He rewards and punishes with equal justice).

Were the libretto only a theater-piece, Sarastro's judgment and the chorus's comment would be absurd, for to all appearances Monostatos has merely performed his duty as a jailer, and he seems to be receiving punishment for doing what he was told to do. But Sarastro, the incarnation of wisdom, is almost a demigod. As he himself has just told Pamina, he knows what is in people's hearts. Thus he knows what base motives keep this ugly fellow's eyes upon the young girl, and that is what he is punishing by the precisely numbered seventy-seven lashes, seven being the number of wisdom. In that case, it may be asked, why did he himself entrust Pamina to Monostatos? The answer lies in the symbolic nature of the libretto, which does not always coincide with logic: Pamina's first "initiatory death" must parallel Tamino's. The inventiveness of the authors in displaying the symbol was theatrically ingenious and fertile in scenes colored to please their suburban audience: let us not ask them for more.

(d) Judgment of Tamino and of Papageno

The future of the two strangers remains to be decided. It is taken care of swiftly by Sarastro in a simple recitative. But at first it retains the triple beat oo-oo-oo, thus being set against the feminine world's quinary knocking o-oo-oo, which had appeared with Pamina. The meaning of this scene was discussed on pp. 130–1.

"Führt diese beiden Fremdlinge/ In unsern Prüfungstempel ein" (Introduce these two strangers into our Temple of Trials), the Master orders. *"Bedecket ihre Häupter dann"* (Then cover their heads)—a descriptive descending line— *"Sie müssen erst gereinigt sein"* (They must first be purified) —this last phrase, *adagio a tempo*, which is to say sung as measured despite the recitative, which by its nature cannot be so sung. The descent of Sarastro's voice to the extreme bass underlines the seriousness of the decision and its oracular aspect.

Tamino thus has completed his preparatory journey. He is now fit to undergo the actual initiation, which will be the subject of Act II. Papageno's fate is more surprising. Everything happens as though this character had from the beginning been introduced for symbolic purposes, for to the degree that his usefulness on that level has now evaporated, he is used as foreign to all internal significance, as a simple comedic supernumerary. The decision concerning him, furthermore, is quickly scamped: he is simply sent off with Tamino.

(e) Final Chorus

"Wenn Tugend und Gerechtigkeit/ Den grossen Pfad mit Ruhm bestreut,/ Dann ist die Erd' ein Himmelreich,/ Und Sterbliche den Göttern gleich" (When virtue and righteousness shall strew the great path of life with glory, then will earth be like heaven and mortals like gods).

A Masonic morality analogous to those attached to other episodes, and notably to that of the duet *"Mann und Weib."* But instead of being spoken *sotto voce* to the audience in confidence, it is proclaimed syllabically in C major by a large chorus with full orchestra, including Masonic basset horns, trumpets, timpani, and, finally, with trombones doubling the voices, as they often had doubled them in Salzburg Cathedral. We note the figuralism of the exposed part (soprano, then bass) as it evokes the earth and the sky in a sort of fugal response—and, in the traditional final cadence, another affirmation of the 3×3, this time in even rhythm.

"Den Göttern gleich" (like the gods): this is the act's final phrase. It is also the supreme goal toward which all the action leads. Act II will show how it is reached.

21

The Second Act

First Scene

SARASTRO'S SACRED WOOD

In Chapter 16, we saw the significance of this scene, a transposition of the ritual deliberation that leads to embarkation upon the trials. For easily understandable theatrical reasons, the framework is not that of a "real" temple, but a symbolic décor in which every detail is specified and has a meaningful intention. The rubric says:

"The scene represents a palm grove. All the trees are of silver, their leaves of gold. There are eighteen seats made of leaves. Above each seat, there are a pyramid and a large black horn encrusted with gold. The largest pyramid and largest tree are in the middle. Sarastro, surrounded by other priests, enters in solemn raiment; each priest carries a palm-frond; their entrance is accompanied by a march played by the wind instruments."

That rubric must be explained first of all.

"The scene represents a palm grove." The palm, as we have noted, is a solar plant. In addition, in the universal symbolism it is both the sign of victory and, according to the definition in the *Dictionnaire des antiquités chrétiennes*, the symbol of the "triumph over death by resurrection." For a Christian, that is the way to eternal life, above all when achieved through martyrdom. Masonically transposed, the same meaning becomes the resurrection into the initiate life after the symbolic death represented on the stage by a swoon. The same dictionary (under *arbres*) tells us that "trees ornamented with leaves, of whatever nature, generally signify Paradise—that is, the eternal felicity into which the just are admitted." The transfer is easily made.

"Trees of silver, leaves of gold." The javelins with which the Three Ladies killed the serpent, as well as the palm-fronds held by the Three Boys, were also of silver. Note the hierarchy of foliages. Further, silver corresponds to the Moon (and thus to the feminine world), gold to the Sun (masculine world). The silver trunk produces golden leaves, infinitely more precious. We are in the assembly of Men, certainly, but they are issue of Woman, and the initiate dominates the world of women as well as that of men: in the Temple of the Sun, both Isis and Osiris are invoked.

"Eighteen seats made of leaves. Above each seat there are a pyramid and a large black horn encrusted with gold." Nettl [1] thought eighteen the mystic number of the Rosy Cross, but that exegesis remains risky because the libretto of *Die Zauberflöte* never touches upon the symbolism of the higher degrees; furthermore, the number eighteen was not associated with the degree in question until early in the nineteenth century. The pyramid allocated to each seat recalls the "Egyptian" initiation, the horn the right to deliberation, it being by a blast of horns that the initiates manifest their approval. As for the color of the horns, it may be another allusion to the universal-

ism of masculine supremacy over the two sexes, already mentioned: the feminine black and the masculine gold.

"*The largest pyramid and largest tree are in the middle.*"
This is evidently meant to emphasize the greater wisdom of
Sarastro in relation to the other priests. The precaution is necessary, for though Tamino's initiation is deliberated according
to the rules and is approved by all, Pamina's is apparently decided upon by Sarastro alone against the advice of the college
(one will note, later, the hostile silence that greets her entrance as a future Initiate into the sacred college).

No. 9 / MARCH OF THE PRIESTS

Solemn and meditative, it immediately locates this act in a
quasi-liturgical ambience. The orchestration for wind instruments is asked for by the librettists for a symbolic reason: the
winds are the favored instruments of the Masonic "columns of
harmony"; the significant basset horns figure among them.
Sotto voce, the score says: as we have seen, that direction may
have had a double meaning.

There is no contradiction between the rubric's specification of
"a march for wind instruments" and the score, in which the winds
are doubled by the strings. The latter reinforce the sonority, but the
harmony is complete in the winds, and it is certainly the latter
that give the piece its character. Such reinforcements, further, were
frequent.

Like the beginning of the finale No. 8, this number starts in a
meditative tone and ends in a march in dotted rhythm. The initial
phrase, beautifully plastic in line, seems, furthermore, to be derived from the one that follows the entry of the Priests of Wisdom
in that same finale. One notes certain analogies with the celebrated *Ave Verum*, composed at more or less the same time.

This march often has been compared to the "religious march"
in Gluck's *Alceste*. And in fact, it has the solemn rhythm, the
very simple structure AABB; the plan TD, then DT; the dactylic
rhythm, the reprise of the theme in T at the opening of the final
coda. But all of that is the common nature of the genre, and does

not necessarily imply direct influence. Nonetheless, Kufferath demonstrated that Mozart had followed very closely a march in the *Oberon* (the famous "model" that Schikaneder gave him) of Wranitzky, who, in turn, had copied several passages from the *Alceste* march. Because the similarities did not occur in the same locations, one can say that A came from B and B from C, but not that A came from C—and add that eighteenth-century listeners were struck by a family resemblance from which a link is now missing. One knows that the march from *Alceste* was played on November 28, 1778, during the funeral ceremony held in honor of Voltaire in the Loge des Neuf Soeurs, into which he had been initiated on April 7 of that year, two months before his death.[2]

In turn, Mozart's march has begotten numerous imitations. One of the most curious doubtless is the Canadian hymn *O Canada*, by the Canadian composer Calix Lavallée (1841–1891), the beginning of which reproduces almost textually its first two measures.[3] We note the series of sixth chords, an integral part of the religious vocabulary of the epoch (a remnant of the old-time *fauxbourdon*), the cadence preparations through sixth and fourth, and the finales by feminine appoggiaturas.

No. 9a / SPOKEN SCENE:
Deliberation of the Initiates

The ritual nature of this scene was noted in Chapter 11. Here, so as not to repeat what was said there, I shall sum it up with reference only to the action. Sarastro recalls that his interlocutors have received illumination in the Temple of Wisdom and are servants of the great gods Osiris and Isis. One may be amazed here to find Isis, goddess of the Night, associated with Osiris, god of the Sun, in his temple; but so it will be to the end: although the lodges were exclusively masculine, they were nonetheless decorated with the two symbolic columns J and B, representing respectively the masculine, solar principle of Osiris and the feminine, lunar principle of Isis. Further, the priests, though they form a privileged, exclusively masculine society, nonetheless have moral sway over all of humanity, women included (Pamina's father said that in clear terms to his wife in his testament, quoted in No. 13A). Thus they receive the double illumination of the two principles (*cf.*, on this question, pp. 86–8).

Sarastro now explains that an adolescent, son of a king, has presented himself at the "north portal of the Temple." On p. 133 we saw that the North signifies "the side that the light does not reach" (*cf.* the facsimile overleaf). The same idea sometimes is expressed in a variation. "The Apprentices," Jules Boucher wrote, "are placed at the North because they need to be illuminated: there they receive the light from the South window." The dialogue of investigation follows the ritual very closely. The postulant is declared "virtuous, discreet, and charitable." Then Sarastro asks those present to declare with him whether they judge the postulant worthy of admission.

The response, which is affirmative, is a "knocking" of the Master's degree: 3 x 3 in anapestic rhythm—which we heard in the middle section of the Overture. It is considered as being played by the eighteen horns on the stage; in actuality, they merely pretend to play it; the knocking is orchestrated for the pit, with trombones, horns, and woodwinds.

Sarastro thanks them "in the name of all humanity." Digression on the benefits of the unanimity just manifested, which protects the Temple against "all the calumnies that the prejudiced weave around us" (clearly an allusion to the attacks then being made on Freemasonry); an affirmation of confidence in the Order's final victory.

After which Sarastro turns to the case of Pamina. He explains that the gods destine her for Tamino; for that reason, he has taken her "from her proud mother." That woman, he says, "believes herself powerful" and wants "to overthrow the Temple" by setting the people against us "through imposture

D. Pourquoi ?

R. Comme le Soleil termine le jour à l'Oc-
cident, les Surveillans s'y tiennent pour
fermer la Loge, renvoyer les Ouvriers
contens, & faire bon accueil aux Freres
Vifiteurs.

D. Où vous a-t-on placé après votre réception ?

R. Au Septentrion.

D. Pourquoi ?

R. Parce que c'eſt la partie la moins éclairée,
& qu'un Apprentif qui n'a reçu qu'une
foible lumiere, n'eſt pas en état de fup-
porter un plus grand jour.

D. A quoi travaillent les Apprentifs (1) ?

R. A dégroſſir & ébaucher la pierre brute.

D. Où font-ils payés ?

R. A la colonne J.

D. Quels font les plus grands devoirs d'un
Maçon ?

R.* C'eſt de remplir ceux de l'état où la

---

(1) Comme les anciens Chevaliers enſeignoient
à leurs nouveaux Initiés, non-ſeulement la Morale
& la Religion, mais encore toutes les connoiſ-
ſances utiles au genre humain, ils comparoient les
hommes à une pierre brute, & diſoient que leurs
ſentimens dépendoient preſque toujours des pre-
mieres impreſſions qu'ils recevoient, comme la
forme plus ou moins précieuſe d'une pierre dépend
des coups que l'Artiſte lui donne. Voilà ſeulement
pourquoi la pierre brute doit être l'emblême des
Apprentifs. *Voyez l'Origine de la Maçonnerie.*

I   Providence

The "North Portal of the Temple." Same source as page 88,
1809 edition (signed), at the Grand Orient de France,
Bibliothèque de la Grande Loge de France.

and superstitions. She will not succeed!" Another allusion to a then-contemporary situation, which, as we have said, some commentators have dilated upon, to the point of wanting to make the Queen of the Night the stage personification of the Empress Maria Theresia, who was hostile to Freemasonry. But if one refers back to the central idea—that is, the opposition of the sexes—one may see in that diatribe against the imposture and superstitions spread by women the idea that "clerical" religion (for that certainly is what is meant by "superstition"), though theoretically masculine in hierarchy, was upheld above all by the society of women. That exegesis (which in no way excludes the political allusion mentioned) will also explain the forthcoming intervention by the Three Ladies, who mention the Order in terms that might have emanated from the Roman Holy Office.

Sarastro, then, says that he has decided to confound the Kingdom of the Night, for which reason he must remove the virtuous Pamina from it. As for Tamino, once initiated, he will be the best support of the edifice.

Again approval (second blast of 3 x 3).

The "Speaker" then rises (we are dealing here with a very specific function so denominated in the hierarchy of the lodges) and sets forth his fears that Tamino, who is very young, could not succeed in the trials: "Life has prepared him so little: he is a prince." Sarastro's answer is: "He is more than that, he is a man [Mensch]." If he is destined to die, "it will be given him to be received by Isis and Osiris before us and to taste the divine joys" (affirmation of the Masonic faith in the future life).

Third and final triple ternary approval by the horns (note the abundance of threes).

Then Sarastro gives the order to conduct Tamino, "as well as the companion of his journey" (who, it must be said, has been disregarded completely; note the word "journey," which is related, as we have already said, to the symbolism of the trials), toward the forecourt of the Temple (scenic transposition of the Cabinet of Reflection of the first trial, that of Earth). And, addressing the Speaker (who, we have seen, incorporates the Expert in the libretto so as to economize on one role), he orders him to perform his official duty according to the rite.

No. 10 / SARASTRO'S PRAYER, WITH CHORUS OF PRIESTS

This is an invocation of Isis and Osiris, the text of which is very closely derived from the Abbé Terrasson's *Sethos*. The "Egyptian" ritual, as we have seen, includes an analogous prayer in the ceremony that opens the proceedings.[4]

Orchestration for Masonic winds (with doublings by the strings without violins). Style of the religious canticle in *fauxbourdon*, in which abound series of parallel sixths and thirds, modal degrees of religious evocation (VI), the depths of the voice doubling the harmonic bass, as often in the older repertoire (bass particularly shored up on the word "*Grabe*" [tomb]).

The first phrase, which asks Isis and Osiris to give wisdom to the "*Neue Paar*" and to watch over the postulants during their dangerous journey, singularly recalls (in the quintet No. 5) the episode of the gift of the flute ("*O Prinz . . .*"), as well as the moral of the same episode (on the words "*Sind zu eurem Schutz vonnöten*" [are necessary for your protection]). The ideas are so close that this scarcely can be a coincidence.

This piece in two strophes TD and DT is constructed on the principle of the oldtime *virelai*: both of the (different) verses end on the same melodic phrase, taken up as a refrain by the chorus (dominant DO the first time, TP FA the second). The short prelude is slightly reminiscent of the "canticle" accompaniment to the entrance of the Three Boys in No. 8A, and presents a bass in the style of a chaconne which persists through what follows, in addition to which it will often be followed by the voice. Observe the differing vocal dispositions of the two refrains of the priests (the theme given to the second tenor the first time, to the baritone the second).

Second Scene

THE CABINET OF REFLECTION

At the entrance to the Temple, a desolate scene of "terrestrial" symbolism. It is night. This represents both the Cabinet of Reflection of Masonic initiation and Tamino's trial by Earth commented upon earlier (Chapter 11). *Cf.* the stylized realization of this scene as the frontispiece of the first edition of the libretto (Plate 33).

No. 10a / SPOKEN SCENE

Ritual scene: the priests bring in the postulants, their heads veiled, remove the veils, and give them instructions before leaving them alone in darkness. These instructions deal mostly with the law of silence, an absolute virtue in a secret society, but at the time also considered specifically masculine (we remember the mouth-sealing ritual in the feminine initiation, reflected by Papageno's padlock).

See the analysis of the dialogue on p. 139.

No. 11 / DUET OF THE PRIESTS

This duet clarifies the special application of the law of silence: it deals above all with knowing how to remain silent in the presence of the fair sex. *"Bewahret euch vor Weibertücken:/ Dies ist des Bundes erste Pflicht"* (Beware of women's deceptions: that is the Brotherhood's first duty). Then follows a detailing of the miseries that await any man who displays weakness toward women.

Musically, the duet, in C major, develops without much complexity, most often at the third or the sixth, underlining the accord of the characters, in the syllabic style required for every moralizing piece and, despite the allegretto, in the general atmosphere of a canticle marked principally by feminine cadences. Some "realistic" touches in this passage, as for example the descent of the double-basses at the words *"Er fehlte"* (He erred): this refers to man's fall in the face of feminine onsets; or, again, the dotted rhythm of the march, with an affirmative cadence marking the last sentence, *"Tod und Verzweiflung war sein Lohn"* (Death and despair were his reward)—this spoken *sotto voce* like most of the moralities in the libretto. In a letter to Constanze (see p. 23), Mozart admitted having composed one piece in *Die Zauberflöte* in a state of boredom: there is every reason to think that he was referring to this one, which contains nothing of great musical interest.

Except, perhaps, for one detail: the striking apparent modulation on the word *"Vergebens"* (in vain). The classical analysis, which knows nothing of this class of phenomenon, would find a modulation here—brutal and in defiance of the rules—to the major third (from C to E). In fact, it is not a modulation at all, but, according to the oldest treatises, the use of a IIIrd degree with an altered third.*

No. 11a / SPOKEN SCENE

The priests depart, leaving the postulants in darkness (allusion to the bowels of the Earth and to the Cabinet of Reflection, as well as to the night of ignorance from which the profane now must emerge gradually). Distant thunder (which symbolizes the dark forces: further, it is one of the elements of the ritual of initiation). Tamino and Papageno remain alone on the stage. Papageno calls for light: *"Das ist doch wunderlich,*

---

* The harmony treatise of Gustave Lefèvre, director of the École Niedermeyer (1885), exemplifies this kind of "false modulation" by a passage in Rossini identical with this one, with the analysis I-III-I in C major, without any movement to E. As early as 1803, Momigny had spoken out against the analyses showing constant "shiftings" that lacked musical reality, affirming the tonal unity of such instances. *Cf.* Jacques Chailley, *"Un Grand Théoreticien belge de la musique: Jérôme-Joseph de Momigny (1762–1842),"* in the *Bulletin de l'Académie Royale de Belgique*, 1966, 2–3, p. 80.

*so oft einen die Herren verlassen, sieht man mit offenen Augen
nichts"* (It's strange, whenever the gentlemen leave, one can
see nothing with open eyes). Here again, despite the comic
tone, the double meaning is clear. Tamino urges him to be
patient. Then the Three Ladies appear, rising from below
through a trapdoor (temptation from the Earth).

No. 12 / QUINTET

The meaning of this unexpected irruption already has been
pointed out (pp. 111–12, 136, 140). On the one hand, it deals
—by transposition of the "philosophic Testament" that the postulant must compose in the Cabinet of Reflection—with
verifying his feelings toward Freemasonry; on the other, with
putting to a test the strength of his silence when faced with
the tittle-tattle of the fair sex. Conceived as a function of
Tamino's trials, the symbol doubtless introduces some illogi-
cality into the character of the Three Ladies, who were presented in Act I as imperfect initiates into the Masonry of
Adoption. But we already have noted that this incoherence is
more apparent than real.

That is why the Three Ladies must attempt to discredit the
Order in the mind of Tamino; but he, carrying out the orders
that he has been given, faces them in obdurate silence.

The symbolism has evolved with respect to Tamino too.
In the first act, he was the ignorant stripling who, reacting to
his first emotions, underwent a first, imperfect initiation ema-
nating from the nocturnal kingdom: he discovered the world
of women, sensed their spell, and accepted their orders. He
did not yet suspect that Pamina could escape from their grasp
or that he himself would change. He is already changed. He
no longer needs to discover Woman, for he has found her in
her most elevated aspect. But it remains for the Queen of the
Night and her Ladies to try to divert him from the plan of
pursuing an initiation that, by drawing Pamina in his wake,

would cut her off finally from her mother's world. It was a fine opportunity for the creators of the opera to refute in public the attacks then being launched against Freemasonry by putting their own arguments into the mouths of the protagonists. In this scene (No. 12), the libretto moves very close to then-contemporary references. Opportunity, too, in passing to launch some darts at the influence of the Roman Church on feminine society, which is implicitly accused of being ordered to spread in the salons the anti-Masonic slogans in ecclesiastical style which are heard caricatured in this spot.* Perhaps, also, some barbs flew in the direction of the Empress Maria Theresia, who was said to have inspired them. Given that opportunity, the creators could happily sacrifice apparent psychological unity—which bothered them very little in any case.

Breaking away from the tonalities of the preceding scenes, which tended toward flats, the key of G major at once removes us from the meditative climate in which we have been evolving. The Ladies begin by pointing out to Tamino the dangers that he runs; they express themselves strongly, but the short inter-phrase interludes suffice, by their sly syncopations— revealed in the meshings of the first violin and the flute—to show how tortuous their thoughts are.

Papageno is determined to talk; Tamino does his best to keep the Birdcatcher silent (comedic style). Then the Ladies reveal that their Queen just has entered the Temple surreptitiously (descriptive ascending line). Stupefaction on Papageno's part, marked by incisive trills. Tamino imposes silence

---

* On this subject, see chapters 8–10. The possibility has led to conjecture by some musicologists, notably Dent (p. 231), that it could have been an allusion to condemnations of Freemasonry by the pope. But if that was the case, it was not an allusion to contemporary events, as that condemnation had been made more than fifty years earlier—and the last Roman document of that sort had been Benedict XIV's *Providas*, dating from 1751, forty years before *Die Zauberflöte*.

upon him (not that he himself observes the rule by not making any sound, but that he refuses to converse with the Ladies, which is something altogether different).*

This sly interlude leads to a new intervention by the Ladies: *"Tamino, hör du bist verloren!/ Gedenke an die Königin!/ Man zischelt viel sich in die Ohren/ Von dieser Priester falschem Sinn"* (Tamino, listen, you are lost! Think of the Queen! It is often whispered in one's ears that these priests are false).

"Ein Weiser prüft" (A wise man weighs matters), Tamino replies, *"und achtet nicht/ Was der gemeine Pöbel spricht"* (and pays no attention to popular gossip). The Ladies again repeat their allegations: they have learned a lesson, and they repeat it *ad nauseam.* Here the repetition of motives has a particular meaning, as does the rapidity of the chatter—one could call it tittle-tattle—that marks their words, however serious. To the point at which Papageno can continue without a break in their childish style. *"Sag an, Tamino, ist das wahr?"* (Tell me, Tamino, is this so?). The answer is significant: *"Geschwätz von Weibern nachgesagt,/ Von Heuchlern aber ausgedacht"* (Idle chatter, spread by women, but devised by hypocrites). But Papageno comments: *"Doch sagt es auch die Königin"* (But the Queen says it too). Tamino: *"Sie ist ein Weib, hat Weibersinn"* (She is a woman and has a woman's mind). And, this time in peremptory fashion (significant cadence), he curtly orders Papageno to keep quiet—this after having asserted in ecclesiastical style (marked by the parallel sixth-chords of *fauxbourdon*) that his word should suffice to reassure Papageno.

The Three Ladies fretfully complain of his rudeness to

* This fact renders unnecessary the interpolations of J. G. Prod'homme, who, in his translation, found it flatly contradictory that Tamino should speak and yet win the test by silence, and therefore punctuated almost all of Tamino's replies with "Aside."

Papageno, who would have succumbed if Tamino had not imposed silence upon him a final time. The Three Ladies nonetheless recognize their defeat, and the five singers, setting their roles aside as usual, unite for the moral of the episode: *"Von festem Geiste ist ein Mann,/ Er denket, was er sprechen kann"* (A man has a strong spirit. He thinks and then speaks). This is in a sense the reply to the preceding morality, which dealt with the Ladies' chatter. Here again, the word opposed to *"Weib"* is *"Mann."*

The moral seems to end the episode: the Three Ladies prepare to depart. At this moment, however, a sort of coda intervenes. From inside, voices are heard crying (the very word of the rubric: *"Schreien"*) a maledictory apostrophe: *"Entweiht ist die heilige Schwelle,/ Hinab mit den Weibern zur Hölle!"* (The holy precinct is profaned. May the women go to Hell!) Note the nature of the sacrilege: what profanes the Temple is the presence of women as women, not as adversaries.

It would be pointless to wax indignant over the point: the conception was held by almost all of the ancient religions.* I remember having been present, in a synagogue of Mea-Shearim, the holy quarter of Jerusalem, at a similar cursing, a woman in our party having been so foolish as to look through the window when I went in with a friend without being bothered in any way despite the fact that I was obviously only a tourist.

"A terrible chord, using all the instruments, thunder, flashings, and lightning; two simultaneous loud thunderclaps" (such is the rubric). *"O weh!"* (O woe!), the Three Ladies cry three times (successions of diminished sevenths), after which they vanish through a trapdoor into the depths of the

---

* It is not hard to find a parallel close to home, even in the Catholic religion. Not until the instruction *Musicam Sacram* of 1967 was the presence of women in parish choirs officially proclaimed licit (until then they had been merely "tolerated"). Even in that 1967 instruction, an interdiction was included against having the chorus sing in the choir itself.

Earth whence they came, while the first violins represent their disappearance by a descent in tremolos on the final diminished seventh.

The scene concludes very swiftly: Papageno repeats the Three Ladies' tragic *"O weh!"* and falls to the ground. Is that ending truly comic? One could think so, given the usual character of Papageno's scenes. Thus it would be somewhat analogous to Sganarelle's final reply in Molière's *Dom Juan,* after he is swallowed up with the Commandeur. Nevertheless, it is very possible that this time Papageno should be taken seriously. Unlike Tamino and Pamina, he has not yet experienced the required symbolic swoon before facing the real trials—and here it is. Everything that he has done as a supernumerary to Tamino thus does not "count." But has he really "succeeded"? The rubric is not decisive, and his behavior could well be as wretched during his own trials as it was during those at which he was only a witness. . . .

We note the refined writing of the final measure, in which the orchestra falls silent after a single quarter-note while Papageno holds his final note through the duration of a whole-note: a subtle way of emphasizing the resulting swoon.

No. 12a / SPOKEN SCENE

The rubric indicates another triple chord, but it does not appear in the score.

That chord announces the arrival of the Speaker accompanied by the other priest, both of them carrying lanterns. The Speaker salutes Tamino's success in his first-act trial and invites him to continue the long journey (we have seen the word's ritual significance). He puts back Tamino's veil, a translation of the blindfold placed over the postulant's eyes as he emerges from the Cabinet of Reflection, and then leaves with him.

The second priest remains alone with Papageno, and proceeds in a more familiar style: "*Auf! Sammle dich, und sei ein Mann!*" (Get up! Pull yourself together and be a man!). This refrain, which surreptitiously supplies the key of the swoon, awakens this sort of reflection in Papageno: "*Aber sagt mir nur, meine Herren, warum muss ich denn alle diese Qualen und Schrecken empfinden? Wenn mir ja die Götter eine Papagena bestimmten, warum denn mit so viel Gefahren sie erringen?*" (But tell me, gentlemen, why must I suffer these dangers and horrors? If the gods will grant me a Papagena, why must I work so hard to get her?). The priest puts Papageno's veil back on without answering him, and leads him out.

Third Scene

PAMINA'S TRIAL BY EARTH

The trial is symmetrical with the one that Tamino just has undergone. See the commentary on pp. 105 and 148. The symbolic décor evokes the Earth (trees trimmed in horseshoe shape, grassy banks), the Night (moonlight), and the feminine initiation (beds of roses upon which Pamina lies asleep).

No. 12b / SPOKEN SCENE

Enter Monostatos, who, in the monologue already discussed (pp. 148–9), proclaims his contempt for Pamina. Nonetheless, seduced by her whiteness, he cannot resist hiding himself from the Moon and taking the stars as witness to his temptation to steal "just one little kiss" from her.

No. 13 / MONOSTATOS'S VERSES

This whole aria, the rubric specifies, is to be played and sung so quietly as to give the impression that the music is coming from a distance. Perhaps to suggest that for Pamina it is a sort of dream? We easily distinguish the sprightly character and the couplet form, identical with Papageno's in Act I: like Papageno, Monostatos is a comic character. Much identified with "Turkish music," * Monostatos is a Negro, and that fact sufficed, at a time when no one was very demanding about the geography of exoticism, to justify this style,† which is affirmed by the piccolo, the particular accentual rhythm, the characteristic formulas. All that is lacking is the regular beats of the side drums, cymbals, and triangle, which, though absent from the scoring, are nevertheless sufficiently hinted at by the musical context. It is equally amusing to note the resemblance of this beginning to Figaro's celebrated aria in Rossini's future *Il Barbiere di Siviglia.*

The first stanza expresses Monostatos's revolt against the fact that because he is black and a Negro is ugly, he must renounce love and live without a woman, though he is made of flesh and blood. The second stanza approaches the symbolism still more frankly: it is a White woman who has conquered this Black man: *"Weiss ist schön, ich muss sie küssen:/ Mond, verstecke dich dazu!/ Sollt es dich zu sehr verdriessen,/ O so mach die Augen zu!"* (White is beautiful, I must kiss her. Moon, veil yourself, and if it embarrasses you too much, close your eyes!). Thus Monostatos implicitly avows his allegiance to the Kingdom of the Night. He silently glides toward Pamina. At this moment, the Queen of the Night rises

* By this designation, the eighteenth century indicated a special type of piece that was used to furnish local color in Oriental scenes. Mozart made frequent use of it (*Die Entführung aus dem Serail*, the "*Rondo alla turca*," etc.), and the march in the Ninth Symphony is a borrowing from "Turkish music." It is curious that the fact of this aria's belonging to a very well-known genre has passed so unobserved to this day that Denés Bartha could write that "*Die Zauberflöte* is absolutely devoid of all exoticism"—this in a study especially documented with regard to "Turkish music" itself ("*Mozart et le folklore musical de l'Europe central*," in *Influences étrangères dans l'oeuvre de W. A. Mozart*, p. 157). Carl de Nys mentions it on p. 180 of that book.

† Perhaps also because Monostatos, as his name hints, is foreign to the milieu in which he is living?

suddenly from below (always the Earth, as with the Ladies for Tamino); the two scenes are perfectly symmetrical.

No. 13a / REVELATIONS OF
THE QUEEN OF THE NIGHT

The Queen motions Monostatos back with one word, "Zurück," and then ceases to pay attention to him. In short, she restricts herself to getting rid of an intruder who is preventing her from talking to her daughter, and gives no thought to protecting the girl or punishing the shabby fellow. Monostatos takes advantage of that: he conceals himself and watches the scene without the Queen's noticing him.

Waking Pamina, the Queen asks, not about her well-being, but about the mission that she herself has entrusted to Tamino. Learning that he has "given himself to the initiates of Isis," she realizes that her daughter is lost to her: she has no power to protect the girl in the temple where she is imprisoned. And in the long recitative already discussed (p. 93), she tells Pamina how the power once held by her father was divided, upon his death, between Sarastro and herself. Either the young man will deliver Pamina or he will remain a prisoner of the Initiates and will be lost to her. Pamina rejects her mother's insinuations as Tamino rejected those of the Three Ladies.

"Liebe Mutter, dürft' ich den Jüngling als Eingeweihten denn nicht auch ebenso zärtlich lieben, wie ich ihn jetzt liebe? Mein Vater selbst war ja mit diesen weisen Männern verbunden; er sprach jederzeit mit Entzücken von ihnen, preiste ihre Güte, ihren Verstand, ihre Tugend. Sarastro ist nicht weniger tugendhaft" (Dear Mother, why can I not love the young man when he is among the Initiates as tenderly as I love him now? Was not my Father allied to their Brotherhood? I myself remember hearing him speak enthusiastically of its Brothers. He praised their goodness, their understanding, their virtues. Sarastro seems to me to have all those qualities).

These words, by means of which—without knowing it—Pamina is about to pass the Masonic examination of the Cabinet of Reflection, unloose the Queen's fury. If she is to regain her power, only one solution remains: to kill Sarastro. As her daughter now lives in his empire, she must be charged with the murder. And the Queen gives her the dagger (an object of terrestrial metal, this being the trial by Earth) with which to carry out that necessary act.

The order to kill Sarastro is easy to understand: by marrying, and thus entering the kingdom of men, woman finds herself in possession of a strong weapon that can, if she wishes, kill in them the element that is theirs. That is why the Queen of the Night hands her daughter a dagger. Pamina's initiation will lead her to refuse this role and render herself worthy of the new society into which she is entering, even though, because of that refusal, she will find herself rejected by the society that she is leaving.

The Queen's order to murder Sarastro is now to be commented upon musically, accompanied by the curse that the mother places upon her daughter if she should fail.

No. 14 / ARIA OF THE QUEEN OF THE NIGHT:
Her Malediction of Pamina

This celebrated two-section aria—each section ending in formidable *fioriture*—is very often denatured by sopranos who make it resemble the "Bell Song" from *Lakmé* as an exhibition of their virtuosity. Nevertheless, it is primarily an expressive and an angry aria. *"Der Hölle Rache kocht in meinem Herzen"* (Hell's vengeance burns in my heart)—those opening words set its character, and Mozart rarely achieved such dynamic force. The wide vocal intervals, often treated in ascending arpeggios, the brilliance of the extremely high tessitura—which seems less like a banal, stereotyped element from the virtuosic arsenal of coloraturas than like authentic cries of rage prolonged by the renowned staccato vocalises so feared by sopranos—the constant motion of the orchestration; the absence of any repetition, which avoids the formalistic aspect of so many arias (Mozart's included) of the epoch; the abrupt ending after a somber Neapolitan sixth on a recitative cadence that the voice does not complete, but which the orchestra brings to a brutal, raging termination as the Queen of the Night vanishes underground—all of that contributes to making this aria not the featherbrained vocal exercise that it too often has become, but one of the most extraordinary depictions of character ever achieved in music.

On the symbolic level, one notes in the prelude (measures 4–6) the presence of the rhythm of the "five even little beats" common to nearly all the numbers of nocturnal-feminine significance, and perhaps it is no pure coincidence that this rhythm recurs in anacrusis in the first series of grand vocalises (*cf.* p. 160). It may also not be a coincidence that the phrase *"So bist du mein!"* (second time) textually reproduces the *"Sie ist vollbracht"* with which, in the first scene, the Three Ladies announce the accomplishment of the "heroic act": the text of the maternal curse is in effect the inevitable outcome of the process then set in motion: *"So bist du meine Tochter nimmer mehr!"* (Then you will never again be my daughter!), the Queen of the Night says. Pamina's drama is that of being wrenched from the nocturnal kingdom, and this phrase of the Queen's expresses it strikingly.

No. 14a / SPOKEN SCENE

Left alone with the dagger in her hand, Pamina ponders the command that she just has received. Kill Sarastro? She could never do it. And while she remains pensive, Monostatos materializes. At once he begins, as an aside, a rapid monologue in which he reports his thoughts about what he has overheard. Now he knows that Sarastro's solar circle has magic virtues (*cf.* Plate 31) and that in order to appropriate it the young

princess must commit murder. *"Das ist Salz in meine Suppe!"*
(That is salt in my soup, meaning that it beautifully helps his
plans). He is going to try to blackmail Pamina: either she will
give herself to him or he will reveal everything to Sarastro, in
which case her mother will be drowned *"in diesem Gewölbe,
in eben dem Wasser, das die Eingeweihten reinigen soll"* (in
the underground cavern, in the very water intended for the
purification of the Initiates). This is no mere figure of speech:
water is known to represent the feminine element. Pamina
refuses, horrified. Monostatos snatches the dagger from her
and threatens her. *"Nein? Und warum? Weil ich die Farbe
eines schwarzen Gespenstes trage? . . . Liebe oder Tod!"*
(You refuse? And why? Is it because I have a black face? . . .
Love or death!). Pamina answers: *"Mein Herz hab ich dem
Jüngling geopfert"* (I have pledged my heart to the young
man). *"Was kümmert mich dein Opfer?"* (What difference
does your promise make to me?) is Monostatos's answer. And
he would strike Pamina if Sarastro did not appear at this
crucial moment. *"Ich weiss . . . dass deine Seele ebenso
schwarz als dein Gesicht ist"* (I know that your soul is as black
as your face), the Master says. But he will not punish
Monostatos because he knows that the dagger was forged by
a woman as wicked as her daughter is virtuous. That woman
alone is to blame. And Monostatos, muttering a threatening
word, runs away. He has decided that as the daughter refuses
his help, he will turn to the mother. Translation: as love removes from the world of debauchees the women whom it
enlightens, for that world there remain those women who, not
having undergone that transformation, are ready to welcome
the basenesses of the black world of the Night.

Pamina, left alone with Sarastro, asks him to have pity on
her mother and not take revenge upon her. Sarastro answers
that he knows everything; he even knows that at this moment
the Queen is wandering through the underground passages

of the Temple plotting vengeance against him and against mankind; as for him, he knows nothing of vengeance. He hopes that the gods will permit Tamino to triumph in his trials, and that Pamina will then be enabled to enjoy happiness with him. Her mother will be confounded, and will have no choice but to retire to her castle and never again involve herself in men's affairs. "As for you," Sarastro concludes, "learn to know us and do not flee our sacred halls."

No. 15 / SARASTRO'S ARIA

Growing out of those last words, this is an idyllic description of the abode of the Sages, where vengeance (*"Rache,"* the term used by the Queen) is unknown, where fraternity reigns. The tonality selected, breaking with the preceding alternations, is that of E major, full of clear sharps. The aria is treated in couplets, in a diatonicism without asperity and almost devoid of modulations (except, in the middle, something of an inflection toward the dominant). The phrases occur symmetrically two by two, and the tranquillity of the happy abode is evoked by the abundance of notes tied two by two on the same syllable: a procedure that others (notably Weber) would abuse later, and the origin of which perhaps harks back to the famous description of Renaud's dream in Lully's *Armide*, *"Ce fleuve coule lentement."* The phrase by which Sarastro describes the "hand of friendship" supporting the repentant sinner is accompanied, during its long, mounting line, by a unison (more exactly, a doubling at the octave) of the first violins, which "accompany" the voice as the hand upholds the weak: this musical image was also used in the priest's reply to Tamino before the portal of the Temple. A refinement: when the voice descends, the violins continue upward. And the effect of the low notes, magnified by the deepness of Sarastro's voice, contributes to the solemn gravity of the description.

The aria ends in a moralizing sentence like the sentences that end episodes throughout the libretto: *"Wen solche Lehren nicht erfreuen,/Verdienet nicht ein Mensch zu sein"* (He who rejects teaching of this sort does not deserve to be a man). But this time man is *"Mensch,"* not *"Mann"*: it refers to mankind, not to the struggle of the sexes. The scheme is as elevated as the symbolism of the key signatures. Is it a coincidence that a seven-note theme begins the prelude and that at the end, enhanced by a return of the horns—which have been merely filling in up to this point—the concluding phrase also is punctuated by a formula of seven notes, the number of Wisdom?

Fourth Scene

TAMINO'S TRIAL BY AIR

The stage, the rubric says, represents "a passageway in which the flying machine can move" (it symbolizes the trial by Air). "This flying machine will be covered with roses and other flowers" (symbols of feminine initiation: the trial also involves Pamina). "A door opens into the vestibule. At the extreme front of the stage, two grassy banks" (recalling that Tamino and Pamina already have undergone the trial by Earth).

The essence of this tableau, as the rubric foretells, will be Tamino's trial by Air, but it will also include various trials of Papageno and Papagena, treated as a comic interlude.

No. 15a / SPOKEN SCENE:
Papageno's and Papagena's Trial by Water

The two men, their heads unveiled, are again brought in by their guide and then are left alone. Tamino (but not Papageno, who has not yet passed his trial by Earth) seats himself on the grass. Papageno tries to engage him in conversation, but at each remark Tamino reminds him of the rule of silence. One of the replies specifies that this rule is with regard to women: "*Mit mir selbst werd' ich wohl sprechen dürfen; und auch wir zwei können zusammen sprechen, wir sind ja Männer*" (I am allowed to talk to myself, and also we can talk to one another because both of us are men). And because Tamino prevents him from speaking, he begins to sing (an allusion to the role of music in the trial by Air), after which he complains of being thirsty and of not having even a drop of water to drink: only a figure of speech, as he dislikes water heartily. But here it is a question of introducing his trial by Water, which will soon follow.

As soon as Papageno utters those words, an old woman enters holding a goblet and a ewer of water. We have noted (p. 108) what her role signifies: because the future couple has not yet passed any of the necessary trials, the Birdcatcher's dream-woman cannot appear to him clothed in any of the seductions that will render her desirable. Comically calling Papageno "*mein Engel*" (my angel), she takes him at his word, offering him water to drink. Not accepting it, Papageno persuades the old woman to sit down near him to pass the time—and asks her how old she is. She answers that she is eighteen years and ten minutes old (this is her "physical" age despite her appearance, not the "Masonic age" of the Three Boys) and that her love is none other than Papageno himself. Flabbergasted, Papageno throws the water at her and asks her her name. "*Ich heisse . . .*" (I am called . . .), the old woman says. At that moment, a clap of thunder interrupts her and she disappears without completing the sentence. In despair Papageno decides: "*Nun sprech' ich kein Wort mehr!*" (I won't utter another word!).

This scene always has been judged to be a meaningless

episode, farce. But it very evidently was included for a reason. Papageno, who likes only wine, has been offered water. He has not drunk it, but has thrown the liquid at his companion's head. As remarked earlier (p. 154), he has thus refused to be marked with the feminine sign (complement of the masculine sign, Fire) essential to fulfillment of the couple, and it has marked only his future wife. As she will not pass the trial by Fire, each of them will remain, in their menage, marked by his own sign, but not by that of his mate. Contrary to what will happen to Tamino and Pamina (who will pass together the trials by Fire and Water), this future couple will remain forever incomplete.

No. 16 / TRIO OF THE THREE BOYS

We return to the main action: the trial by Air of the two principal protagonists. The Three Boys enter on the flying machine covered with roses.*

One holds the magic flute, the other the glockenspiel in its case (the latter is mentioned especially to recall the sign of Earth: the instrument is hidden, as if buried).

The Boys cause to descend from their flying machine a table abundantly set with appetizing dishes. They return the enchanted instruments to the candidates, invite them to eat and drink if they do not disdain the repast provided, and disappear after encouraging them: "*Tamino, Mut! Nah ist das Ziel*" (Tamino, take courage, your goal is at hand!); "*Du, Papageno, schweige still!*" (You, Papageno [they promise him nothing], be silent and say nothing—the pleonasm is in the text: *schweige still*).†

---

* The rubric mentioning the flying machine is often simply omitted in various editions and translations—and overlooked in the staging. However, it is the *raison d'être* of the scene, from which its omission removes all significance. Indispensable to the symbolic understanding, it is equally indispensable to musical comprehension of the trio that follows.

† And not "continue to be silent," as this is often translated. The loquaciousness will begin soon enough . . .

The entire scene is traversed by a light, almost impalpable motive that mounts, undulates, and soars, sometimes rising, sometimes descending without ever touching the earth, almost without support from the double basses; it strikingly represents the aerial flight of the machine.* The syllabic trio (necessity of understanding the words) ends with a postlude reprise of the descriptive prelude and shows the Boys flying away as they had arrived.

The A-major tonality may seem surprising. Coming after the E of Sarastro's aria, it can be explained in several ways, no one of which is conclusive. The most believable explanation is that the preceding E major precluded a return to the symbolic flats (the linking-up would have been too harsh even after a spoken scene), and that the tonality was therefore selected because its lightness fitted the subject matter well. The explanation remains valid for the pieces that follow, which return to the middle of the scale of tonalities by gradual progression, after which the balance between "profane" and "mystical" tonalities, respected up to this point and abandoned only temporarily, can be restored.

Same coincidence (?) as in the preceding aria: the bassoons, doubled by flutes or oboes, emphasize the frequently repeated injunction *"Schweige still!"*—first by a figure of seven beats, then with one of seven notes.

No. 16a / SPOKEN SCENE:
The Trial by Air Properly Speaking

At first the trial (explained on pp. 141 and 150) is for Tamino only: the Boys have brought him, on the one hand, his magic flute and, on the other, a well-stocked table. Which will he choose? Faced with the same dilemma, Papageno does not hesitate a second: without giving a thought to his glocken-

---

* Jean-Victor Hocquard (*La Pensée de Mozart*, p. 507) explains these features by "an orientation toward the upper atmosphere, toward light too violent to gaze upon, facing the Sun." Thus one sees the danger of trying to substitute philosophy for musicology.

spiel, he falls upon the victuals and stuffs himself with the delicacies. It matters little to him: he is associated with Tamino's trials only for form's sake or, rather, to show in caricature what not to do: his real trial will take place later.

Tamino, on the contrary, has the proper reaction. Paying no attention to the good food (antithesis of the idealistic Air), he concentrates upon the flute and—not uttering a word because of the rule of silence—plays upon it, thus associating his wind instrument with the trial by Air.

The second section of the trial will be more painful: attracted by the magic melody (not notated in the score), Pamina runs joyfully to Tamino. He sighs sadly, but nonetheless firmly refuses to answer. Not speaking a word to her, he goes on playing the flute and motions her to leave. Naturally, Pamina does not understand the reason for his unexpected attitude and thinks that he is rejecting her love, not realizing that his action is associated with his trial by Air, which she herself also is undergoing. In justified despair she speaks to Papageno, who, for reasons certainly different from Tamino's —his mouth is full—makes the same gestures of rejection (Plate 18). In despair, Pamina then sings of her sorrow.

No. 17 / PAMINA'S ARIA

Again a very famous aria, this one—strikingly in its relation to her first interventions—reveals the transformation taking place within Pamina. By means of a regular accompanying rhythm in four that evokes her breathless sighing, the princess, believing herself abandoned, expresses her anguish in a continuous musical line at once sweet and ardent, marvelously continuous melodically, and of an expressiveness that is the more intense because it is reserved—all the while also expertly displaying the soprano's voice.

The atmosphere is established, beginning with the second measure, by a troubling appoggiatura sustained by a chromaticism of

"false modulation" in the violas, and then by the expressive clash—
so logical that one cannot speak of "dissonance"—of the harmonic
F sharp of the orchestra with the F natural of the voice. With the
exception of the second phrase, in the relative major (B flat),
from which one returns to TP (G minor) by harmonic march, the
entire aria is practically devoid of modulation. Nevertheless, because of the constant play of eloquent harmonic or melodic con-
strictions that translate her sorrow, no monotony results: note
particularly the beautiful Neapolitan sixth on the word *"Ruh'"*
(repose), which, when it is repeated, culminates in a long-held
note, only to fall suddenly to the other extremity of the voice, to
murmur in the depths the explanation of what that repose will be:
"im Tode sein" (in death).

As with the portrait aria, one cannot speak of a definite form,
but only of continuous melody without reprise or development.
Yet the piece is traversed by defined and characterized cells that
make each measure immediately recognizable, so that it could not
be moved elsewhere. If one must relate it to a classic scheme, one
can—as with the corresponding aria—speak of a supremely supple
form of the triptych ABA, the restatement of A being no more
than suggested by the repetition of some inflections from the first
section: *"der Liebe sehnen,"* measure 29, after *"der Liebe Glück,"*
measure 6, followed by a vocalise (*"so wird Ruhe"*), its beginning
also repeated, from the first section, measure 12, where it was in
the relative key. In the same way, 34–6 can be taken as an expressive variation of 5–7. In that hypothesis, one considers as A the
first fifteen measures, formed of two large phrases TP-RM *—
leading to the vocalises on the word *"Herzen"* (heart) and ending
in the relative major; B will be the harmonic march leading back
to TP and introducing new inflections (16–26), with a hesitant
conclusion on a broken cadence. The end will be a final section
in G minor, including the random repetitions from A just mentioned.

At many points, one's attention is caught by the refinement of
the orchestration, though it is very simple. Thus, in measures
4–7, the ravishing octave relationship of the bassoon and the oboe,

---

* I repeat the abbreviations used here: TP—principal tonality, RM—relative
major, Rm—relative minor, D—dominant, SD—subdominant.

then of the oboe and the flute; or, again, the alternating echoes between voice and flute-oboe in measures 16–24. And also the very curious rhythmic disposition of the postlude, in which violins and violas continue the preceding 6/8 while the first violins, doubled by the woodwinds, transform it for two measures into 3/4.

No. 17a / SPOKEN SCENE

At the end of her aria, Pamina leaves. Tamino and Papageno remain on stage. The latter is very pleased with himself and delighted to have been able to remain silent at last, quite forgetting that the reason why he could not speak was that his mouth was full: ". . . *bin ich Mann*" (I am a man), he proclaims proudly, swallowing several glasses of wine.

A non-notated triple trombone call is heard. Tamino recognizes the signal that was described to him, and wants to leave, taking Papageno, who resists because some food remains uneaten. He will stay where he is, he says, even if Lord Sarastro uses the combined strength of his six lions to remove him from this place.

That statement produces the result that might have been foreseen: in come the lions of which Schikaneder was so proud, and which move menacingly toward the terrified Papageno. Tamino puts his flute to his lips and plays a non-notated melody; appeased, the lions turn back. Doubtless the episode is related to the trial by Air, for the flute (a wind instrument) plays a preponderant role in it. It is nonetheless incongruous, having no meaning on the symbolic level, being merely a purposeless repetition of the appearance of the animals at Tamino's first flute-playing. Perhaps it was a "gag" thought up by Schikaneder (during the rehearsals) in order to make use of his menagerie and at the same time add a comic effect to the original plan.

Papageno has learned his lesson and is now ready to follow Tamino. Second sounding of the trumpets. Guided by the gestures of the still-silent Tamino, Papageno obeys regretfully. The two men leave.

The conclusion of this scene will be discussed at the beginning of the following one.

Fifth Scene

VAULT OF THE PYRAMIDS
No. 18 / CHORUS OF PRIESTS

On stage are Sarastro, the Speaker, and some priests. Two priests bear on their shoulders an illuminated pyramid. Each priest carries a transparent pyramid the size of a lantern.

The pyramids seem not—at least unless further information is brought to light—to play any symbolic role in the libretto beyond that of calling up an Egypt of which they symbolize the mystery and the wisdom (whence their illumination). One notices the insistence with which, here as elsewhere, the specification of a central pyramid larger than the others is repeated (*cf.* p. 235).

The chorus that begins the scene (and closes the preceding episode) provides the clues that at intervals help us to follow the scheme of the trials. Not dealing with Papageno (who does not interest them at all), or even with Pamina, the priests announce the end of the second trial (that by Air) and foretell Tamino's final victory.

Invoking Isis and Osiris (here there is a short interlude for winds alone), the priests rejoice over seeing the Sun's brilliance frighten away the dark Night (somber inflection toward the flats of the *"düst're Nacht"* [dark Night], radiant ascent toward the sharps for the brilliance of the Sun). They say: *"Bald fühlt der edle Jüngling neues Leben,/ Bald ist er unserm Dienste ganz ergeben./ Sein Geist ist kühn, sein Herz ist rein,/ Bald* [an enthusiastic ascent in arpeggios on the triple repetition of the word *"bald"*] *wird er unser würdig sein"* (Soon the noble young man will feel new life; soon he will be given over to our service. His spirit is bold; his heart is pure; soon he will be worthy of us) (3 times).

This chorus, in D major, is the last of the short series that supplies an exception to the general symbolism of the tonalities. Its orchestration is that of the religious scenes, with the horns, the trumpets, and the three trombones. Here again we find the syllabic canticle style, with the series of sixth chords in *fauxbourdon*, the feminine cadences on 4–6, the chords on modal degrees. One of its phrases (*"Sein Geist ist kühn"*) is astonishingly close to the religious choruses in *Parsifal*.

No. 18a / SPOKEN SCENE:
Preparation of the Final Trials

Tamino is brought in, and Sarastro harangues him: *"Prinz, dein Betragen war bis hierher männlich* [always *"männlich"*] *und gelassen; nun hast du noch zwei gefährliche Wege zu wandern"* (Prince, your actions up to now have been manly and prudent; you still have two final trials to undergo). In fact, Tamino has passed two of the four trials by the Elements: that of Earth and that of Air. He still must face those of Water and of Fire. Sarastro calls down the help of the gods upon him, takes him by the hand, and orders that Pamina be brought in. The priests, who are not at all enthusiastic over the initiation of a woman, preserve a hostile silence as Pamina is led in covered with the same veil that covers the Initiates. Sarastro unties the ribbons of the veil; frightened by the silence in which she is received, Pamina asks where her fiancé is. *"Er wartet deiner"* (He awaits you), Sarastro answers, *"um dir das letzte Lebewohl zu sagen"* (to bid you his last farewell). Troubled by the *double entendre* of these words, Pamina again asks for him. Sarastro has Tamino appear, and Pamina runs toward him. But Tamino, not yet freed of the rule of silence, spurns her.

The meaning of this scene presents no difficulty in so far as it concerns Tamino, but it is more obscure in relation to Pamina. If one concedes that she has participated in the trial by Air without really having undergone it (which seems to be indicated by a new scene under that sign at the beginning of the finale), this is the point at which the neophyte appears before the assemblage after leaving the Cabinet of Reflection. But it may conceal a deeper meaning.

In fact, the admission of Pamina to the "regular" trials—not merely to the trials of Adoption—presents an anomaly. That possibility has never been mentioned during the deliberations of the Initiates: she is not only a woman, but also the daughter of the Queen of the Night, and therefore was destined, upon her mother's death, to inherit the rule of the enemy kingdom. But she has been borne off, separated from her milieu. Her mother has disowned her: *"So bist du meine Tochter nimmer mehr"* (Then you will never again be my daughter). Subjected by accidental circumstances to a trial by Earth analogous to Tamino's, she has displayed equal strength of character. Associated despite herself (and always without preliminary deliberation) with the young prince in the trial by Air, she has been the one to suffer (though she has not undergone her own trial by Air). She is, then, as much prepared as Tamino. In giving her, as the rubric says, exactly the veil that covers the Initiates, the priests, without having even deliberated, accept an already accomplished fact: the Woman, having left the Kingdom of the Night, has become the equal of the Man, and can, like him, be admitted officially to the final trials. The veil that Sarastro unties is a victorious answer to the veils that hide the faces of the Queen and her Ladies, which will not be removed. This is the first sign of the Woman's victory, of her redemption, and of her future glorification.

This appears to be a carrying-out of Sarastro's own policy, and the superiority of his wisdom over that of the other priests is symbolized by the larger pyramid. It is Sarastro who has Pamina brought in; the other priests greet her with an icy, disapproving silence that dismays her. The initiation of a woman was a revolutionary decision, and no deliberation had preceded it. Sarastro's gesture in untying Pamina's veil is therefore of primordial importance in the action.

No. 19 / TRIO: Tamino, Pamina, Sarastro

Not dwelling upon Tamino's seeming coldness, Pamina voices her fears of the dangers that he is to face. Supported by Sarastro, Tamino answers that the gods will protect him. Sarastro announces that the hour has arrived. And Tamino, this time supported by Pamina, declares himself ready. Farewells.

Musically, this piece is rich in symbolic touches. In its first section, Pamina stands alone facing the Sarastro-Tamino combination, their good relationship being indicated by the frequent parallelisms in thirds. In the second section, the musical disposition is wholly different: Pamina is associated with Tamino, and it is to their *duo concertante* that Sarastro addresses his words: *"Die Stunde schlägt"* (The hour strikes).

The first section—solos and duos, T to SD—opposes Pamina, eager to learn whether she will see her beloved again (the gracious curve of the major phrases does not accord very well with the feeling expressed), to the Sarastro-Tamino combination; without answering her directly, they at least reassure her about Tamino's fidelity. The sense of this section is well established by the tonality of E-flat major in which it ends.

"*Der Götter Wille mag geschehen*" (May the gods' will be done), Tamino says, accompanied by Sarastro: "*Ihr Wink soll mir* $\begin{cases} mir \\ ihm \end{cases}$ *Gesetze sein!*" (Their bidding shall be $\begin{cases} my \\ his \end{cases}$ law!). The phrase repeats almost literally the second theme in E major of the Clarinet Quintet (K.581) composed two years earlier for a lodge brother, Anton Stadler. Is there some allusion here to which we have lost the key? One is the more inclined to think so because the first theme of the Quintet is not unlike another religious piece in *Die Zauberflöte*, the March of the Priests that opens Act II (No. 9). Be that as it may, the relationship of the two men is marked strongly by the fact that they speak simultaneously, frequently in thirds: in that way we are informed clearly that Tamino's love is an invincible reality, but is nonetheless subordinate to his internal progress, symbolized by the initiatory trials.

A uniform accompaniment formula—violas, bassoons, and cellos—supports this dialogue: Mozart first had composed it more tritely, for violins alone. The difference is remarkable: from a simple filler in current usage, he makes a personalized pattern, the insistent repetition of which, cast into relief by register inversions, summons up the inexorable fatality of the imminent sacrifice: "*Die Stunde schlägt*," Sarastro repeats throughout the second section.

In that second section (trio, SD to T), Tamino is no longer associated with Sarastro, but with Pamina. "The hour strikes," the Master says over a long, harmonically moving chromatic progression; that warning at once brings together the two young people, who, forgetting the rule of silence (for the purposes of the libretto, the librettist forgets it with them), bid each other a tender farewell punctuated by *twelve* imposing chords that fall like the twelve strokes of the clock. Five chords form the final cadence.

The five chords are easy to understand. The twelve strokes

also are very significant: the initiation cannot begin without the "opening of the labors," which cannot take place without the symbolic proclamation: "It is noon." That is the hour for which Pamina has been longing since her first meeting with Papageno (*cf.* p. 208).*

A certain likeness can be detected between the beginning of this piece and that of the Queen of the Night's vengeance aria: what is being prepared for here is in effect the accomplishment of her prediction: Pamina will *"nimmer mehr"* be her daughter. The Queen was angry (the phrase was in the minor); here the subject is one for rejoicing (it is in the major).

No. 19a / SPOKEN SCENE:
Papageno's Trials by Fire and Earth

Like Papageno's trial by Water, these trials are dealt with as an interlude. Once everyone has left and the stage remains empty, one hears from outside the voice of Papageno, forgotten during the trio: he is calling Tamino. He enters and goes toward the portal through which Tamino has been led away. But a voice from inside cries out *"Zurück!"* (Go back!),

---

* At least if the twelve strokes do not, on the contrary, represent the midnight of the termination of the labors, the one at which, Freemasonry having completed its mission, will open the Age of Gold symbolized by the ordination of the Tamino-Pamina couple. That is perhaps what is to be deduced from the verses of Zacharias Werner, initiated in 1792, in his poem *"An ein Volk"*:

> Ich sehe Weisheit, Schönheit, Macht
> In ewig unzertrenntem Bunde
> Schon tönet mir die Feierstunde
> Der höchsten Mitternacht.
> (I see wisdom, beauty, might
> In an imperishable fellowship.
> Already sounds for me the hour of celebration
> Of the supreme midnight.)

The "supreme midnight," Louis Guinet comments, "is when Jesus will be born here below for the last time, when men will celebrate their last Christmas, the midnight when the bells will sound the beginning of the Kingdom of God" (*Zacharias Werner et l'ésotérisme maçonnique*, Caen, Caron, 1961, p. 69. See also note 30 in the same work, p. 71).

as earlier it had cried out to Tamino. Thunder, a brutal chord in the orchestra (not notated in the score). A flame bursts forth and drives back the poor man, who retreats in terror toward the portal through which he entered. The same result: *"Zurück!"* Thunder, orchestra, and flames. Collapsing, Papageno comically bursts into tears.

His trial by Earth follows immediately, cryptically announced by the Speaker, who, carrying his luminous pyramid, comes on stage as soon as the Birdcatcher displays his cowardice. *"Du hättest verdient, auf immer in finsteren Klüften der Erde zu wandern"* (You deserve to end your days in the depths of the Earth), he says. Papageno certainly is incapable of understanding what that means.

Scarcely has the Speaker gone, leaving the candidate alone despite himself, when an immense glass filled with wine rises from the Earth. More sensitive to the allure of the "divine juice" than to its latent symbolism, as I mentioned on p. 155, Papageno drinks delightedly, and at once begins to ramble sweetly on. He grasps his glockenspiel without realizing that he is thus activating an instrument of the Earth, as Tamino with his flute had activated an instrument of the Air—and begins to sing and play, demanding the Papagena whom the wine fumes make appear more and more desirable to him.

No. 20 / PAPAGENO'S COUPLETS
WITH GLOCKENSPIEL

Accompanied throughout by the crystalline tintinnabulation of the magic bells mixed with the orchestra, their variations increasing from one strophe to the next, *"Ein Mädchen oder Weibchen"* is a charming aria in couplets, in the same vein as Papageno's song in Act I. Its first phrase was derived in direct line from a popular song, the first-known state of which appeared in 1590 as adapted for religious use in a chorale by Antonio Scandello:[5]

Er rett dein ar-mes Le- ben Nimmt dich in sei- nen Schutz, etc.

The air was especially popular from 1780 to 1795: Christian Friedrich Schubart presented it in 1782 as a Swabian song under the curiously coincidental title *"Lied eines Vogelstellers"* (Song of a Birdcatcher); in 1786, Christoph Rheineck, a composer of songs, copied the air into a collection of songs.[6] Less than a year after *Die Zauberflöte*, at Paris— where the Revolution blocked recognition of Mozart's work —one of the popular airs was the *"Rondeau des Visitandines,"* from the *opéra-comique Les Visitandines* composed by François Devienne and first performed on July 7, 1792.* That *rondeau* begins as follows:

En-fant chéri des Da - mes, je fus en tout pa - ys Fort

bien avec les fem - mes, Mal a - vec les ma - ris

The relationship of the two is obvious: if one merely dots the sixteenth-notes of Devienne's air, as was normally done, they become identical in places.

---

* This *opéra-comique* was clearly very disrespectful toward the nuns it dealt with: the time demanded that. By a curious coincidence, there figured in the *Zauberflöte* exposition organized in 1967 by Roger Cotte the original of an anonymous eighteenth-century poem, parodistic and somewhat bawdy, describing in equivocal terms a Masonic initiation of Adoption, fantasized but well documented, which occurred in the same Visitandine convent in which this *"rondeau"* in turn was unknowingly to reproduce one of the most celebrated arias of the Masonic *opéra-comique par excellence, Die Zauberflöte*.

In his aria, Papageno naturally sighs after the woman of his dreams, "*ein Mädchen oder Weibchen*," whom in passing he calls "*Täubchen*" (little dove). Two sections, one in binary rhythm and restated as a refrain with the same words, the other in ternary rhythm, three couplets with different words to the same music. The only musical change from one couplet to another is in the part for glockenspiel, which increases its variations each time; the rest of the orchestra does not change.

No. 20a / SPOKEN SCENE:
Papagena Takes Part in Papageno's Trial by Earth

Like Tamino's flute bringing Pamina to him, Papageno's glockenspiel brings him the little old woman who had made such curious advances to him during the trial by Water. Now those advances become a formal declaration, which Papageno receives without enthusiasm. But when the old woman assures him that the only choice he has is to grant her his love or remain in this prison, with nothing but water to drink, he resigns himself to the situation; saying that he is ready to love her (while awaiting something better, he adds in an aside).

In true fairy-tale manner, his declaration instantly transforms the ugly little old woman into a resplendent young girl dressed exactly like Papageno—who, stuttering in ecstasy, at once recognizes her as his Papagena.

Alas! at the moment when he is about to embrace her, the Speaker appears and interrupts (Plate 19): "*Fort mit dir, junges Weib! Er ist deiner noch nicht würdig! Zurück! sag' ich*" (Away with you, young woman! He is not yet worthy of you! Away with you! I say). Papageno protests: "*Eh' ich mich zurückziehe, soll die Erde mich verschlingen*" (I won't go away even if the Earth should open up and swallow me). Naturally, the Earth opens and he disappears.*

* The French translation by Prod'homme and Kienlin specifies (p. 52): "He

The explanation of the scene lies in a detail of the rubric which is easily overlooked: the little old woman enters dancing and striking the earth with her staff. In that way, she partakes with her future mate in the consecration of the Earth. For the rest, see pp. 155 and 157.

Sixth Scene

AN EXIGUOUS GARDEN

No. 21 / FINALE

The long finale now begins: it is made up of five linked episodes grouped in four scenes with three different settings. No further pause occurs in the music.

A. Pamina's Trial by Air

We have considered (pp. 150-1) the significance of this very mysterious scene, which cannot be explained in terms of its apparent meaning, as nothing has been told us to justify Pamina's being so distracted after having said farewell to Tamino with confidence and hope—to Sarastro's encouraging *"Wir sehn uns wieder"* (We shall meet again), punctuated by the lovers' repeated *"Lebewohl."*

The E-flat major tonality, the *sotto voce* sonority of the wind instruments, the religious-canticle style, with its series of sixths and its characteristic cadences—all of that suddenly plunges us back into the climate of the big initiatory scenes that we have forgotten somewhat. The beginning of this second finale is closely analogous to that of the first one. Here too the prelude ends on a march rhythm resembling that of the entrance and duet of the priests (No. 11).

---

bounds up out of the hole and disappears to the left." Nothing of that appears in the original text.

The Three Boys come and go in the background. Repeating the prelude in trio, they announce that soon "the sun will shine with all its fire to herald the morning."

After the hymn, the syncopations in the orchestra take us back to Pamina's distress. Falling to the relative minor, the Three Boys evoke her sorrow: she is beside herself (expressive figure of the augmented second in the doublebasses after the word *"Leiden"* [sorrows]), and they pity her fate (no less expressive chromatic descents by the doublebasses). Ah, if only her lover were present! (the Neapolitan sixth of regret). But here she is—they will hide and watch her (increased activity in the doublebasses).

Pamina enters. She is holding a dagger (is it the one that her mother gave her to kill Sarastro? the text does not say) which she is on the verge of turning against herself. In a monologue punctuated by asides from the Boys, she blames her mother for having cursed her and thus caused this loss— and prepares to rejoin her beloved by dying. The scene is dramatic, with its very free recitative, halfway between arioso and aria; its wide, disorderly vocal motions; its expressive orchestral syncopations. When Pamina speaks of *"Liebes-gram"* (love's grief), a stiff string rhythm rages on the re-proachful diminished seventh.

The Three Boys reveal their presence and try three times to dissuade Pamina, who does not heed them. *"Ha, des Jammers Mass ist voll!"* (Ah, the cup of sorrow is full!), she cries on a chromatic descent: *"Falscher Jüngling, lebe wohl!/ Sieh, Pamina stirbt durch dich"* (False youth, fare thee well! See, Pamina dies for you)—a chromatic ascent in the orchestra, interspersed with alternate comments by Pamina and the silences of her sobbing (even the name *"Pamina"* is cut in two). She is about to stab herself.

The Three Boys stop her in time, and the arresting entry of

the horns introduces the sonority of the Masonic winds in the symbolic key of E-flat major—not heard since Pamina's entrance—and makes clear the meaning of their intervention. They assure her that her lover loves no one but her, and in turn would perish if he were to see her in her present condition. The series of sixths in the violins and the doubling of the Boys' notes by the characteristic woodwinds give their remarks oracular meaning.

Pamina cries: *"Was? Er fühlte Gegenliebe,/ Und verbarg mir seine Triebe,/ Wandte sein Gesicht von mir?/ Warum sprach er nicht mit mir?"* (What? He returned my love and kept it hidden from me? Why did he turn his face from me? Why did he not speak to me?). The Three Boys answer: *"Dieses müssen wir verschweigen"* (We must not reveal the reason), *"Doch wir wollen dir ihn zeigen,/ Und du wirst mit Staunen sehen,/ Dass er dir sein Herz geweiht"* (But we will lead you to him, and you will see that his heart is devoted to you). *"Führt mich hin, ich möcht' ihn sehn!"* (Take me there, I must see him!). (This last phrase, sung three times, recalls almost exactly the one with which, in No. 19, Pamina expressed the complementary idea: *"Soll ich dich, Teurer, nicht mehr sehn?"* [Shall I never see you again, my dearest?]). The triple statement of *"Ich möcht ihn sehn"* in the key of E-flat major is not a banal operatic repetition: its insistence well indicates Pamina's firm resolution.

The action of the scene stops there: the quartet ends with the singers stepping out of their roles and, in E-flat major, addressing the moral to the audience: *"Zwei Herzen, die vor Liebe brennen,/ Kann Menschenohnmacht niemals trennen./ Verloren ist der Feinde Müh',/ Die Götter selber schützen sie"* (No mortal power can separate two hearts united in love. Every enemy threatens them in vain, for they are protected by the gods themselves). These last words are treated solemnly, avoiding the syllabic manner of the earlier moralizings: Pamina's soprano voice dominates the ensemble, culminates in a long-held high B flat on the word *"Götter,"* and then curves sweetly through a caressing descent of almost two octaves to express the protection of *"schützen sie,"* which is repeated insistently. The orchestral postlude ends, in an affirmative cadential rhythm, on three unambiguously stated E-flat major chords.

Seventh Scene

B. Tamino's and Pamina's Trials by Fire and Water

The symbolism of this magnificent scene has been discussed at length (pp. 117, 142), but there is no less to say about the music than about the libretto.

(a) Prelude

The scene opens in C minor, with the three ritual beats. It is orchestrated for strings and trombones, but the strings are used only to reinforce the sonority: the trombones create the religious and oracular character. In response, the woodwinds sketch a sort of religious march in the style of the hymns in parallel sixths (*fauxbourdon*).

Note that, despite the care taken by Mozart not to sound the fundamental and the ninth simultaneously, the chord opening the second period, written as a diminished seventh, is heard as a ninth, a rare occurrence with Mozart.

The terminal reprise DT is necessitated by the TD structure of the first period. The symmetry could have been banal, but an un- obtrusive interior counter-line for the cellos prevents that: the orchestration is masterly.

Despite the apparent simplicity of these six measures, they are full of meaning, and are not unrelated to the *Maurerische Trauermusik* (K.477).* Beyond the obvious significance of their tonality, rhythm, harmony, and orchestration, they warn us that what we are about to see on the stage is to be understood symbolically. Unlike the common procedure, the music eschews all descriptive comment, which would have been easy to make and must have been tempting for the evocation of Fire and Water (we are very far from the final moments of *Die Walküre*). The descriptive aspect was entrusted entirely to the stage manager, who was charged with evoking it in sound without "respect" for the music, which he probably had to cover during the original presentation: one "hears," the rubric specifies, the roaring of water and the spitting of flames. A machinist's sound effects: but the orchestra, unlike the décor, applies itself entirely to the inner meaning. Cascade and volcano are only images. If man really confronts danger, it is not during a few minutes of his "trial," but throughout his existence, when such dangers are less harmless than in the good Schikaneder's terrifying stage effects.

(b) Fugato and Chorale of the Men in Armor

After that short, packed introduction, the scene properly speaking starts with a sort of canonic fugato in staccatos in fours; in it has been found the theme of the third Kyrie from a *St. Henry Mass* by Heinrich Biber, a Salzburg musician of the generation preceding that of Mozart, who had become

* Which, contrary to what one often reads about it, is not a funeral deploration, for it was composed in July 1785, whereas the two Brothers for whom it was said to have been destined did not die until November. We should probably see it, as Paul Nettl and Roger Cotte[7] have suggested, as initiatory music composed in July for rites of funerary evocation accompanying installation in the rank of Master—and repeated later (after November) during a Lodge ceremony in memory of the two aforementioned Brothers.

familiar with Biber's works in the Cathedral.[8] Was the borrowing intentional? That is very possible, and we shall soon
see the meaning that it might take on.

Here I use the word "fugato" as best fitting the character of
the passage, though all theoreticians will consider it incorrect:
the entries, most often at the octave, do not follow the traditional
scheme. This "fugato" will be developed at length in chords, and
its diatonic theme, soon diluted to a harmonic march, will not be
long in giving rise to a descending chromatic "countersubject"
marked by silences. In this last, one may be surprised to discover,
almost textually, the future subject of the fugue of César Franck's
Prélude, choral et fugue, even including the *stretta* responses that
such a theme would demand imperiously from both composers.
Thus one has the equivalent of an exposition, be it four entries
at the octave, diversely combined with the large, then larger, amplifications of the countersubject: second violins, then first violins
(shortened theme), violas, and finally doublebasses. In the orchestra of the period, the entry of the violas would have risked
sounding too weak: for the sake of sonority, they are doubled by
the cellos—without doublebasses: with the entry of these last,
the cellos again assume their "real role."

On the terminal cadence of that "exposition," the two Men
in Armor begin to read the inscription discussed on p. 143 (it
is not enough to say, as is said too often, that "they sing a
chorale"). This famous passage is completely without prece-
dent in Mozart's works, less because of its technique—which
is related to that of the religious pieces on a liturgical *cantus
firmus* which Mozart worked out during his Italian and Salzburg years (examples: *Jubilate*, K.117, *Benedictus*, K.342) and
took up again in 1785 in the *Maurerische Trauermusik*—
than for the originality of its orchestration and, above all, the
particular use of the *cantus firmus*, clearly expressing an intention that apparently never has been discussed.

In fact, Mozart adapts the text of the inscription—the score
explicitly emphasizes this—to the melody of a Lutheran

chorale: *Ach, Gott, vom Himmel sieh' darein*. The number of syllables does not fit; he solves that problem by compromise, changing the value of the uniform half-notes of the model as required. Although this somewhat distorts the chorale, the correct musical text is sounded by the winds (*cf.* illustration, p. 144).

Except for those value-changes, the quotation of the chorale conforms to the traditional melody, though the B-natural on the word "*himmelan*" is sensitized by tonal antimodalism. The original stops at the penultimate phrase ("*im Stande sein*"); Mozart added a final phrase ("*sich den Mysterien*") for two reasons: because the original is not long enough for the text being adapted to it; then musically because the chorale is nontonal in conception and therefore lacks the tonal conclusion felt necessary at the time of *Die Zauberflöte*. That final phrase does not follow well what has just preceded it: it breaks the regular procession of half-notes (altered or not), and the Neapolitan sixth—doubtless introduced out of reverence for the name of Isis, to which it corresponds—frankly is not in the same style. Mozart was personally too remote from it to be able to imitate it.

When examining this passage during the explanation of the trial (pp. 144-5), we posed two questions: "Why a chorale? Why this one?" We proposed an answer to the second question; we still must try to answer the first. Mozart was both a Catholic and a Freemason, but he seems to have had no connection with the reformed religion,* which had much less influence in Austria than in Germany. The chorale belonged specifically to the Protestant cult. So, once again, why a chorale?

Two answers can be suggested, I believe. One is practical: having had the idea of associating Terrasson's text with Psalm XI for the reasons already advanced, Mozart could not find in the Catholic liturgy any specific timbre adaptable, simply

---

* We may even wonder how he came to know its repertoire. Paul Tinel, replying to that question, pointed out to me that this particular chorale figured as an example in the treatise on composition by Johann Philipp Kirnberger, with which Mozart certainly must have been familiar.

as music, to the text of that Psalm. In the Church, the Psalms are sung in timbres of psalmody which vary from one feast to another but are identical for whatever Psalms may be selected.* On the contrary, reformed usage, having adapted each Psalm to a melodically independent chorale, made the musical quotation clear in reference to it.

The second answer is more risky, and I advance it tentatively. Freemasonry officially admitted (and in numerous rites still admits) belief in God, the "Great Architect of the Universe"; but it refused to support any single religion,† venerating equally as "books of the Holy Law" the Bible, the Koran, the Vedas, and holy books of other religions. If one considers that this *reformed* chorale is a literal translation of a verse from a *Hebrew* Psalm and is developed by adaptation to an ancient text of a *pagan* religion (whether or not it is authentic is unimportant) on the orchestral base of a Kyrie by a Salzburg *Catholic Kapellmeister*, one will form an idea of the extraordinary attempt at synthesis which, long before the ecumenism of the second half of the twentieth century, Mozart's admirable music illustrates, thus representing, consciously or unconsciously, an idea dear to Freemasonry: the union of the cults and dogmas beyond their particularisms, in a sort of philosophic super-religion, which Masonry tried to be.

Equally remarkable in this scene, as we have already noted, is its orchestration, both instrumental and vocal. The two men

---

* The single exception is the Psalm *In exitu Israel*, given a special tone called the *tonus peregrinus*, which enabled the Reformed Church to adapt a chorale to it and Bach to quote the Psalm instrumentally in the *Suscepit Israel* of his *Magnificat* in a manner comprehensible both to Protestants (because of the chorale) and to Catholics (because of the Psalm-tone).

† "A Mason is obliged, by his membership, to obey the Moral Law, and if he understands the Profession well, he will never be either a stupid atheist or an irreligious libertine. But . . . it is now considered more expedient to bind them only to that Religion on which all men are agreed, leaving to each one his own opinions—that is to say, to be good men and loyal . . . whatever may be the denominations or confessions that help to differentiate them" (*Anderson's Constitutions*, in Palou, p. 315).

—tenor and bass—chant the chorale in parallel octaves; flutes, oboes, and bassoons set it forth over four octaves (in half-notes, which is to say in the authentic version, without the changes necessitated by the syllables of the words); two trombones, in unison with the two singers, emphasize it in quarter-notes followed by silences, in a way that accentuates the attacks and distinguishes, in the singing, between the "real notes" of the borrowed chorale and those which have been changed out of necessity. All that above the "animated background" of the strings as they develop, most often staccato, the subject and countersubject of their fugato.

(c) Tamino's Determination (F minor, SD of the Preceding Chorale)

"*Mich schreckt kein Tod*" (No fear of death can terrify me), Tamino cries, "*als Mann* [always *Mann*, not *Mensch*] *zu handeln*" (into not acting like a man); "*Den Weg der Tugend fortzuwandeln*" (and following the road of virtue). An ardent vocal phrase rising progressively to the word "*Tugend*" (virtue) and a simple formula of emphasis by the strings.

Then Tamino gives the decisive order: "*Schliesst mir die Schreckenspforten auf*" (Open the Gates of Terror to me [descriptive string tremolo for the "*Schreckenspforten*"]); "*Ich wage froh den kühnen Lauf!*" (I shall risk the dangerous journey joyfully). (In fact, the voice undulates joyfully against the orchestral background of a peremptory cadence on the Neapolitan sixth.) And he starts toward the Gates.

(d) Pamina Demands to Join Him (D-flat major to A-flat major)

Now we hear a voice from outside: "*Tamino, halt! Ich muss dich sehn!*" (Tamino, wait! I must see you!). The phrase seems to prolong Tamino's, of which it is in a sense the retrograde. "*Was hör ich?*" (What do I hear?), Tamino asks, to gentle syncopations by the strings. *"Paminens Stimme?"* (Pamina's voice?). The Men in Armor reply affirmatively. Tamino's joy, echoed by his guardians, leads to its expression in trio: *"Nun trennet uns kein Schicksal mehr,/ Wenn auch der Tod beschieden wär!"* (Now no fate can separate us [them], even if death should await us [them] here).

But Tamino is bothered by scruples: *"Ist mir erlaubt, mit ihr zu sprechen?"* (Am I allowed to speak with her?), he asks in a voice broken by emotion and again accompanied by orchestral syncopations. Again the guardians reply affirmatively, and again joy is expressed in trio: *"Welch' Glück, wenn wir uns wiederseh'n,/ Froh Hand in Hand in Tempel geh'n!"* (What joy for us [them] to see each other again and enter the Temple hand in hand).

(e) Moral in Trio: Tamino and the Men in Armor (A-flat major)

"Ein Weib, das Nacht und Tod nicht scheut,/ Ist würdig und wird eingeweiht" (A woman who fears neither Night nor Death is worthy and deserves initiation). We noted earlier (p. 152) the importance of this sentence to the overall evolution of the libretto. Starting off within the framework of the preceding trio, Tamino's voice abandons the voices of his guardians in the background and returns, on *"Ist würdig,"* to the homophonic style of the morals sung at the ends of earlier sections.

A short transition by the strings without doublebasses appears to lead from the A-flat major of the trio to its relative, F minor.

(f) Pamina Rejoins Tamino, and with Him Prepares for the Trials (F major)

The formulas of the orchestral transition seem, as we just noted, to be leading toward F minor. But a gate opens; Pamina

enters and falls into Tamino's arms. With extraordinarily il-
luminating effect, it is in the major rather than the expected
minor that the ecstatic song of love blooms softly: *"Tamino
mein! . . . Pamina mein! . . ."*—the earliest of three famous reunions, foreshadowing the *"Tristan! . . . Isolde! . . .
Geliebter!"* and the *"Pelléas! . . . Mélisande! Est-ce toi,
Mélisande?"* each with its own illumination, which complete
the trilogy thus begun by the masterly hand of Mozart. Further, it is perhaps no accident that the moment of this re-
encounter, when for the first time Tamino sees the uncovered
features of his beloved, is almost a repetition of the melodic
design of the opening phrase of the portrait aria (No. 3):
"Dies Bildnis ist bezaubernd schön." The reality has not be-
lied the depiction. Nor, probably, is it accidental that the *"O
welch' ein Glück"*—which the lovers sing one after the other
—echoes the *"Ich glaub' es kaum"* of their first meeting.[9]
"Hier sind die Schreckenspforten" (Here are the Gates of Terror), Tamino says, with an inflection shaded toward the flats
of the subdominant (B flat). *"Die Not und Tod mir dräu'n!"*
(That threaten me with danger and death!). Sweetly and
firmly, Pamina raises the tonality toward F major: *"Ich werde
aller Orten/ An deiner Seite sein;/ Ich selber führe dich,/
Die Liebe leitet mich!"* (I want always to be at your side; I
myself will follow you; love leads me on!)—a sustained ascent,
step by step, to high A). *"Sie mag den Weg mit Rosen streu'n"*
(Love will strew our way with Roses [we have noted the sym-
bolism]), *"Weil Rosen stets bei Dornen sein"* (For where
there are thorns there always are roses).

Then Pamina takes Tamino's hand (see pp. 123, 142, and
151 for explication of this) and, on the arpeggio of majesty
repeated from her *"Tamino mein!"* orders him to play on his
magic flute (*ibid.*), which will guide them through their trials.
As earlier, when support of the friendly hand was evoked for
entry into the Temple (No. 8) and in Sarastro's aria (No. 15),

the voice is "supported" by a unison suggestive of the protection (*"sie schütze uns"*) that it will provide. But note the
discretion of Mozart: not wanting an overfacile image here,
he entrusted its expression not to the flute, but to the oboe.

It is here that Pamina reveals the real origin of that enchanted flute, which her father—Sarastro's predecessor as Master of Wisdom (see p. 123) magically carved from a millenary
oak during a storm. A fully descriptive musical narration, in
which two brief tremolo sforzandos represent the storm.

The sequence concludes with an admirable quartet (Pamina, Tamino, the two Men in Armor), which Wagner
seems to have remembered well while composing the quintet
in *Die Meistersinger: "Wir wandeln durch des Tones Macht/
Froh durch des Todes düstre Nacht"* (By the power of music
we travel joyfully through Death's dark night).

"The Gates," the rubric says, "open before them. Tamino
and Pamina advance amid the crackling of fire, the roaring of
wind, and at moments the muffled sound of thunder and the
murmuring of water." All of that (which will continue during
the flute-playing to follow) to a very simple instrumental accompaniment without imitative element: the sound effects
are left to the stage machinist. A simple transitional chord introduces the modulation toward the C major of the trial
properly speaking, to the sound of the magic flute.

(g) Tamino and Pamina Undergo the
Trials by Fire and Water (C major)

Fire and Water, as we know, are the two symbols of Man and
Woman. Henceforward, united in the indissoluble Couple,
the Man and the Woman must be dealt with together and
without distinction as they pass their trials together.

The music is impressive in its simplicity. Barely sustained
by a few rare religious brass chords immediately answered by

a kettledrum sounded softly like a reverberating echo, the magic flute plays a solemn march from which virtuosity is excluded. Meanwhile, the gates into the mountain of fire open and then close behind the couple. We do not witness the trials—which thus remain secret—and nothing in the music illustrates them: imperturbable, the magic flute pursues its lonely march. Pamina and Tamino return very quickly (a little too soon even in view of theatrical convention); they embrace, and stop in midstage. Now the flute falls silent and the orchestra resumes its role.

In parallel thirds and sixths (the traditional expression of concord and union), still in C major, the now indissoluble Couple proclaims its victory over Fire thanks to the music of the magic flute. May it, they say, protect them equally during the trial by Water.

The trial by Water is presented similarly—a simple musical repetition of the flute's march, unchanged. Perhaps a symbol of the new equality of the Man and the Woman in the Perfect Couple, putting finis to the temporary inferiority of Woman. Once the trial has been passed, the same victory song, slightly abridged. *"Ihr Götter, welch' ein Augenblick!/ Gewähret ist uns Isis Glück!"* (You Gods, what a moment! Isis' joy is granted to us!).

(h) Chorus of Priests Announcing the Victorious Conclusion of the Trials (C major)

A chant of triumph in traditional style, with fanfare arpeggios in honor of the "Noble Couple" (*"du edles Paar"*), which is now invited to enter the Temple and be consecrated to Isis.

A curious coincidence: the phrase *"der Isis Weihe ist nun dein,"* like an analogous chorus in Haydn's *Die Schöpfung,* differs by only a few notes from the beginning of the *Marseillaise,* which Rouget de Lisle was to compose the next year, very probably without being familiar with *Die Zauberflöte.** But that is also true—with the syllabic amplification that draws it close to the *Marseillaise*—of the Queen of the Night's *"So bist du meine Tochter nimmer mehr"* and of the *"sie ist vollbracht"* of the "heroic act" of the Three Ladies in Act I. That we are dealing, after all, with a very banal triumphal formula does not suffice to explain the link of meaning among the three fragments. Nor that the words *"Heil sei euch, Geweihten"* so much resemble the prelude to the trial.

Eighth Scene

AN EXIGUOUS GARDEN

C. Papageno's and Papagena's Trial by Air;
   the Outcome for These Two Characters

The matter of the unhappy Papageno has been forgotten during the preceding scenes. Having failed in all his trials, he will, in the words of the Speaker, have "to end his days in the bowels of the earth in a dark pit." But he could not, as a comic character, be left to so tragic a fate. Also, we have been told that the gods will grant him grace. He will have to be content not to experience the joys of the Initiates, which is all the same to him: he never asked to undergo these damned trials, but only to find a companion befitting his amiable mediocrity. Now that Tamino has his Pamina, Papageno must win his

---

* And probably also without knowing Mozart's Piano Concerto K.503, written five years before, but then unpublished, in which the same motive appears, as it occurs several times in the sketches for the *Marseillaise*. I have had occasion to point out that the resemblance occurs not in the initial version of the hymn, but in the version reshaped by Gossec, so that if there was influence, it is to Gossec that we must look for it, not to Rouget de Lisle (*"La Marseillaise, ses transformations,"* in *Actes du 99ᵉ Congrès des Sociétés savantes,* Lyon, 1964, p. 13). It is different in the case of Haydn, who could have known the *Marseillaise* in Gossec's version.

Papagena. Just as Tamino played on his magic flute, Papageno must make use of his magic glockenspiel. And as Tamino passed his final trials, Papageno must do the same. Such symmetry was a theatrical convention of the period.

In No. 20, the Speaker foretold that Papageno would see Papagena again when he was fit for her—an oblique way of telling us that Papageno had not yet completed his trials. Let us list them: he experienced the preliminary swoon in No. 12; he went (very badly) through the trial by Water in No. 15A; that by Fire in No. 19A; that by Earth in Nos. 19A and 20. What remains ahead of him is the trial by Air. The reappearance of the Three Boys in their flying machine tells us that we are about to witness that last trial.

(a) *Papageno Weeps for His Papagena and Wishes to Hang Himself*

The light key of G major and a happy 6/8 rhythm summon us back, in contrast, to the climate of the Birdcatcher's scenes, without regard for his despair, which remains a comic emotion.

As with the other "servant arias" in the score, Papageno's aria is of strophic cut; but it differs from its predecessors: four different stanzas in couplets followed by a common refrain (in the music, not in the text). For the fourth stanza, a trio for the Three Boys replaces the refrain.

The prelude introduces the opening call: *"Papagena!"* of the first couplet. It is followed by a five-note call on the syrinx (accessory of Air), which accompanies its orchestral cadence (it is the veritable Leitmotiv) and by the first singing of the refrain.

The first two stanzas are all but identical. In the first, Papageno, accompanied by an almost obstinate five-note figure, grieves over the loss of his "little dove" and makes his *mea culpa*: his excessive babbling has done him no good (short melancholy inflection on the word *"Unglück"* [unhappiness]).

In the second, he remembers the magic wine that aroused his desires, and excites himself by recalling "*das schöne Weibchen.*"

The more developed third stanza shows Papageno ready to hang himself—Mozart paradoxically creates tormented music without abandoning the tone of light comedy: orchestral somersaults, numerous modulations, light grazings of the minor. A ravishing violin interpolation, doubling the voice with a different phrase (on the words "*Kind zubandelst*"), introduces something like a reminiscence of the marvelous duet of the two women in *Le Nozze di Figaro*. Note also the significant accompaniment (after "*Nun, ich warte noch*") in persistent formulas of five violin notes. Time is also handled strikingly: when the stanza has equaled the length of the two preceding stanzas, the listener feels that its "time" has been filled, and awaits the refrain. But it does not come: the orchestra tarries, foolishly jabbering on the dominant chord of the expected key: "Nobody comes," Papageno says (he has been waiting for Marius's famous "Stop me"); "all is silence." And only then does the refrain recur. Osmin's lines at the end of *Die Entführung aus dem Serail* had made use of a similar procedure.

The fourth stanza shows Papageno ready to hang himself, but not without first gaining a few instants on his own terms. He counts: "One, two, three . . ." and waits for the sign from Heaven which will stop him. As it does not come, he takes his syrinx and plays his call three times. This whole scene of "threes"—does it have a symbolic background like that of the "five" rhythm of the orchestra? Possibly, but not certainly. A comic effect is created by the absence, in the orchestra, of the expected cadence (which the prelude has suggested to us); its place is taken by a fermata. Decidedly, the miracle-producing machine is out of order. With fitting bitterness, Papageno says: "*Gute Nacht, du falsche Welt!*" (Good night, false world!). He climbs a knoll and, without knowing that he is about to make the essential gesture of his remaining trial, prepares to leap off into space. At once—naturally—his intention produces the sought-for miracle: the Three Boys appear on their flying machine to stop him, interrupting the aria. The last stanza thus is deprived of its refrain, which is replaced by the trio of the Three Boys.

(b) The Three Boys Stop Papageno and Advise Him to Play on His Glockenspiel

The irruption of the savior-Boys transforms the light key of G major into the more serious one of C major. Papageno answers —and returns to G major! He wants to see his *Mädchen* again. The Boys, in C major: "*So lasse deine Glöckchen klingen*" (Then let your bells ring). "*Ich Narr vergass der Zauberdinge!*" (How stupid I was to forget the magic bells!), Papageno says, suddenly leaping to C major. And happily, now in that key, he looks around for his magic instrument, the counterpart of the flute at the time of Tamino's final trial.

(c) Playing of the Glockenspiel; Papagena's Reappearance

Suddenly the glockenspiel is heard alone, without orchestra, for eight measures as it weaves fantastic arpeggios around a melody of popular character. Doubtless it was here that Mozart played on Schikaneder-Papageno the joke described on p. 125; the details of that joke prove that in performance, so as to give the illusion that Papageno is playing the glockenspiel himself, it should be played on stage, or at least in the wings—rather than, as most often today, in the orchestra pit. In gay dialogue with the crystalline tintinnabulations of his magic bells, Papageno—as earlier, when he faced Monostatos —encourages his sounding talisman and begs it to bring him his "*Mädchen*," his "*Weibchen*." Meanwhile, the Boys have started toward their flying machine. *"Nun, Papageno, sieh dich um!"* (Now, Papageno, look over here!). And from the chariot descends the petite Papagena, all befeathered.

Note that the "woman-bird," who has arrived by Air and who is the counterpart of the Birdcatcher, from whom even her name is taken, has undergone the baptism by Water (feminine sign) and that of Earth—which, refreshed by the wine spilled over it, has given her her graceful appearance— and who just has alighted from the flying machine (sign of Air, which remains hers)—but that, unlike Pamina, she has neither experienced the pre-initiatory swoon nor undergone the masculine trial by Fire, complementary to her sex. Thus the difference between the two couples is established: the one of Perfect Love, uniting hearts and spirits in complete shared initiation, and the other, which—restricted in meaning be- cause it leaves each individual within the exclusivity of his sex—never brings about in the man or the woman much more than the futilities of the feathered folk: an imperfect couple born of the Air-Earth dyad (the glockenspiel), not from the Fire-Water dyad.

(d) Papageno-Papagena Duet

Returning to the G major of his ingenuousness, Papageno looks at his *"Weibchen."* The rubric specifies that during the ritornello, they both indulge in comic miming. The famous stuttering duet, very amusing in its innocence (but we pointed out, p. 108, that this innocence should not be taken too liter- ally), only just succeeds in carrying out the tour de force of remaining interesting during 130 measures without going be- yond the most closely associated cadential chords or modulat- ing within any of its three sections.

First section of the duet, in G major. The initial ritornello an- nounces, in staccato notes representing the chatter of the two turtledoves, a sort of *chansonette*, of which Chopin was reminded involuntarily in his Étude in F major, op. 10, and Charles Lecoq in the renowned "solfeggio lesson" in his *Le Petit Duc*. It is played a second time, accompanied by the hesitant *"pa-pa"*'s of the two lovers as they strive to call one another by name; then a third time, when the syllables accelerate and lead to the much-desired names. Finally, a coda, in which the stuttering of the *"pa-pa"*'s is heard only in the cellos, then in the violas, while the singers speak of their happiness in dialogue and then in a short duet. Another entry in the dossier of the Leitmotivs: the initial motive is almost identical with that of the allegro in C major in the first trio of the Three Ladies (No. 1).

The Central section, in the dominant key (D major), is a duet of more sustained tone. Their present joy is mixed with the hope of producing many little children who will resemble them (when one thinks of the couple's symbolic meaning, the satirical intention of that is obvious). That forecast of an unending multiplication of little Papagenos and Papagenas is commented upon by the orchestra in a whole series of overflowing ascensions: woodwind scales, dotted string arpeggios preceded by the familiar flourish-group, slow diatonic mounting of the double basses—and leads to a *stretto* riot of descendants of both sexes (Papageno claims the *o*'s, Papagena the *a*'s).

Third section: return to G major and the original ambiance (the same ideas). Observe the three measures in which Papagena holds an immense *"viele"* (many) that covers the swarm of little Papagenos and calls out her partner's serried eighth-notes (the same effect inverted a little farther on).

No change of scene. The duet completed and their dénouement reached, the two leave, and the next episode begins.

D. Assault by the Queen of the Night, Her Ladies, and Monostatos; the Outcome for These Five Characters

The Moor and the Queen of the Night, with all her Ladies, rise through trapdoors, all carrying black torches in their hands.

Monostatos, we see, has kept his word: "rejected by the daughter," he has gone "to offer his services to the mother." Thus the Black, who had wandered by error into the Kingdom of Light, has returned to his true homeland. Symbol of treachery and of the terrestrial sign, he will play his role by guiding the Queen of the Black Kingdom through the underground passages of the Temple, which she plans to destroy. But he is also the symbol of vulgar and degraded love—far below Papageno's love, which is naïve and lacking in nobility, but decent. That is why—this is much insisted upon during the scene—if the Queen succeeds in wresting her daughter from Sarastro's kingdom—which is to say from the sublimation of perfect love that will place her above and beyond the imperfect society of women—she will become Monostatos's wife, thus returning to her condition of low femininity.

To attempt that "rescue," the Queen, her entourage, and the traitor, all bearing black torches representing the artificial light of the Night, use the subterranean passageways that befit their nature and are well known by their guide, Monostatos, man of the Earth, as they move secretly toward the Temple.

They will all be swallowed up, after which, on the diminished seventh of the curse, the orchestra will go back opportunely to the rhythm of five notes of the feminine knocking that inaugurated the opera at the beginning of the Overture and accompanied Pamina's first appearance before Sarastro.

The final assault upon the Temple may also clothe another significance: in the context of the rivalry between the sexes, it is the final attempt of the rebellious feminine world to steal men's hegemony; and perhaps, in the more restricted world of Masonic history, of the pretensions of feminine Masonry to attain the fullness of rights and of Wisdom which only the traditional masculine Masonry can possess. The outcome of the adventure tells us clearly what the authors of the libretto thought of such a claim.

A subtle phrase runs throughout this whole C-minor scene. It translates into music the apprehensive march of the conspirators, broken by precautionary stops and sudden dashes toward the next shelter; the whole prelude thus is a genuine mimodrama, as precise in its descriptiveness (very rarely understood by stage directors) as Beckmesser's entrance into Hans Sachs's house after his caning. Monostatos leads the foray, whence the general comic tone of the scene despite its serious meaning. To a question by him, the Queen replies by confirming her promise to him regarding Pamina, and the Ladies serve as witnesses to her oath. At her words *"es ist mein Wille"* (it is my will), a disquieting chromaticism in the double basses comments upon the political seaminess of that promise.

Now we hear distant, unsettling sounds of thunder, as well as echoes of Water and of Fire—the two trials that remove the Couple from the power of the Night. These noises are made *ad hoc* by a machinist, but the animation of the quartet's eighth-notes helps in depicting the anxiety that they arouse in the attackers.

Nevertheless, they prick up their courage and, solemnly invoking the "great Queen of the Night," swear to offer her their vengeance. Scarcely have they uttered those words when the orchestra bursts into a blinding flash that sets loose the diminished seventh of the big terrors, with the maximum orchestration, trombones included. On the stage, "thunder, lightning, tempest." And on that seventh, stressed by the violins, THE FIVE NOTES OF THE FEMININE ORDER, in the rhythm of the beginning of the Overture and of Pamina's first appearance before Sarastro (this allusion, upon which no one has ever commented, is of great importance here). *"Zerschmettert, zernichtet ist unsere Macht"* (Shattered and destroyed is our might), the black quintet cries in an impressive double vocal descent; *"Wir alle gestürzet in ewige Nacht!"* (We are all plunged into eternal night). And when they have disappeared, the orchestra is calmed and cleansed, dissipating the bad taste of the final ritardandos of the strings, and a beautiful, unexpected F-major chord, which will lead us to B flat, marks the return of light. The scene changes: the whole stage is bathed in sunlight.

Final Scene

E. Apotheosis of the Couple

In a dazzling light, "Sarastro sits enthroned at the highest point. On either side of him, Tamino and Pamina, both clothed in sacerdotal vestments. To the sides, near them, Egyptian priests. The Three Boys are bearing flowers"—this last symbol well demonstrates the importance of that truly new idea, the advancement of Woman: like Tamino, Pamina wears "sacerdotal vestments."

In a B-flat major that soon leads into the hieratic E flat, Sarastro announces his victory in a solemn recitative preceded (after a descent in ritardandos, a last echo of the disappearance of the Night) by an ascending violin fanfare: "*Die Strahlen der Sonne vertreiben die Nacht,/ Zernichten der Heuchler erschlichene Macht*" (The Sun's rays have conquered the Night, destroying hypocrites' furtive might [this last word, underlined by a brutal fall of tessitura—a tenth!—recalls the then-contemporary anti-Masonic campaigns covertly referred to by the Three Ladies in the scene of the Earth]). This recitative has been likened to Mozart's Masonic cantata *Dir, Seele des Weltalls*, K.429, of unknown date, which is also a hymn to the Sun in E-flat major.

The chorus, supported by the religious trombones, now begins its final hymn, naturally also in E-flat major. It opens andante with a salutation to the new Initiates in which we again find almost verbatim a quotation from the Masonic *Thamos* (final chorus), which is still another hymn to the

Sun: *"Höchste Gottheit, milde Sonne."* It has been remarked that the same theme occurs at the end of *Le Nozze di Figaro,* where it illustrates the Countess's pardoning of the Count; and the Massins (p. 1015) see it there as an "indisputable Masonic signature" upon *Le Nozze:* "An invitation to universal fraternity in tolerance, the mutual forgetting of injuries, and universal good will." The chorus continues: *"Ihr dranget durch Nacht"* (You have traversed the Night)—the phrase was copied shamelessly by Schwarzendorf-Martini in his renowned song *"Plaisir d'amour"*); *"Dank sei dir, Osiris, dank dir, Isis, gebracht!"* (We offer thanks to you, Osiris, and to you, Isis!).

The final allegro, celebrating, in the dactylic rhythm often used for such pieces, and with the syllabism of the moralities that were meant to be understood, the triumph of the three Masonic Virtues: Strength, Beauty, and Wisdom (*cf.* No. 5E), the pillars of the Temple. A central section, piano, particularly evocative of beauty and wisdom, supplies contrasting repose and clearly recalls—in the way the voices undulate in vocalises against the syllabism of strength—the quartet of Pamina, Tamino, and the Men in Armor. Then the dactylic chorus again takes over and ends the opera with a traditional apotheosis in the symbolic E flat, punctuated by three terminal chords of the quartet.

22

<hr/>

Conclusion

Far from being that "fable pieced together like Harlequin's cloak" which, with complaisant scorn, it is still accused of being, the action of *Die Zauberflöte* is a remarkably constructed symbolic story rigorously developed. In order to see it so, however, we must approach it on its own terms, not with the criteria of Henry Bernstein's theater. If the word "Symbolist" had not acquired so precise a meaning in literary history, we could say that *Die Zauberflöte* is, in its way, as "Symbolist" as *Pelléas et Mélisande*. In both operas, the events represented upon the stage are only images and reflections of an invisible reality that alone supplies the background for the real action. More here than in *Pelléas*, all the logic flows from the linking of symbols, not from a psychology from which all realism has been eliminated. Like Debussy, Mozart applied all the force of his genius to the musical translation of those symbols: his music explores the words and the "hidden words," and is not content until it has used its magic power to the full. *Die Zauberflöte* must "transform the passions of men, fill the

melancholy with joy, turn amorous the misogynist." And because of it, the Man and the Woman, hand in hand, will be
able to face Water and Fire, and thus to attain the illumination of the great syntheses of the Golden Age.

Although the libretto is violently antifeminist in effect, it
nonetheless attacks Woman only in order to exalt her transformation in the mystery of the Couple and so to restore the
ideal of true love which the society of the period scoffed at
so readily; that Ideal Love which we are free to believe that
Constanze's husband must often have sought. So *Die Zauberflöte* is the successor and antidote to *Così fan tutte*. The Masonic justification is evident throughout the libretto, not just
something extra, something somehow tacked on: it is the
raison d'être of the announced transfiguration, the only means
by which the authors believed it could be accomplished—the
reason, finally, why it broke out into a concluding hymn of
universal brotherhood to which the events of 1791 in France
gave extraordinary resonance.

Understood in that way, Mozart's last work ceases to deserve its reputation as a musical masterpiece based upon an
inept libretto. The libretto and the music coalesce into an in-
divisible whole of high inspiration and rare density. For which
reason the libretto's obvious weaknesses of expression are
gladly forgiven. They weigh little against the loftiness of
views toward which the libretto, in concert with the music,
seems to lead us, views that are not common in the lyric repertoire of the eighteenth century—or of any other century.

Eight days after the première of *Die Zauberflöte* (September 30, 1791), Mozart wrote to his wife, as he did almost daily
after she went to take a cure at Baden: "I have this moment
returned from the opera, which was as full as ever. As usual,
the duet '*Mann und Weib*' and Papageno's glockenspiel in
Act I had to be repeated, and also the trio of the Boys in Act

II. But what always gives me the most pleasure is the *silent approval*. You can see how this opera is becoming more and more esteemed." [1]

Mozart wrote another letter to Constanze on returning from the theater the next evening. In it, he says that his brother-in-law Hofer "has given her [Mamma—i.e., Constanze's mother, Frau Weber] the libretto to read," and he proposes to take her to see the opera the next day. "In her case what will probably happen will be that she will *see* the opera, but not *hear* it." * Then he reports that at the performance he just has left, he found himself with some people in a loge. "——[name deleted—it may well have been Leitgeb] applauded *everything* most heartily. But he, the know-all, showed himself to be such a thorough *Bavarian* that I could not remain or I should have had to call him an ass. Unfortunately, I was there just when the second act began, that is, at the solemn scene. He made fun of everything. At first I was patient enough to draw his attention to a few passages. But he laughed at everything. Well, I could stand him no longer. I called him a Papageno and cleared out." †

Our age suffers from the strange infirmity of wanting to consider the libretto as a negligible element in an opera. In the neologism "pure music" there is a latent element of deprecation of "impure music," and that is both unjust and unpleasant.[2] When Mozart tries to guide an acquaintance toward appreciation of his *Zauberflöte*, he draws the man's attention not to a "particular B flat," but to "certain words." Where, in all that, is our inordinate taste for works heard in a language that we do not understand?

* This in advance of Goethe's phrase quoted on p. 7.

† Letter dated October 8–9, 1791. It is also in that letter, and concerning the same performance, that Mozart recounts the joke that he played upon Schikaneder by going into the wings to play the glockenspiel in his own way. That joke may well have been a way of "sublimating" the exasperation aroused in him by the man in the loge.

As concerns *Die Zauberflöte*, the problem has been doubled by protracted incomprehension. The lesson that it is meant to impart is too lofty and too difficult to be learned easily. The Aristarchuses most often have preferred to shrug their shoulders and accuse Mozart of having composed beautiful music to a very naïve story. Perhaps this book has showed that those terms were ill chosen.

And, as Goethe once remarked forcefully and succinctly to all the Papagenos of the succeeding century and a half: "More knowledge is required to understand the value of this libretto than to mock it." [3]

APPENDIXES

1

Letter from Seyfried
to Treitschke
(unsigned, undated)

Very dear friend,

With profound thanks, I return to you the manuscript that you
entrusted to me . . . and in which I have taken great pleasure, re-
juvenating to some extent, and which must surely have historic interest
for every lover of art. Responding to your wish, I again permit myself
the following remarks, of which I can certainly be the guarantor.—The
personal relations of Schikaneder with Mozart—also those, later, with
Zitterbarth—find their origin in a Masonic lodge—not, certainly, in
Born's very famous lodge, which counted among its members the
highest dignitaries of Vienna and the elite among the literary caste
of the epoch,—but simply in one that is called a "chestnut lodge" or
Fressloge [glutton lodge], in which, during the weekly meetings, they
were occupied above all with amusement, with music, and with the
delights of a well-furnished table, as was often recounted to me by
Giesecke, who, with Schikaneder, plundered the *Dschinnistan* of Wieland, taking from it the subjects for several of his operas.—The composition of *Die Zauberflöte* did not really begin until the spring of 1791,
for the reason that Mozart never worked long at the same thing, and in
any case worked very fast. It was above all in Gerl's apartment or in
Schikaneder's garden that he wrote; few sections were composed at the
theater. I myself often was a guest at the same table, and I was present
at many rehearsals in the same salon, or, to speak more exactly, in the
same cabin in the woods. The prompter Haselbeck had to put
Schikaneder's rough prose lines into verse, and a certain number of
passages may very well have been his own invention, such as the verse:
"*Schön Mädchen, jung und fein, Viel weisser noch als Kreide,*" following: "*Aha; Da seh ich Leute! Gewagt, ich geh hinein!*"

The libretto had been completed up to the first finale when the
Leopoldstadt gave "*Die Zauberzither, oder Kasper der Fagottist.*"
Perinet also was inspired by that same Wieland story, but he had followed the original faithfully except for the locales of the action. This
did not fail to trouble our Emmanuel somewhat, but he was not long
in finding a remedy, that of reshaping the plan entirely; and that for

the happiness and good health of the whole work, as without it, it would have been difficult for Mozart to bequeath us, as his swansong, so marvelous a model of poesy and romanticism.—Mozart went to the coronation at Frankfort in order, by means of some concerts, to repair again the holes in his broken-down finances; when, responding to the invitation from the States of Bohemia, he undertook the trip to Prague, the ensembles up to the first finale already were finished—that is to say, the vocal sections, the bass, and the notation of the chief musical motives; it was that score which my friend Hotteberg studied in the interim. When Mozart returned—the 10th or 12th of September—he began to do the instrumentation and to complete the whole with the little pieces that follow; it was only on the 28th that the March of the Priests and the Overture issued from his pen; the latter reached the dress rehearsal in the state of wet manuscript. . . .

[Some details follow about the first performance in Italian at Prague during the winter of 1793, with remarks about its cast.]

On the evening of December 4 [1791], Mozart, in his delirium, thought himself present, at the Wiednertheater, at the performance of *Die Zauberflöte.* He whispered to his wife—and these were almost his last words: "Silence! Silence! Now Hofer is taking her high B-flat";—at that moment his sister-in-law was singing her second aria: *Der Hölle Rache;* with what power she attacked and held the B-flat: *Hört! hört! hört! der Mutter Schwur!*

The second part of *Die Zauberflöte,* "*Das Labyrinth, oder Der Kampf mit den Elementen,*" was composed by Winter all by himself. The opera composed in collaboration with Gallus bore the title: *Babylons Pyramiden.*

2

Anonymous Article in the *Monatsschrift für Theater und Musik,* Vienna, 1857

The Birth of *Die Zauberflöte*[1]

It was on March 7, 1791, at eight o'clock in the morning, that Emmanuel Schikaneder, director of the Theater auf der Wieden, im Freihause, went to see Mozart, who was still in bed, so as to address him in these words: "Friend and Brother, come to my assistance or I am certainly lost!" Still drunk with sleep, Mozart sat up and said: "How can I help you? I am only a poor devil myself."

SCHIKANEDER: I need money. My enterprise is going badly, the Leopoldstadt is killing me!

MOZART (bursting into laughter): If that's what you've come to see me about, Fraternal Brother, you have knocked on the wrong door.

SCHIKANEDER: Not at all! Only you can save me. H—— the wholesaler has promised to lend me 2,000 florins if you write me an opera. With that amount, I'll be able to settle my debts and give my theater a new brilliance such as it has never known. Mozart, save me from ruin, and the world will regard you as the noblest of men. Moreover, I'll pay you very well, and the opera, which will undoubtedly earn great success, will fill your pockets well too. Schikaneder is said to be a frivolous fellow, but ungrateful he certainly is not.

MOZART: Have you a libretto?

SCHIKANEDER: I have one under way. It's a fairy-tale libretto after *Lulu,* from Wieland's *Dschinnistan,* and I flatter myself about its poesy. I'll do the dialogues, but because I'm afraid that the pieces to be sung wouldn't be to your liking at all, I'll leave them to my friend Cantes, who has a marked interest in me and my theater. You can be confident, then. In a few days it will all be finished; I'll give it to you to read. Well, my dear friend—your answer—do you say yes?

MOZART: I don't say yes or no. First I'll have to think it over. You'll have my answer in a few days.

Having once again placed his welfare in Mozart's hands, Schikaneder left. While he was still on the stairs, a bright idea struck him, and without stopping to catch his breath, he ran as fast as his great corpulence would allow him from the Rauhensteingasse to the

Wieden, Kapaunergasse—to the "*Kapäundl*," then still in existence. There lived Frau Gerl, who, with her husband, the basso Gerl, belonged to Schikaneder's troupe. She was not, it was said, without influence upon Mozart. The artful Schikaneder won her over to his cause, and that same evening Mozart went to see Schikaneder on stage and told him: "Well, arrange it so that I'll have your libretto quickly, and in the name of God, I'll write you your opera. If we come up with a fiasco, I'll not be involved at all, as I've never written a fairy-tale opera." About a week later, Mozart had the libretto, which delighted him because it contained really poetic, even romantic, ideas, which Schikaneder, who totally lacked intellectual background, certainly had not developed, but at least he had furnished them. Mozart quickly set to work, but he had to interrupt his composing even before the end of March: his duties called him to Prague to compose *La Clemenza di Tito* on the occasion of the coronation at Frankfort. He finished that in a few weeks, and then returned to Vienna to finish *Die Zauberflöte*. That great work was brought to light half in Mozart's house in the Rauhensteingasse, half in the little garden that Schikaneder rented in the large central courtyard of the Freihaus. Today one can still see that little pavilion—half in ruins, to be sure—[and] the table and chair that Mozart used for composing. During dinner (it was midsummer), which Mozart most often took in company with Schikaneder himself, spirit was never lacking for work, laughter, and drinking champagne. There you have the conditions under which that masterpiece, *Die Zauberflöte*, came to light.

Scarcely had Mozart composed the first pieces of *Die Zauberflöte* when Josef Schuster, one of Schikaneder's actors, went to see Schikaneder to tell him some disagreeable news: quite by accident, he had attended a rehearsal of the fairy-tale opera that the Leopoldstadt theater was mounting, *Kasper der Fagottist, oder Die Zauberzither*, by Perinet, to the music of Wenzel Müller, and he had become sadly certain that Perinet had taken his subject from Wieland's *Lulu* and that the characters, as well as the way the action proceeded, showed a close resemblance to those of *Die Zauberflöte*. There was nothing to do but to alter the section already written and give a new orientation to the opera. Sarastro, who had originally been a tyrant and villain, now took on the lineaments of a noble, wise priest, a friend of humanity; the Queen of the Night was transformed from a Princess of Love and tender mother into a monster, an intriguer, an inhuman woman. The Three Ladies, who were companions of the Night, [and] the Moor— what a happy allegory of the dark fury of evil!—were given her as aides. Thus was born an entirely new work, of which the author himself had had no inkling before. That was how it happened that, on their first appearance, when they save Tamino's life, the Three Ladies indicate the Three Boys who will be his guides, themselves remaining in the service of the Queen, whereas during the course of the opera the Boys become creatures devoted to Sarastro who protect Tamino and Pamina against the Queen's black designs. Schikaneder did not see that inconsistency at all, and the great Mozart, fully conscious of his musical power, paid no attention to it. A large number of pieces composed by Mozart were altered at Schikaneder's request. Papageno's song, which Schikaneder—who had reserved the role for himself—could not sing as it was because of his very limited vocal capabilities—or, rather, because of his total lack of voice—and it had to be kept in extremely simple form—and see how melodious it still is in that form, how exquisitely lovable! Mozart had to change the duet *"Bei Männern, welche Liebe fühlen"* three times. Schikaneder kept on repeating: "Brother, it is very beautiful, but it is too learned for me." Finally, Schikaneder began to hum an air in his cracked voice, and the good Mozart said to him indulgently: "Good, don't worry, that's all you need to do." But it is a shame that Mozart had destroyed his first rough sketches.

Most of the opera was composed then. Mozart worked without respite, Süssmayr, a pupil of Mozart, did more than half of the instrumentation—he was so closely aware of his master's wishes that more than one supplementary piece may be by him (working out preliminary indications by the master, be it understood). The chorus of priests *"Isis und Osiris,"* Papageno's songs, and the second finale were composed on September 12, the March of the Priests and the Overture not until September 28, [when they were] brought still damp to the orchestra rehearsal.

Finally, on September 30, 1791, after many rehearsals, the first performance took place. It is interesting to note that the audience for that *première*, probably surprised, disconcerted by the beauties of the music and the richness of its motives, gave it a welcome totally unrelated to the unprecedented success that the work has had since then. At each performance, the enthusiasm grew, and that musical masterwork was understood and appreciated at its true value, so much so that *Die Zauberflöte* was given sixteen evenings in a row. Mozart personally directed the first three performances; Süssmayr, seated beside him, turned the pages; Henneberg, leader of the orchestra of the Freihaustheater auf der Wieden and organist *"bei den Schotten,"* played the glockenspiel. We shall report here a circumstance that well illustrates Mozart's modesty: on the first evening, the composer was insistently called for in a tempest of bravos. He kept hiding so as not to have to show himself, until Schikaneder and Süssmayr went to drag him from his hiding place and pushed him onto the stage by force.

Because the first cast of *Die Zauberflöte* was recently cited in this review, we shall refrain from repeating it, and shall mention only some later changes. The second genie having fallen ill, the part was entrusted to little Maurer—who sang the role of Sarastro four years later and became one of the great bassos of Germany; Sebastian Mayer, a brother-in-law of Mozart, alternated with Schikaneder as Papageno on the evenings when the latter, physically unwell or out of sorts, was prevented from doing it; when Fräulein Gottlieb went over to the enemy at the Leopoldstadttheater, she was replaced by Fräulein Wittmann; finally, after Herr Nosseul was engaged by the Burgtheater, it was Herr Haibel—another brother-in-law of Mozart and a member of Schikaneder's troupe at the time—who took up the role of Monostatos.

The opera was presented twenty-four times in October 1791; despite the smallness of the auditorium and the not very high price of the seats, up to November 1, it brought in the amount of 8,443 florins, which was thought to be fabulous. It continued to be given steadily. But the Master, often ill after his return from Prague, grew weaker and weaker, and the uninterrupted intellectual tension to which he had been subjected (he composed *La Clemenza di Tito*, *Die Zauberflöte*, and the Requiem almost simultaneously) had literally used him up. He heard only echoes of his triumph. By then, he rarely left his bed, and in no case left his room.

On November 20, 1792, when *Die Zauberflöte* was given for the eighty-third time, Schikaneder, for selfish reasons, announced it as the one-hundredth performance, although that [statement] was false. Similarly, one read on the posters announcing the performance of October 22, 1795, "two-hundredth," whereas the opera had been played only one hundred thirty-five times.

Die Zauberflöte did not earn Mozart a great deal, as Schikaneder paid him only meager honoraria; further, he sold the score to various theaters without any share being received by the genius who had created it. When that injustice, which was all the greater because he had saved Schikaneder from ruin, was pointed out to Mozart, that noble, good man said only: "What would you have me do? He is a scoundrel!" and the reasoning was understood. It is beyond doubt that—coming on top of the precarious state of his health—the forced labor to which Mozart lent himself, the late nights, and his abuse of strong drink to keep himself awake had brought nearer the hour of his death. The very day before he died, he said to his wife, the future Frau von Nissen (it was from her own mouth that the author of these lines heard it): "I would much like to hear my *Zauberflöte* once more." And he sang in a scarcely perceptible voice "*Der Vogelfänger bin ich ja.*" The late Kapellmeister Roser, who was seated near his bed, rose, went to the piano, and sang the aria, which seemed to bring great joy to Mozart. The following morning, he died; it was 1 a.m., December 5, 1791. The funeral procession took place on December 7 in a terrible snowstorm. The only ones who accompanied the coffin were Kapellmeister Roser, the Hoftheater cellist Orsler, and Süssmayr. His wife, who was ill, had to remain in bed. Schikaneder was not there. As Mozart had been born on January 27, 1756, he was not yet thirty-six years old. How many immortal masterpieces he would still have been able to create! But [only] his entourage and posterity could complain: as for him, one must judge him happy not to have experienced the infirmities of age and the inevitability of showing them in later works. He had arrived on Earth wholly equipped, armed, and quit our world in all the splendor of his gifts.

Let it be said in conclusion—and this is to Schikaneder's honor—that the author of this article, who often had occasion to talk with him toward the end of his life, never heard him utter Mozart's name without having tears in his eyes.

COMMENTARIES
ON THE PLATES
NOTES
BIBLIOGRAPHY
INDEX

Commentaries on the
Plates (following page 146),
with Sources

1 Mozart wearing Masonic insignia of the degree of Master. Anonymous painting, probably nineteenth-century, reproduced without reference by J. Kuéss-Scheichelbauer in his book *200 Jahre Freimaurerei in Österreich*. Reproduced by kind authorization of the publisher, O. Kerry, Vienna.

2 Ignaz von Born, 1742–91. Masonic portrait: the cartouche is mounted upon a base evoking the ancient Operative Masonry, held up by a sphinx and a lion and flanked by a palm and a branch of true acacia. Above it, an eight-pointed star in a wide oval shines with the brilliance of the Sun. The portrait is surrounded by a serpent with its tail in its mouth and looking toward the East. All of these symbols are doubtless attributes of degree, independent of *Die Zauberflöte*; nevertheless, one finds a number of them in the opera, notably with reference to Sarastro. Same source as for Plate 1. Reproduced by kind authorization of the publisher, O. Kerry, Vienna. Photograph from the Historisches Museum, Vienna.

3 and 4 Masonic tarots of Etteilla (an anagram of Alliette), almost contemporary with *Die Zauberflöte*. In the explanatory note these two tarot cards or "tiles," evoking respectively the domain of Sarastro and that of the Queen of the Night (the evocation is still more striking in the original polychromes), bear the names, which are not reproduced on the tiles themselves: *Maçonnerie d'Hiram* and *Ordre des Mopses*. They replace, with a different order of numbering, the Sun and the Moon of the classic tarots, an example of which is reproduced with them. The differences are considerable, particularly for the "*Maçonnerie d'Hiram*," about which see the commentary on p. 101: naked children of indeterminate sex, alchemical oven, flaming five-pointed star instead of the Sun, etc. Paris, Bibliothèque Nationale, B. P. Grimaud legacy (modern republication).

5 and 6 Ordinary tarots, tiles 18 (the Moon) and 19 (the Sun), cor-

responding to tiles 3 and 2 of the Etteilla tarots shown above (note the inversion). See the commentary on Plates 3 and 4. Fifteenth-century wood engravings reproduced by R. Merlin in 1869. Paris, Bibliothèque Nationale, Estampes, IC. 178. 4°.

7 The Three Boys, engraving attributed to François Boucher and often reproduced on Masonic diplomas. This is a "Lowton" or "adopted child" diploma (cf. the "wolf-cubs" of the French Boy Scouts) of the Lodge "La Rose Écossaise." The device, not reproduced here, is *Post tenebras lux,* the major theme of *Die Zauberflöte.* Early nineteenth-century painting by Tessier. Paris, Collection Alain Serrière, plate from Éditions Robert Laffont, Paris.

8–10 Masonic aprons bearing various symbols found in *Die Zauberflöte.* Plates 8 and 10 are Master's aprons, both of them bearing the Flaming (five-pointed) Star with the G (cf. Plate 33, frontispiece of the libretto of *Die Zauberflöte*), the Sun and the Moon corresponding to the columns J and B, but reversed (on this reversal, see p. 99), and the three-portaled Temple at which Tamino will knock. On the more recent Plate 8 (beginning of the nineteenth century), numerous symbols also figure, among them the Egyptian pyramids and sphinx, the sandpile, the shovel and the pickax of the frontispiece of *Die Zauberflöte* (Plate 33), the broken column from that frontispiece, Monostatos's chains, etc.

Plate 9 (epoch of Louis XV) is a woman's apron for the rite of Adoption, embroidered like the one in Plate 8. Its central motive is the rose of the feminine initiation, which appears so often in *Die Zauberflöte* (the bank of roses where Pamina sleeps, the Three Boys' flying chariot covered with roses, etc.), supported upon a five-leaved branch. On the bib, the dove evoked by Monostatos with reference to Pamina: it bears a five-section olive branch in its beak.

Plate 8: from the collection of the G.·.L.·.D.·.F.·. (Grande Loge de France), impressed on leather in blue on a white background with red braid, nineteenth century, plate from Éditions Robert Laffont, Paris.

Plates 9 and 10: from the Collection Alain Serrière, silk embroidered in colors (eighteenth century), plate from Éditions Robert Laffont, Paris.

11 and 12 Schikaneder in the role of Papageno. This engraving, which illustrates the libretto of *Die Zauberflöte,* was announced in the program publicity as "representing H. Schikaneder in his true costume." In fact, as can be seen in Plates 23 and 24, he has been made to appear somewhat younger. As for the costume,

compare the design in the first edition, 1791 (Plate 11), with that of the second, 1794 (Plate 12), which shows several modifications: suppression of the tail, decoration of the cage, syrinx hung around the neck, etc. The décor also has been adjusted slightly.

Plate 11: Paris, Bibliothèque Nationale, Music Department.

Plate 12: Paris, Musée de l'Opéra. Photo Schnapp: *Réalités*.

13 Illustrated title page of a nineteenth-century edition. The illustration by Karl Christian Glassbach, representing Tamino's encounter with Papageno near the dead serpent in the first act, manifestly was inspired by the preceding illustration and completed with Tamino and the serpent. Note, about the latter, that the prescription in the rubric that it has been cut into three pieces has been forgotten. This was respected in the 1794 design, Plate 15. Paris, Institut de Musicologie. Photograph from the Bibliothèque Nationale, Paris.

14 The sword and the serpent, Belgian Masonic medal of 1838. From the collection of the Grande Loge de France, plate from Éditions Robert Laffont, Paris.

15–20 Scenes in *Die Zauberflöte* from Schikaneder's staging. Six colored sketches by Josef and Peter Schaffer published in 1794 in the *Allgemein-Europäische Journal*, Brünn. For the authenticity of the attribution to Schikaneder, see Plates 23 and 24 and the comments upon them.

Plates 15, 17, and 20: Bildarchiv. Öst. Nationalbibliothek, coming from the Historisches Museum der Stadt Wien. Photograph by the Historisches Museum, Vienna.

Plates 16 and 18: photographs by Rudolf Stepanek, Vienna.

Plate 19: Paris, photograph from the Bibliothèque Nationale, Paris.

21 Backstage scene of the performances of *Die Zauberflöte* at the Weimar Hoftheater in 1794, under Goethe's direction (*cf.* Alfons Rosenberg, *Die Zauberflöte, Geschichte und Deutung*, Munich, 1964, Plate II). At the left, preparation of the menagerie; hanging from the ceiling, Papageno's birdcage. Tamino is being dressed. Papageno is quenching his thirst, Sarastro trying out his voice. Between them is Monostatos; in the background, the priests converse. At the right, the Three Boys with their palm-fronds. An assistant is bringing the Ladies' javelins through the open door. Aquarelle by George Melchior-Krauss at the Castle of Tiefurt. Photograph Int. Stiftung Mozarteum, Salzburg.

22 Allegory of the birth of Freemasonry, 1857. Symbols of symbolic Masonry and Egyptian Masonry: the two columns, the Sun and

the Moon, the Temple of Solomon and "Brass Sea" (purification basin), the Boys carrying the acacia and the compass, pyramids, sphinx, reversed statues, the serpent with a woman's body in the Tree of the Knowledge of Good and Evil, the Egyptian sages, the Sky and the Earth, Strength with the lion, the Truth, the ladder, etc. Polychrome lithograph by the FF.∴. Vayron and Viette, Paris, from the Collection Alain Serrière, plate from Éditions Robert Laffont, Paris.

23 and 24 Two portraits of Schikaneder. The first of the portraits is probably Masonic: the word *"Fremdling,"* usually translated as "stranger," is the one by which, at the end of Act I, Sarastro designates Tamino and Papageno, in the sense of their being "profane"; *"als Fremder"* doubtless signifies that Schikaneder is represented without the Masonic attributes to which he would have had the right.

The second portrait is precious because it authenticates the Schaffers' designs (Plates 15–20) as closely related to Schikaneder's staging. As in the various Papagenos of those designs, here shown in sequence, one is struck by the actor-author's low forehead and characteristic jaw. One re-encounters them confirmed by other portraits that we cannot reproduce here, but which can be found in the following publications: Fritz Brukner, *Die Zauberflöte*, Vienna, 1934, plate on p. 128; Paul Stefan, *Die Zauberflöte*, Vienna, 1937, p. 89; and *Neues Mozart-Jahrbuch* I, 1941, plate on p. 152. Schikaneder was forty-three years old when he created *Die Zauberflöte*; he must have been flattered and rejuvenated by the famous sketch of Papageno reproduced here as Plate 11. Sketch by Philipp Richter, photograph from the Bibliothèque Nationale, Paris.

25 Introduction of the Apprentice Mason into the Temple of Truth. If the engraving is symbolic, the postulant's attire is ritual: left breast and knee bared, feet shod in slipper style, eyes blindfolded, etc. It is the "light raiment . . . without sandals" specified for Tamino by the libretto. The "Apprentice" is led by the Brother Expert, as Tamino is led by the Speaker. Eighteenth-century engraving, Bibliothèque Nationale, reproduced in Serge Hutin, *Les Francs-Maçons*, Éditions du Seuil, Paris, 1960, plate from Éditions Robert Laffont, Paris.

26 Eighteenth-century feminine initiation in a Lodge of Adoption. The postulant with bandaged eyes and chained arms (*cf.* Monostatos). Note the presence of the masculine officers and, on the Grand Mistress's table, among other accessories, the bisected apple.

Engraving of the eighteenth century, Bibliothèque Nationale, reproduced in Serge Hutin's *Les Francs-Maçons*, Éditions du Seuil, Paris, 1960, plate from Éditions Robert Laffont, Paris.

27 Trial by fire, represented upon an admission token of the Lodge "La Clémente Amitié." Silver; date not known. Collection G.·.L.·.D.·.F.·. (Grande Loge de France), plate from Éditions Robert Laffont, Paris.

28 Admonition to silence, in the form of a statue putting a finger to its mouth; showing at one side the column J, as motive on a diploma of the Grand-Orient de France. Beginning of the nineteenth century, engraved by Canu, 37, rue des Noyers, chez le F.·. Michalet, 47, rue de Grenelle. Collection Alain Serrière, plate from Éditions Robert Laffont, Paris.

29 and 30 Medal of a Paris Masonic lodge, 1807. On the obverse (Loge de Saint-Michel, Orient de Paris), Egyptian pyramid, acacia (the tree planted on Hiram's tomb and often employed in Masonic symbolism), beehive, columns J and B. The date (5807 in Masonic usage) is inscribed on the trowel. On the reverse, under the device *Dispersit superbos* (taken from the *Magnificat*), the Luminous Delta strikes a three-headed serpent. The close relationship with *Die Zauberflöte* is easy to grasp. Original relics preserved at the Monnaie de Paris, reminted in 1967. Collection of the author, plate from Éditions Robert Laffont, Paris.

31 Authentic solar circle, in bronze, of the Hittite or pre-Hittite age (second half of the third millennium B.C.). The circles were not "borne on the breast," as by Sarastro, but as standards at the end of staffs, and were presented during sacrifices. Ankara, Arkeoloji Muzesi (Archeological Museum), called the "Hittite Museum," plate from Éditions Robert Laffont, Paris.

32 Masonic jewel, female: five-pointed flaming star and rose on a T-square and compass. Paris, nineteenth century. Collection G.·.L.·.D.·.F.·. (Grande Loge de France), plate from Éditions Robert Laffont, Paris.

33 Frontispiece of the original libretto of *Die Zauberflöte*, published in 1791 by J. Alberti at Vienna. This engraving, representing allegorically the Cabinet of Reflection of the trial by Earth, is discussed on p. 138. Remark the five-pointed star with the G (purposely not very clear), the broken statue, and the reversed columns (*cf*. Plates 10 and 22), the shovel and pickax in front of the ewer, and the sandpile (*cf*. Plate 34), the funerary urn, the pyramid covered with signs. Photograph from the Mozarteum, Salzburg.

34 The symbols of the Cabinet of Reflection, which are to be found, as they are or as transposed, on the frontispiece of *Die Zauberflöte* (Plate 33). Comment on pp. 134–9. After Jules Boucher, *La Symbolique maçonnique*, Paris, 1953. Bibliothèque Nationale.

35 Ritual trowel of the Grand Mistress, used during the rite for sealing up the mouth—transformed in *Die Zauberflöte* into Papageno's padlock. The fingers of the hand indicate the scale. Massive gold. Collection E. Linval, plate from Éditions Robert Laffont, Paris.

36 Cabinet of Reflection. Stool and table, with a tibia, a candlestick, and writing materials (pen and ink) beneath macabre and moralizing inscriptions. Photo from Serge Hutin's *Les Francs-Maçons*, Éditions du Seuil, Paris, 1960.

37 Diploma of Master Mason, sometimes said to be Mozart's. Richard Koch reproduced it as such and gave a translation of the text into German in which all the blanks were filled in, demonstrating how little faith he had in the document as such. In fact, it comes from the Viennese Lodge "L'Espérance Couronnée" (notice the text in French), but the name has been left blank, the diploma prepared but not signed, and the date (Year of the Light 5792, 22nd of the IIIrd month—signifying May 22, 1792) five months after Mozart's death. Salzburg Museum, photograph from the Bibliothèque Nationale, Paris, plate from Éditions Robert Laffont, Paris.

38 The "Basin of Mesmer," the propagandist of animal magnetism and an active Freemason. Mozart's *Bastien und Bastienne* was presented in his garden. Bibliothèque Nationale, Paris, plate from H. Roger Viollet.

39 *Les Mystères d'Isis*, "revised" version of *Die Zauberflöte*, for a long time the only version of it presented in Paris. End of the Overture. Paris, Institut de Musicologie, plate from Éditions Robert Laffont, Paris.

40 The same passage in the authentic version (beginning with measure #3). Note, in *Isis*, the modifications of the orchestration and, above all, the insipid prolongation of the three terminal chords of symbolic value into an interminable series of perfect chords devoid of meaning. Paris, Bibliothèque Nationale, plate from Éditions Robert Laffont, Paris.

41 The Grotto of Aigen, near Salzburg, with its entrance decorated as a temple portal and its nearby cascade. According to Richard Koch, Masonic and Illuministic meetings were held here at which Mozart could have been present, and the memory of which, Carl de Nys thought, could have affected the conception

of the Cavern of Water during the trials in *Die Zauberflöte*. We have seen (*cf.* Plate 37) that Koch's testimony must be accepted circumspectly. Photograph from the Museum Carolino Augusteum, Salzburg.

Notes

For bibliographical data
on the works cited, see the
Bibliography, p. 333.

Chapter 2

[1] Goethe's phrase really referred to his own drama *Helena*, but as he added "as is true of *Die Zauberflöte* and other plays," our citation is justified. *Cf.* Otto Jahn, *Mozart*, IV, 1859.

[2] Edward J. Dent, *Mozart's Operas*, p. 255; Paul Nettl, *Mozart und die königliche Kunst*, p. 146.

[3] Jahn, IV, p. 653.

[4] Nicolas Slonimsky, "The Weather at Mozart's Funeral," *The Musical Quarterly*, January 1960, pp. 12–21.

[5] Mathilde Ludendorff, *Mozarts Leben und gewaltsamer Tod*. The publication place and date of this work—Munich, 1936—relate it to the Nazi atmosphere. According to it, Mozart was assassinated, "like Luther, Lessing, Schiller, and many others," for having invaded *"den Tempel Salomos, das heisst die Judenherrschaft"* (p. 222). The thesis had been sketched out earlier in *Der ungesühnte Frevel an Luther, Lessing, Mozart, Schiller, im Dienste des allmächtigen Baumeisters aller Welt* (Munich, 1928, republished 1936).

[6] Kuéss-Scheichelbauer, *200 Jahre Freimaurerei in Österreich*, p. 86.

[7] Carl Baer, *Mozart, Krankheit, Tod, Begräbnis*.

[8] Dieter Kerner, *Mozarts Todeskrankheit*.

[9] First of all, M. Roger Cotte, author of a thesis in preparation on Masonic music in France in the eighteenth century, whose constant help has been invaluable to me; then M. Charles-Henry Chevalier, Grand Chancelier de la Grande Loge de France and general secretary of Foreign Affairs; M. Jean Baylot, Grand Surveillant de la Grande Loge Nationale Française; M. Guy Thieux, specialist in esoterism; M. Pierre Morlière, editor in chief of the review *Le Symbolisme*; MM. Alain Serrière and E. Linval, who spontaneously opened their valuable collections to me; as well as the Bibliothèque de la Grande Loge de France, and many others. With respect to another category of ideas, I must also thank the

French Institute of Vienna, and especially M. Espiau de la Maëstre, professor, and Mlle E. Petertil, librarian, as well as Dr. Novak, chief of the department of music in the Stadtbibliothek, Vienna, who all facilitated my access to official documents. Finally, I must thank my pupil Jean-Marie Gouélou and Mlle Guy, who effectively helped me in analyzing some of them.

[10] A good bibliography on Masonic matters can be found in Jean Palou, *La Franc-Maçonnerie*.

[11] See the works of Komorzynski, and J. and B. Massin, p. 550.

Chapter 3

[1] J. and B. Massin, pp. 306–7.

[2] The imbroglio doubtless began with Ignaz von Seyfried's gossiping to Treitschke (see letter in the Appendix, p. 301; *cf.* Richard Koch, *Mozart, Freimaurer und Illuminaten, nebst einigen freimaurerischen kulturhistorischen Skizzen*, p. 13). Lewis, *Geschichte der Freimaurerei in Österreich*, pp. 39–40, cites Mozart and Schikaneder together as members of the Loge zur neugekrönten Hoffnung, but without dates or references. Komorzynski does the same in the 1901 edition of his *Emanuel Schikaneder, ein Beitrag zur Geschichte des Deutschen Theaters*, p. 29, confusing that lodge with the Loge zur gekrönten Hoffnung. Richard Koch (*Br.'. Mozart, Freimaurer und Illuminaten, nebst einigen freimaurerischen kulturhistorischen Skizzen*, p. 13) repeats Lewis's assertion, but remarks honestly that he has not found Schikaneder's name in any of the three lodge lists that he has been able to consult. Same absence in the documents published by Otto Erich Deutsch. Koch devotes a chapter to the Loge zur Führsicht in Salzburg, in which he points out "*nach meinen Forschungen*" the names of Archbishop Colloredo as a member—and, as visitors or guests, "Amadeus Mozart, Leopold Mozart, Emanuel Schikaneder," but without dates or reference. The assertion is surprising; Mozart and his father could not have been received as visitors until they had been initiated—that is, until after 1785; but Wolfgang never returned to Salzburg after 1781. Further, it is difficult to believe, when his relations with Colloredo are taken into account, that he would have visited the Archbishop's lodge.

[3] Paul Nettl, *Mozart*, pp. 87–90.

[4] Dent, p. 210. See Otto Erich Deutsch, *Das Freihaustheater auf der Wieden 1787–1801.*

[5] Alfons Rosenberg, *Die Zauberflöte, Geschichte und Deutung*, p. 328.

[6] This fact, apparently never noted before, is proved by the existence

in the Stadtbibliothek at Vienna (685.928 AM.) of a copy of the original edition of the libretto bearing his signature as owner and having tipped-in pages in his handwriting containing many stage directions such as appear in a prompt-book. For details about Giesecke and his "revelations," see Dent, pp. 306–16; the critiques by Komorzynski; and Otto Rommel, *Geschichte der altwiener Volkskomödie.*

7 Koch, p. 13, it is true, names Giesecke, as a member of the Loge zur neugekrönten Hoffnung at an unspecified time, but he is not to be trusted blindly. He says that Giesecke's name bears "the number 46," but does not say where. Dent's information on this subject much postdates *Die Zauberflöte.* The frequently repeated statement that Mozart and Schikaneder belonged to the same Viennese lodge doubtless dates from Seyfried's letter cited on p. 301; Edgar Istel (*Die Freimaurerei in Mozarts Zauberflöte*) says that they were together there "in 1790," but cites no reference, and his work seems uncritical. He was contradicted by Nettl (*Mozart und die königliche Kunst,* p. 90).

8 Julius Cornet, *Die Opern in Deutschland,* pp. 24–5. Komorzynski (*Schikaneder,* p. 123) denied this testimony, which he was later eager to destroy; at the time, however, he did not know Cornet's book, and mentioned only an article that appeared in the *Ostdeutsche Post* in 1857, seven years later (p. 196).

9 Since Komorzynski's violent criticisms, which were reiterated in his article "*Die Zauberflöte*" (*Neues Mozart-Jahrbuch* I, pp. 147–74), attacks on Cornet's narrative have increased; cf. notably Castle, "*K. L. Metzler von Giesecke, der angebliche Dichter der Zauberflöte,*" in *Chronik des Wiener Goethe Vereins,* vols. 48–50, 1946; Otto Rommel, *Geschichte der altwiener Volkskomödie,* pp. 496 ff.

10 The delay does not seem a conclusive argument: much time elapsed between 1791 and 1818, the date of the "revelations" to Cornet, and then from 1818 to 1849, the date of Cornet's "revelations." But there is nothing unusual in the fact that a onetime actor who has become a scientist should remain discreet about his earlier career, which was looked down upon in his new milieu; further, a ghost writer is called upon to remain silent about his collaboration as long as his "patron" is active. Nor is there anything anomalous about a man who is preparing a book and who waits to put into it whatever concerns his subject, even though it happened long before. The only surprising thing would have been if nothing of it all had filtered out in the interim; but much seems to have filtered out. Jahn mentions remarks about it made

to him by Neukomm (this passage, judged too favorable to Giesecke, was changed by the editors of later editions), and public gossip, though hesitant over the names, had not waited for Giesecke to insist that Schikaneder had not written his texts unaided. Cornet mentions that before 1818, "many people thought that the prompter Helmbock had been his collaborator," Seyfried suggests another prompter, Haselbeck, and the 1857 notice mentions "his friend Cantes" in that role. That errors in detail should slip into a story told from memory so much later is inevitable; to a historian, this signals the necessity for care, not for rejection. Finally, that Giesecke's *Oberon* is an impersonal plagiarism is perhaps a fact, but is of no importance: Schikaneder had not asked him for anything else. Further, with regard to *Die Zauberflöte*, Giesecke never claimed to have conceived the libretto, but only to have prepared the serious parts; that does not place the arrangement itself in doubt.

[11] Georges de Saint-Foix, *Wolfgang Amédée Mozart*, V, p. 217.

[12] Nettl (*Mozart und die königliche Kunst*, p. 105) pointed out that simultaneously with Born's article there appeared, without signature or place of publication, a similar work entitled *Crata repoa, oder Einweihungen in der alten geheimen Gesellschaft der Ägyptischen Priester* (1785).

[13] Documents reproduced in Otto Erich Deutsch, *Mozart und die Wiener Loge*, passim.

[14] Dent, p. 218.

[15] J. and B. Massin, p. 564.

Chapter 4

[1] Here I must thank my pupil Jean-Marie Gouélou, who, while working on a university study of this subject, helped me in my attempt to unravel the tangled skein of this little problem in detection.

[2] A copy of a modern republication by Fritz Brukner is in the Mozarteum at Salzburg.

[3] Complete text in the Appendixes, p. 303. The Massins (p. 551) translate *umwerfen* as *détruire* (destroy).

[4] Letter to Constanze of June 12, 1791, describing the preceding day. The première of *Kaspar* had taken place on June 8.

[5] Dent, pp. 218–19. The book was written in 1913 and revised and brought up to date in 1948 (and translated into French in 1958 without modification of this passage).

[6] Dent, p. 225.

Chapter 5

1 Jahn, IV, pp. 596–7.
2 Jahn, IV, p. 599.
3 Saint-Foix, IV, p. 227.
4 *Arlequin Franc-Maçon* was recorded by Roger Cotte in 1967 (Pathé-Marconi record DTX.348). *Cf.* that writer's article in the *Revue internationale de musique* No. 11, Autumn 1951, p. 493: in a note he cites five plays of the same sort from the same period.
5 Wagenseil's name was added in pencil to the copy in the Stadtbibliothek, Vienna (Theater Department).
6 Dent, p. 225.
7 Nettl, *Mozart*, p. 159. These sources are set forth in detail in Rosenberg.
8 Dent, pp. 225–6. The quotation is from Thomas Lediard's English translation of 1732.

Chapter 6

1 Stadtbibliothek. ms. Ja N 8. 355.
2 J. and B. Massin, p. 541.
3 *Berliner musikalische Zeitung*, 1793; *cf.* Massin, p. 561.
4 Rosenberg, p. 331, supposes, without being sure, that they may be of the first performance. But a comparison of our plates 11 and 12 shows that this hypothesis must be excluded: Papageno's costume is that of the 1794 design, not that of 1791.
5 An analysis of the mutilations that Lachnith inflicted upon *Die Zauberflöte* will be found in Georges Servières's *Episodes d'histoire musicale* ("Les Mystères d'Isis," pp. 147–70), Paris, 1914.
6 Berlioz's article, some fragments of which he incorporated into the *Mémoires*, was included by André Hallays in the posthumous collection of Berlioz's critiques published in 1903 as *Les Musiciens et la musique*.
7 For information about that abundant, curious repertoire, parodies, pamphlets, etc., see Fritz Brukner, *Die Zauberflöte, unbekannte Handschriften und seltene Drucke aus der Frühzeit von Mozarts Oper*.
8 A detailed analysis of Goethe's project can be found in Paul Nettl's *Mozart und die königliche Kunst*, pp. 146–60.
9 Nettl, *Mozart und die königliche Kunst*, p. 122.
10 Seventh dialogue, between Thalia and Momus. On this exegesis, see *Neues Mozart-Jahrbuch* I, 1923 ("Aus Deutungen der Zauberflöte," by Emil Karl Blümml).

[11] Nettl, *Mozart und die königliche Kunst*, p. 122. Nevertheless, in 1848, one finds in a ritual of "Masonic baptism" (a ceremony now fallen into desuetude) published by N.-C. des Etangs, *Œuvres maçonniques*, p. 217 (Bibliothèque Nationale H.5 293), the instruction to play during the offertory an aria from that deformation of *Die Zauberflöte*, *Les Mystères d'Isis* (*"Soyez sensible à nos peines"*).

[12] *Ibid.*, pp. 124–8.

[13] Maurice Kufferath, *La Flûte enchantée*.

[14] Giuseppe Leti and Louis Lachat, *L'Esotérisme à la scène: La Flûte enchantée, Parsifal, Faust*, preface by Antonio Coën.

Chapter 7

[1] It should be remembered that *Le Devin du village* was not originally conceived as an *opéra-comique*, but as an operatic intermezzo without spoken text. The Overture and the final divertissement were added later.

[2] The term Venerable is relatively modern. It is an abbreviation of "Venerable Master," the title normally employed when addressing the presiding officer of the lodge as he is performing his duties, as well as new initiates of the third degree. The older term had been "Master of the Lodge" or "Grand Master" (now reserved for a different officer).

[3] Massin, p. 283.

[4] At least according to some writers. The question is discussed in Chapter 8.

[5] More accurately, discovery of a Singspiel with a libretto by Schachtner and music by Josef von Friebert, the action of which Mozart followed step by step. *Cf.* Massin, pp. 858–61.

[6] Girdlestone, *Rameau*, 1957.

[7] I cannot deal here with a subject that would take us too far afield, and which Roger Cotte plans to deal with in a thesis now in work. The list of Parisian Freemasons of the Grand-Orient de France published by Le Bihan covers only the end of the eighteenth century, a period too late for Rameau. On page 411 of that list and—unlike the general usage of the publication—without vital data, there is a Jean-Baptiste Rameau, "professor of music and of violin" who in 1778 was a member of the Loge Saint-Charles du Triomphe de la Parfaite Harmonie. But his relationship to Jean-Philippe is not known.

[8] *Cf.* Pierre-Jean Jouve, *Le Don Juan de Mozart*, 2nd ed., 1968.

Chapter 8

1 It is interesting to note, in almost all the recent works of French historians of Freemasonry either affiliated with the order or sympathetic to it, a tendency to regret its nineteenth-century evolution and to desire a return to the mystic and symbolic sources. *Cf.* Hutin, p. 175, Palou, pp. 314–15, Naudon, p. 57, Baylot, pp. 117 *et seq.*, and even—despite his penchant for scandal—the fictionized but documented study by Roger Peyrefitte, *Les Fils de la lumière*.

2 For the initiate traditions of the operative Masons, see the abundant literature that followed publication of *Mystère des cathédrales* (1925) by Fulcanelli, and notably *Le Nombre d'or* by Matila Ghika.

3 Among them were the Misraïm Rite, Italian in origin, and that of Memphis, of French origin, the joining of which, after various vicissitudes, gave birth in 1959 to the Ancient and Primitive Rite of Memphis-Misraïm. Its ritual, published by Robert Ambelain in 1966 (*Cérémonies et rituels de la Maçonnerie symbolique*), often recalls scenes in *Die Zauberflöte*. It would be interesting to know if it should be considered as having preceded Mozart's opera despite the recent date at which it was brought to light. But the question is very complex: the dates advanced by Ambelain, p. 22, are on the whole distinctly earlier than those given by Palou, pp. 242 and 249–50, and by Paul Naudon (*La Franc-Maçonnerie*, p. 104). For example, Ambelain gives 1782 as the date of the creation of the Misraïm Rite, whereas Palou gives 1805, Naudon "about 1813." If the first is correct—we cannot judge the point here—the texts of that rite could be considered possible sources for *Die Zauberflöte* despite their modern publication, whereas in the opposite case they would have to be excluded. Be that as it may, the details of the Rite, at least of those sections which concern us, remain secondary in comparison with the common usage, so that we shall not scruple at times to refer to this ritual, the only published one available at present; the hope of finding a ritual rigorously conforming to that of Mozart—that is to say, a Viennese ritual of the Strict Observance at the end of the eighteenth century—unhappily remains Utopian under the conditions of research currently permitted to the profane.

4 Dent, p. 242.

5 Serge Hutin, *Les Francs-Maçons*, p. 84.

[6] Kuéss-Scheichelbauer, p. 18.

[7] *Ibid.*, pp. 57–60.

[8] Koch, p. 21.

[9] The text of the regulation will be found in Kuéss-Scheichelbauer, p. 66.

[10] *Ibid.*, pp. 74–5.

[11] *Ibid.*, p. 77.

[12] Naudon, pp. 42, 62, etc.

[13] Kuéss-Scheichelbauer, p. 53.

[14] Palou, p. 174.

[15] J. and B. Massin, p. 1184.

[16] Notably by the Massins, p. 1184. Dent, p. 237, refers to an article of the sort by Hubert Bradley in the English Masonic review *Ars Quatuor Coronatum*, but notes that doubt has been thrown upon Koch's reliability, which Dent's informant had not thought worth taking seriously.

Chapter 9

[1] In a communication to the Société de Musicologie, December 13, 1966. *Cf.* his article *"Une énigme dans la vie de Mozart"* (*Miroir de l'Histoire*).

[2] Naudon, p. 114.

[3] René Dumesnil, *"La Flûte enchantée et la Musique maçonnique de Mozart,"* *Musica*, March 1955, p. 24.

[4] Michel Brenet, *Les Concerts en France sous l'Ancien Régime*, *passim.*

[5] Alain Le Bihan, *Francs-Maçons parisiens du Grand-Orient de France* (*fin du XVIIIᵉ siècle*), p. 308.

[6] *Cf.* J. and B. Massin, and Jacques Chailley, dissertation, *"Sur la signification cachée du quatuor de Mozart K.465 dit 'les Dissonances,' et du 7ᵉ Quatuor en fa majeur de Beethoven."*

[7] See my article "Haydn and Free-Masonry," in the *Festschrift* prepared for Karl Geiringer on his seventieth birthday.

[8] Koch, p. 21. *Cf.* note 2 in Chapter 3.

[9] J. and B. Massin, p. 434.

[10] Translation by Emily Anderson (*The Letters of Mozart and His Family*, II, New York, 1966, p. 907).

[11] Translation by Eric Blom (Otto Erich Deutsch, ed., *The Schubert Reader*, New York, 1947, p. 436).

[12] *Cf.* Jacques Chailley, *"Le Winterreise de Schubert est-il une œuvre ésotérique?"* in *Revue d'Esthétique*, 1965, pp. 283–7.

[13] J. and B. Massin, p. 447. There is disagreement between the Massins

and Koch—according to whom (p. 12) the Venerable was not Gebler, but Graf Wenzel Paar. Gebler is mentioned by Koch (p. 15) as Grand Master in 1784 of the district lodge, the Loge zum neuen Bund.

14 Deutsch, *Mozart und die wiener Loge*, pp. 31 ff.

15 J. and B. Massin, p. 457.

16 *Cf.* Dent, p. 223.

17 J. and B. Massin, p. 573 (Sophie's own account).

18 Paumgartner, *Mozart*, p. 471.

19 Slonimsky, pp. 12–21, and Baer, p. 121.

20 *Cf.* J. and B. Massin, pp. 578 and 583.

Chapter 10

1 Naudon, p. 70.

2 Palou, p. 87. A good popular account will be found in the article *"Loges d'Adoption"* in the nineteenth-century Larousse.

3 Vat, *Étude sur les Loges d'Adoption.*

4 Naudon, p. 70.

5 Vat, p. 10.

6 Kuéss-Scheichelbauer, p. 18.

7 Haven, *Rituel de la Maçonnerie égyptienne, passim.*

8 Vat, initial bibliography and p. 12.

9 The title of Grand Mistress, like that of Grand Master, only later took on the meaning of chief of obedience. In the older sense, it signified only the "Venerable of the Lodge."

10 Mixed Masonry of Human Rights, founded on an international basis. A Grande Loge Féminine de France still exists, but dates only from 1944. The feminine Grande Loge rejected the ritual of Adoption; it operates, with some variations, under the masculine Scottish Rite.

11 Vat, p. 51.

Chapter 11

1 J. and B. Massin, p. 1150.

2 Chailley, dissertation, *op. cit.*

3 As M. Jean Baylot kindly wrote me, *Ordo ab Chao* is one of the mottoes of the 33rd degree in the Ancient and Accepted Scottish Rite. *Cf.* Kuéss-Scheichelbauer, p. 186.

4 Nettl, *"Mozart et la Franc-Maçonnerie,"* p. 221. The context is explicit: in this description, it clearly deals, not with the chords

in the middle of the fugue, for which it would be exact, but with those at the beginning, for which it is not.

[5] Here I want to thank M. Roger Cotte, to whom I am indebted for this important working hypothesis, the more so because he suggested it to me before the work by Palou mentioned later had placed its elements at the disposition of the "profane." Verified by a minute examination of the score, it brought about a complete change of direction in my research, which was already well advanced at that time.

[6] Matila Ghika, *Le Nombre d'Or*, I, p. 36.

[7] *Ibid.*, II, p. 105. On the "enigmatic G," see Jules Boucher, p. 236 ff.

[8] I owe these last reflections to the kindness of M. Guy Thieux.

[9] Palou, pp. 338–9. The source, not cited, is an 1817 ritual reproduced by Vat.

[10] The custom of placing the dots in a triangle or a quincunx is not very old. In the eighteenth century, the three or five dots were most often placed in a line after the name, and at times even replaced it.

[11] Palou, p. 224.

[12] Jules Boucher, *La Symbolique maçonnique*, p. 334.

[13] Information communicated by M. Roger Cotte.

Chapter 12

[1] Ghika, I, p. 38.

Chapter 13

[1] I owe this explanation to M. Jean Baylot.

[2] Boucher, p. 178.

[3] *Ibid.*, p. 180.

[4] Palou, p. 339.

[5] Cf. François Bayle, *Dictionnaire historique et critique*, III, 1715, pp. 925–31.

[6] For the relationship between the character of Sarastro and Ignaz von Born, see Chapter 3.

[7] Nettl, *Mozart*, p. 159.

[8] Marianne Verneuil, *Dictionnaire pratique des sciences occultes*, p. 257.

[9] Vat, p. 63; Palou, p. 341.

[10] J. and B. Massin, p. 1149.

[11] Ghika, II, p. 38.

Chapter 14

[1] Vat, pp. 38–54; Palou, pp. 266–73.
[2] Palou, p. 339.
[3] Alfred Einstein, *Mozart: His Character, His Work*, p. 464.
[4] Gérard de Sède, *Le Trésor cathare*, p. 200.
[5] Boucher, p. 42, after O. Wirth, *Le Livre de l'apprenti*, p. 120.

Chapter 15

[1] J. and B. Massin, p. 1153.
[2] Dent, p. 225.

Chapter 16

[1] Colossians III, 3. On symbolic death in the Masonic doctrine, see Naudon, pp. 76–7.
[2] Serge Hutin, *Les Francs-Maçons*, pp. 145–6.
[3] Robert Ambelain, *Cérémonies et rituels de la Maçonnerie symbolique*, p. 47. See note 3 to Chapter 8.
[4] *Ibid.*, p. 42.
[5] *Ibid.*, p. 46.
[6] *Ibid.*, p. 50.
[7] Hutin, p. 146.
[8] *Ibid.*, pp. 145 ff.
[9] *Cf.* note 5 in Chapter 9.
[10] Boucher, p. 26.
[11] Koch, p. 31.
[12] Dent, p. 228. The anonymous French source mentioned by Dent was probably a *Traité sur les rapports de la Franc-Maçonnerie avec les religions des anciens Égytiens, des Juifs et des Chrétiens*, published at Leipzig in 1836 by R. S. Acerrelos. Boucher mentions in this connection Ragon's *Cours philosophique*, 1841, p. 90.
[13] On this question, see Marius Schneider, "Le Rôle de la musique dans la mythologie et les rites des civilisations non européennes," in *Encyclopédie de la Pléiade: Histoire de la musique*, Paris, 1960, I, pp. 131–214.
[14] Verneuil, p. 452.
[15] *Cf.* Jacques Chailley, "Mythologie et civilisation musicales dans la Grèce antique," in Jacques Porte, *Encyclopédie des musiques sacrées*, I, Paris, 1968, p. 116.

Chapter 17

[1] *Chroniques de ma vie*, 1935, p. 116; *Story of My Life*, New York, 1936, p. 83.

[2] Perhaps, as often happens, the symbolic significances of the keys of B-flat major and E-flat major were given *a posteriori*. These two tonalities were in fact among the easiest to play on the ensembles of wind instruments of the "harmonic columns," taking into account the sometimes perilous pitch relationships of the period: clarinets in B-flat major, horns in E-flat major, bassoons, basset horns in F major or E-flat major. Therefore their frequent use in the repertoire of those ensembles.

Chapter 19

[1] The accusation of plagiarism, discreetly hinted at by Clementi, was made openly by his pupil Ludwig Berger, who cites the first four measures of his teacher's sonata in the *Allgemeine musikalische Zeitung* (1829, p. 470) under the title *"Erläuterungen eines Mozart'schen Urtheils über Muzio Clementi."* It was taken up by Fétis in the Mozart article in his *Biographie universelle des musiciens*, and by J.-B. Weckerlin in his *Nouveau Musicana*, 1890, p. 76.

Chapter 20

[1] Jacques Chailley, *La Musique et le signe*, p. 113, from Françoise Cossart.

[2] Nettl, *Mozart*, p. 160.

[3] Saint-Foix V, p. 227.

[4] Verneuil, p. 452.

[5] Nettl, *Mozart*, p. 160.

[6] Verneuil, p. 448.

Chapter 21

[1] Nettl, *Mozart*, p. 160.

[2] Annals of 5.838 of the Loge des Neuf Soeurs, Paris, Dondey-Dupré (B. N. 16⁰ H. 66 1), pp. 37–8. The march from *Alceste* was played as the opening piece while "the master of ceremonies introduced the visitors two by two." It was followed by "different pieces

from the operas *Castor et Pollux* and *Ernelinde* [*sic*]." During the same ceremony, "the column of harmony plays as a vocal quartet accompanied by the instruments, the *Pie Jesu* of Panseron," father of the composer of the celebrated solfeggios. During the initiation itself, the "columns" of Euterpe, Terpsichore, and Erato, under the direction of "Brother" Capron, a pupil of Gaviniès and soloist of the Concerts Spirituels, will perform the first movement of a symphony for large orchestra by Guénin, which continues "while they move toward the banquet hall" after the interruption by the speeches, itself preceded by the presentation of a ritual laurel wreath, an apron, and the woman's gloves. The Loge des Neuf Soeurs met in the rue du Pot-de-Fer, Saint-Sulpice, in the old Noviciat des Jésuites, also the seat of the Grand-Orient lodge. *Cf.* Fernand Orelli, "*Voltaire franc-maçon*," in the review *La Chaîne d'Union*, Paris, Gloton, 1945–6, No. 5 (February), p. 161.

³ This resemblance was pointed out to me by my pupil Yvon Chartier.

⁴ Ambelain, p. 46. See note 3 in Chapter 8.

⁵ Mentioned by Fétis in his *Biographie universelle*. Text of the chorale quoted by Jean-Baptiste Weckerlin, *Nouveau Musicana*, p. 76.

⁶ Komorzynski, "*Die Zauberflöte*," p. 168. *Cf.* also Ernst Fritz Schmid, in *Influences étrangères*, pp. 78–9. Rheineck's collection is in the possession of the Hotel zum weissen Ochsen at Memmingen. According to Schmid, Komorzynski's hypothesis that Schikaneder could have become acquainted with Rheineck's song at Memmingen and passed it on to Mozart has been proved untenable by Erich Valentin.

⁷ J. and B. Massin, p. 999.

⁸ Saint-Foix (French edition) V, p. 231.

⁹ These two comparisons have also been made by J.-V. Hocquard, *La Pensée de Mozart*, pp. 518 and 583.

Chapter 22

¹ Letter dated October 7–8, 1791.

² Much could be said on this subject: what are we to think, for example, of those "lecture recitals" in which the "singing line" is played with one finger, without the text's even being read, while the principal reader reduces the orchestral part to a piano solo? In view of that sort of thing, ought one to be suprised that, for example, musicians of the Pierre Boulez school follow the example of composers who used to set the verses of M. Scribe?

³ J. and B. Massin, p. 562.

Appendix 1

[1] Seemingly not published. The manuscript is at the Mozarteum, Salzburg. Transcription and translation (into French) by Jean-Marie Gouélou.

Appendix 2

[1] Translation (into French) by Jean-Marie Gouélou. The article begins with a mention of "H²" which is not clarified. Perhaps it contains the key to the author's signature.

Bibliography

Chief works cited:

ABERT, HERMANN: *W. A. Mozart*, 2 vols. Leipzig, 1923.

AMBELAIN, ROBERT: *Cérémonies et rituels de la Maçonnerie symbolique* (Ancient and Primitive Rite of Memhpis-Misraïm). Paris: Niclaus; 1966. About this book, see Notes, Chapter 8, note 3.

BAER, CARL: *Mozart, Krankheit, Tod, Begräbnis.* Salzburg-Kassel: Bärenreiter; 1966.

BARTHA, DENÉS (see *Influences étrangères* . . .).

BAYLOT, JEAN: *Dossier français de la Franc-Maçonnerie régulière.* Paris: Vitiano; 1965.

BERLIOZ, HECTOR: "*La Flûte enchantée et les Mystères d'Isis,*" article of May 1, 1836, reprinted in *Les Musiciens et la Musique*, posthumous collection edited by André Hallays. Paris: Calmann-Lévy; 1903.

BLÜMML, EMIL KARL: "*Aus Deutungen der Zauberflöte,*" in *Neues Mozarts Jahrbuch* I, 1923.

BORN, IGNAZ VON: "*Über die Mysterien der Ägypter,*" in *Journal für Freymaurer*, Vienna, 5784 (Masonic numbering for the year 1784), 1st year, 1st quarter, pp. 15–132. Vienna: Stadtbibliothek; A 24–189.

BOUCHER, JULES: *La Symbolique maçonnique.* Paris: Dervy; 1953.

BRENET, MICHEL (pseudonym of Marie Bobillier): *Les Concerts en France sous l'Ancien Régime.* Paris, 1900.

BRUKNER, FRITZ: *Die Zauberflöte, unbekannte Handschriften und seltene Drucke aus der Frühzeit von Mozarts Oper.* Vienna, 1934.

———: *Mozart und Schikaneder* (edition of an anonymous article published in 1801 by Alberti at Vienna).

CASTLE, ———: "*K. L. Metzler von Giesecke, der angebliche Dichter der Zauberflöte,*" in *Chronik des Wiener Goethe Vereins*, Vols. 48–50, 1946.

CHAILLEY, JACQUES: "*Sur la signification cachée du quatuor de Mozart K.465 dit 'les Dissonances,' et du 7ᵉ Quatuor en fa majeur de Beethoven,*" dissertation in *Natalicia musicologica Knud Jeppesen.* Copenhagen, 1962, pp. 283–7.

————: "*Le* Winterreise *de Schubert est-il une œuvre ésotérique?*" in *Revue d'Esthétique*, 1965, pp. 113–24. A complement to this work is in preparation for the Miscellany dedicated to B. Szabolcsi, Budapest.

————: *La Musique et le Signe*. Lausanne-Paris: Recontres; 1967.

CORNET, JULIUS: *Die Opern in Deutschland*. Hamburg, 1849.

DENT, EDWARD J.: *Mozart's Operas: A Critical Study*. London, New York, etc., 1913; 2nd edn., 1947.

DEUTSCH, OTTO ERICH: *Das Freihaustheater auf der Wieden 1787–1801*. Vienna-Leipzig, 1937.

————: *Mozart und die Wiener Loge*, Edition of the Grand Lodge of Vienna. Vienna, 1932.

————: *Mozart, die Dokumente seines Leben*. Kassel: Bärenreiter; 1961.

DUMESNIL, RENÉ: "*La Flûte enchantée et la Musique maçonnique de Mozart*," in *Musica*, March 1955.

EINSTEIN, ALFRED: *Mozart: His Character, His Work*. London, New York, etc., 1945.

GHIKA, MATILA: *Le Nombre d'Or*, 2 vols. Paris: Gallimard; 1931.

GRADAUR, FRANZ: "*Der Text zu Mozarts* Zauberflöte *und Giesecke*," in *Bayrische Literaturblätter*, 1882.

GUINET, LOUIS: *Zacharias Werner et l'Ésotérisme maçonnique*. Caen: Caron; 1961.

HAVEN, MARC: *Le Maître inconnu, Cagliostro, étude historique et critique sur la Haute Magie*. Paris: Dorbon aîné; 1912.

————: *Rituel de la Maçonnerie égyptienne*, annotated by Marc Haven and preceded by an Introduction by Daniel Nazin. Nice: Cahiers Astrologiques; 1947.

HOCQUARD, JEAN-VICTOR: *Mozart*. Paris: Éditions du Seuil; 1958.

————: *La Pensée de Mozart*. Paris: Éditions du Seuil; 1958.

HUTIN, SERGE: *Les Francs-Maçons*. Paris: Éditions du Seuil; 1960.

Influences étrangères dans l'œuvre de W. A. Mozart, studies collected and presented by André Verchaly. Paris: C.N.R.S.; 1958.

ISTEL, EDGAR: *Die Freimaurerei in Mozarts Zauberflöte*. Berlin, 1928.

JAHN, OTTO: *Mozart*, 4 vols. Leipzig, 1856–9.

KERNER, DIETER: *Mozarts Todeskrankheit*. Mainz-Berlin, 1961.

KOCH, RICHARD: *Br ∴. Mozart, Freimaurer und Illuminaten, nebst einigen freimaurerischen kulturhistorischen Skizzen*. Bad Reichenhall, n. d. (but 1911).

KOMORZYNSKI, EGON VON: *Mozart*. 1941.

————: *Emanuel Schikaneder, ein Beitrag zur Geschichte des deutschen Theaters*. Berlin, 1901; rev., 1951.

————: "Die Zauberflöte," in Neues Mozart-Jahrbuch I, 1923, pp. 147–74.

KUÉSS-SCHEICHELBAUER, ————: 200 Jahre Freimaurerei in Österreich. Vienna: Kerry; 1959.

KUFFERATH, MAURICE: La Flûte enchantée. Paris-Brussels, 1914.

LE BIHAN, ALAIN: Francs-Maçons parisiens du Grand-Orient de France (fin du XVIIIᵉ siècle). Paris: Bibliothèque Nationale; 1966.

LETI, GIUSEPPE, and LACHAT, LOUIS: L'Ésotérisme à la scène: La Flûte enchantée, Parsifal, Faust. Preface by Antonio Coën. Annecy, 1935.

LEWIS, ————: Geschichte der Freimaurerei in Österreich. Vienna, 1861.

LUDENDORFF, MATHILDE: Mozarts Leben und gewaltsamer Tod. Munich, 1936.

MASSIN, JEAN AND BRIGITTE: W. A. Mozart. Paris: Club Français du Livre; 1959.

NAUDON, PAUL: La Franc-Maçonnerie. Paris: P.U.F.; 1967.

NETTL, PAUL: Mozart, with the collaboration of Alfred Orel, Roland Tenschert, and Hans Engel. Paris: Payot; 1962.

————: "Mozart et la Franc-Maçonnerie," in Revue Musicale, Paris, 1930.

————: Mozart und die königliche Kunst. Berlin, 1932.

NYS, CARL DE (See Influences étrangères . . .).

————: "Une énigme dans la vie de Mozart: La Franc-Maçonnerie," in Miroir de l'Histoire, November 1956.

PALOU, JEAN: La Franc-Maçonnerie. Paris: Payot; 1966.

PAUMGARTNER, BERNHARD: Mozart. Berlin, 1927; 2nd edn., Zurich, 1940.

ROMMEL, OTTO: Geschichte der altwiener Volkskomödie. Vienna.

ROSENBERG, ALFONS: Die Zauberflöte, Geschichte und Deutung. Munich, 1964.

SAINT-FOIX, GEORGES DE: Wolfgang Amédée Mozart. Paris: Desclée et Brouwer; 1946.

SCHMID, ERNST FRITZ: "L'Héritage souabe de Mozart" (see Influences étrangères . . .).

SÈDE, GÉRARD DE: Le Trésor cathare. Paris: Julliard; 1966.

SERBANESCO, G.: Histoire de la Franc-Maçonnerie universelle, 3 vols. Paris: Édition Intercontinentale; 1963–6.

SERVIÈRES, GEORGES: "Les Mystères d'Isis," in Épisodes d'histoire musicale, Paris, 1914.

SLONIMSKY, NICOLAS: "The Weather at Mozart's Funeral," in The Musical Quarterly, New York, January 1960.

VAT, G. O.: *Étude sur les Loges d'Adoption*. Paris: Gloton; 1933.

VERNEUIL, MARIANNE: *Dictionnaire pratique des sciences occultes*. Monaco, 1950.

WECKERLIN, JEAN-BAPTISTE: *Nouveau Musicana*. Paris, 1890.

WYZEWA, THÉODORE DE, and SAINT-FOIX, GEORGES DE: W. A. *Mozart: Sa Vie musicale et son Œuvre de l'enfance à la pleine maturité*, 5 vols. Paris, 1912–36.

Of the easily available works in this bibliography, those to which I have turned most often regarding Freemasonry are those of Palou, Hutin, and Naudon for the historic and dogmatic side; those of M. Ghika and J. Boucher for the symbolic side; those of Lewis and Kuéss-Scheichel-bauer for information on Viennese Freemasonry. With respect to Mozart's relations with Freemasonry, the basic source remains Otto Erich Deutsch (*Mozart und die Wiener Loge*), as Koch's assertions apparently remain dubious. See also Nettl and Massin and note 9, p. 319.

The usual Mozartean bibliography is very poor with relation to our subject. The highest authorities habitually glide over it, sometimes without even touching upon it. The only exceptions are Dent, Nettl, and Massin. I have often referred to the Massins' book, which is the most perspicacious of all that I have read despite the sometimes systematic tendentiousness of its anticlerical Jacobinism. The monographs on *Die Zauberflöte* are very disappointing, not excepting Rosenberg's thick book, despite its recent date and the promises of its title, which is useful almost exclusively for study of the sources of *Sethos*. The older Kufferath must not be overlooked: it contains information, notably about Wrantizky's *Oberon*. But nothing, certainly, can take the place of study of primary sources, which I have tried to carry out as much as possible.

Index

A Note About the Author

A composer, Jacques Chailley has been a professor in (and assistant director of) the Conservatoire National Supérieur de Musique, Paris, and is now professor of music at the Sorbonne, director of the Institut de Musicologie, and director of the Schola Cantorum. One of his earlier books, *40,000 Years of Music*, was published in New York with an Introduction by Virgil Thomson.

A *Note on the Type*

This book was set on the Linotype in Electra, a type face designed by W. A. Dwiggins. The Electra face is a simple and readable type suitable for printing books by present-day processes. It is not based on any historical model, and hence does not echo any particular time or fashion.

The book was composed and bound by The Colonial Press, Inc., Clinton, Massachusetts. It was printed by the Halliday Lithograph Corporation, West Hanover, Massachusetts. Typography and binding design by Anthea Lingeman.